THE SHIP
AND THE
STORM

THE SHIP
AND THE
STORM

Hurricane Mitch and the Loss of the Fantome

JIM CARRIER

INTERNATIONAL MARINE / McGRAW-HILL

Camden, Maine • New York • San Francisco • Washington, D.C. • Auckland
Bogotá • Caracas • Lisbon • London • Madrid • Mexico City • Milan • Montréal
New Delhi • San Juan • Singapore • Sydney • Tokyo • Toronto

International Marine
A Division of The **McGraw-Hill** Companies

10 9 8 7 6 5 4 3 2 1
Copyright © 2001 Jim Carrier
All rights reserved. The name "International Marine"
and the International Marine logo are trademarks of
The McGraw-Hill Companies. Printed in the United
States of America.

Library of Congress Cataloging-in-Publication Data
Carrier, Jim.
  The ship and the storm : Hurricane Mitch and the
  loss of the *Fantome* / Jim Carrier.
     p. cm.
  ISBN 0-07-135526-X
  1. Fantome (Schooner). 2. Shipwrecks—Caribbean
  Sea. I. Title.
  G530.F175 C37 2000
  910'.916365—dc21   00-059771

Design by Dede Cummings Designs
Edited by Jonathan Eaton, Bronwen Crothers,
   and Jennifer Comeau

To the men of the *Fantome*—
there but for the grace of God go I.

NOTES ON CONVENTIONS

❧

UNLESS OTHERWISE NOTED, all times are Miami, or Eastern, time—either Eastern Daylight (EDT) or Eastern Standard (EST), as appropriate. In 1998, the switch from daylight saving to standard time occurred at 2 A.M. on Sunday, October 25. Local time in the Gulf of Honduras trails Miami time by one hour.

Tropical storm advisories are issued by the National Hurricane Center every six hours, at 5 A.M., 11 A.M., 5 P.M., and 11 P.M. EDT or at 4 A.M., 10 A.M., 4 P.M., and 10 P.M. EST. When land is threatened by a storm, intermediate advisories are issued at 8 and 2 o'clock EDT or at 7 and 1 o'clock EST.

All distances are in nautical miles; a nautical mile is 1.15 statute miles. Ship speeds, storm travel speeds, and wind velocities are in knots, one knot equaling one nautical mile per hour.

Reported conversations were verified with two or more participants except when only one of the speakers survived.

This is a true story, though truth in journalism is a collection of memories and filters, both conscious and unconscious. Nothing is invented. Any speculation or rumination is signaled in the text.

CONTENTS

Photos appear after page 140

THE SHIP
AND THE
STORM

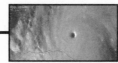

OMOA, HONDURAS
October 4–10, 1998

T HE WATER IN THE BAY was so untroubled, so full of sparkle, that when it lapped against the steel hull it felt like a first kiss. Warm as a bath, rippled by zephyrs into diamond reflections of an afternoon sun, Omoa's small harbor bathed the ship in gauzy silhouette. Four sailing masts towered over a chiseled stern cut with tall windows and a prow sweeping up to a classic bowsprit that jutted into the trade winds. Along her length, nearly that of a soccer field, were what looked like thirty square cannon ports just above the water. From her side, like waterbugs in the shimmering backlight, whaleboats manned by sailors in striped shirts plied to and from shore. Anchored a third of a mile from the beach, in a curve of palms framed by hazy, blue jungle mountains, the *Fantome* imposed herself on the bay.

At 3 o'clock on Sunday afternoon, October 4, 1998, a white Toyota minibus pulled up at the edge of the gray sand beach and spilled rumpled tourists from North America. Cramped from flights and an interminable bus ride, they looked around to find their Caribbean cruise. What they saw through the palms, past children splashing and fishermen seining from dugout canoes, was a scene from *Treasure Island*.

"Holy cow. A tall ship!"

"She's beautiful!"

"I didn't realize it was a schooner that you'd see in a movie!"

One by one they stepped from the sand into the shade of a palm-frond pavilion shaped like a Mayan temple and ordered their first Salva Vida—Life Saver—beers.

Reggae music beat from a sound system. Fish roasted on a grill. Local boys snaked among them, shyly purveying woven bracelets. The bar, six stools long and one long step up from the beach, was soon packed with gringos. One of them opened her trip brochure and marveled that the tableau before them was exactly as promised by Windjammer Barefoot Cruises. Their ship, in fact, was right on the cover.

Built in 1927 for the Duke of Westminster, the 282-foot Fantome *is among the world's largest four-masted staysail schooners. Former owners include the Guinness Brewing family and Aristotle Onassis, who purchased her as a wedding gift for Princess Grace and Prince Rainier. Onassis was not invited to the wedding and the gift was never delivered. She joined the Windjammer fleet as our flagship in 1969.*

"Step on the blue. Grab the crew," Colin August, one of *Fantome's* deckhands, rapped rhythmically as passengers queued up an hour later on a stubby wood dock not far from the bar. August and his brother, Chuckie, grasped the guests' hands, pointed their feet toward a blue strip on the wide wood gunwale of the launch, and directed them to bench seats forward. The whaleboat rocked gently with the weight. They untied lines, revved the diesel to a slow putt-putt, and slipped away. Looking back, one of the tourists snapped a picture. It caught the stern of the whaleboat, the crowded dock and palm-lined shore, and helmsman August, a native of Guyana with shoulders like a linebacker's, smiling beneath a baseball cap turned backward.

Ahead, the *Fantome* loomed. Her masts were as tall as twelve-story buildings. A blizzard of ratlines, stays, shrouds, and halyards ran up their heights. The steel hull, painted white and dark blue, sweated and seeped small rusty rivulets around giant protruding boltheads. Up close the "cannon ports" were recessed glass windows with brass mullions. From the whaleboat, she looked like a floating castle.

"Hands in the boat," August barked as he turned the launch sharply against the bottom of a grated steel stairway that hung amidships off the ship's starboard side. Nine feet up, through a gate in the bulwark, a boyish, blond and barefoot man extended his hand.

"Welcome aboard!" he said in a sharp English accent. "Captain Guyan." The name was sewn on the right breast of his crisp white shirt. Four gold stripes—the insignia of a captain—cut his black shoulder epaulets. He wore shorts and was taut in build, 5-foot-8, like a middleweight wrestler. Next to him stood a towering, imposing, coal-black West Indian.

"Brasso. First Mate," he said, offering a hand and a big smile that melted any intimidation. He directed them aft, along the broad side deck. To their right was a row of cabin doors, to their left a chest-high steel bulwark topped by a varnished mahogany caprail. Overhead, another deck shaded the sun. Fifty feet back, the walkway opened into a breezeway across the width of the ship. This space, thirty-eight by twenty-five feet, had the bustle and feel of a small, elegant hotel lobby. Dark fluted columns framed the entrance to a dining saloon. Above two hand-carved benches, Poseidon, a mermaid, and a Windjammer ship floated around a stained-glass reef. At the forward end of the "lobby," a mahogany bar served as a concierge desk and T-shirt shop. Calypso music oozed from somewhere. The air was rich with old wood, new varnish, brass polish freshly applied, and a seasoned, salty air that blew through from the Caribbean side of the ship. In the middle, on a wood table, stood a bowl of orange punch.

"What's that?" a Canadian guest named Steve Hooper asked.

"You're new, aren't you?" chuckled a tall black steward dressed in a crisp, white tuxedo shirt and black bow tie. His stovepipe Afro erupted from a lanky frame. Chrispin Saunders dipped two plastic glassfuls. "It's rum swizzle," he said, in an island diction that sounded to Hooper like "whumsizzle."

First drinks in hand, Hooper and the seventy-five other guests stowed their gear in cramped, air-conditioned cabins and set out to explore the ship. A few hardy souls even crawled onto the rope netting strung below the bowsprit 30 feet above the water. Looking back, they took in the panorama of the ship.

The *Fantome* was laid out in four decks. The top deck, nearly 20 feet above the water, was the party deck, an open-air gathering spot for buffets, dances and watching the sea go by. The 200- by 40-foot weathered gray wood floor, made of a teak-like angelique, was punctured every 50 feet by four 128-foot steel masts, bigger than two men could reach around at their bases. At the stern sat the ship's bar, itself shaped like a Viking ship with a carved dragon figurehead. The bar and its stools were shaded by a blue tarp. The ship was steered from an elevated bridge forward, between the first and second masts. Built of varnished tongue-and-groove angelique and reached by five wide steps up from the party deck, the bridge spanned the beam of the ship and was surrounded by a brass railing. At its center, in the open air where passengers already were posing for snapshots, stood the large, spoked steering wheel and compass binnacle. Eight feet ahead of the wheel, a chest-high deckhouse blocked all but the long view ahead. Entered through a small French door with sliding overhead hatch, the deckhouse, three steps down, held the chartroom, navigation equipment, and the private quarters of the captain and first and second mates.

One deck down, Deck "A" was considered the main or boarding deck and contained the "lobby" amidships. Its floor was original teak. Double wood doors opened aft to the mahogany-warm, 45-foot-deep dining saloon that filled the *Fantome*'s buxom stern. Large booths upholstered in blue-green cloth lined both sides. Brass lamps swung overhead and natural light poured in through large rectangular windows that circled the room. In the center, a round captain's table shared space with service counters, a dumbwaiter, and an ornate wood staircase that descended to the galley below. Forward, the 100-foot space between the lobby and the forecastle housed sixteen Admiralty Suites, eight on a side, the plushest of *Fantome*'s accommodations, carpeted in burgundy and with doors that opened to the bulwarks and the sea. For $1,075 per person per week, couples got a tightly arranged double bed, armoire, shower, toilet, and small refrigerator. Honeymooners found on their bed a bottle of champagne, two glasses, two T-shirts, a teddy bear, and M&Ms. Tucked in the bow were the crew mess and ship's laundry.

Deck "B," the next deck down, was all business: twenty-four cabins forward, eight cabins aft, almost all with a square portlight, and in the middle, directly below the "lobby," a sparkling galley, walk-in freezer and refrigerator, liquor and dry stores. Rooms on Deck B cost $975 to $1,025 per person per week.

Deck "C" was below the waterline with fourteen passenger cabins, a bow full of crew accommodations—four bunkbeds per room—and a stern packed with engines, generators, fuel and water tanks, and workbenches. Rooms on Deck C cost $875 per person per week.

When full, the *Fantome* held 128 passengers and 45 crew, making her small by modern cruise ship standards but the largest vessel in Windjammer's fleet.

As twilight descended on Omoa Bay, the galley crew laid out a buffet supper on the party deck, and a local band plugged in amplifiers and played salsa, merengue, and a little rock 'n' roll. Passengers dressed in shorts, T-shirts, and bare feet—all that was needed on a Windjammer cruise—began to party. Steve Hooper, from Calgary, asked the band if he could sing "La Bamba." The Spanish-speaking musicians didn't know it. They settled on the Beatles' "A Hard Day's Night." Seen from the top deck, the Honduran shoreline was outlined in lights. Among the palms, Omoa sparkled. Hooper, a burly railroad worker and part-time pro wrestler, had come along on the cruise arranged by his girlfriend, Cathy Stumph, with no idea what lay in store. Six hours after arriving in Omoa, feeling no pain and smitten by the ambience, he got down on his knees in front of several strangers and kissed Stumph's bare feet.

At 11 o'clock, after boarding late-arriving guests and raising the whaleboats into their davits, Captain Guyan March ordered anchors aweigh. Standing atop his deckhouse to see ahead, he spoke quiet orders to the helmsman and engine room and motored the *Fantome* to sea. The Bay Islands, their destination for the week, lay 80 to 100 miles east, but their course would be more northerly for several hours to avoid reefs and shoal ground. Underway, he ordered the sails raised, a thirty-minute ritual involving all nine deckhands and any passenger willing to help haul the rope halyards for three jibs and four immense staysails. As the sails squeaked up under the mast floodlights, the haunting sound of a lone bagpipe floated across Omoa Bay. "Amazing Grace," the spiritual, wailed from deck loudspeakers. Jet lag and rum swizzles notwithstanding, grown men and women shivered and teared up.

Once the bar closed and people fell into swaying bunks, First Mate Emmanuel "Brasso" Frederick took the watch. A native of Antigua, he stood at the wheel, taking in the stars and the distant shoreline that passed as a dull glow to his right. The *Fantome* motor-sailed eastward into the trade winds, its engines a distant murmur, its four staysails pulled tight to the centerline and flapping gently at their edges.

At 4 A.M. a passenger appeared on the bridge, nodded dizzily, and went to the rail. He didn't look good. A few minutes later another man joined him.

"I slept through my own engagement," the first man groaned. "I was going to do it at midnight, after we set sail. Everybody would be in bed. It would be quiet. Moonlight. The stars. The ocean. I figured it was perfect. Five cognacs later, I wake up. It's 3 A.M. I tried to wake her up and couldn't. I'm an absolute idiot."

The stranger laughed. "We're on our honeymoon. What about sunrise? We'll get our champagne and a camera."

At 5:30 A.M. the men showed up again, dragging a sleepy woman to the bridge. "C'mon," her boyfriend said to her, "let's go see the sunrise."

The woman, Deena Kaplan, was still in her boxer shorts. Her hair was uncombed, her teeth unbrushed. She couldn't see without her contacts. She'd known her roommate, Andrew Biewend, all of six weeks. Groggy, she leaned her back against the railing where Biewend grabbed her hand.

"Will you marry me? Here." He thrust a green leather pouch into her palm.

The ship was sailing directly into the sunrise. As they kissed, the stranger snapped a picture that caught a sunbeam streaming between them. The sky was a palette of bright yellow, pink, and green. Higher up, arcing westward over the deck, the colors went from light blue to navy to black. There were stars overhead. Directly behind, over the fantail, the moon was setting. It was the perfect beginning. At the helm, Brasso flashed another big grin and a thumbs-up.

🐚

As a "love boat," the *Fantome* had few equals. Mike Burke, her owner, liked to say she had "balls," and often bragged of unplanned conceptions "under the Caribbean moon." But *Fantome*'s lines also evoked the deeper mystique of seafaring. The Great Age of Sail, a period that lasted four hundred years and ended just before *Fantome* was launched in 1927, packed the English language with enough metaphors to fill books and brochures into the new millennium. During *Fantome*'s seventy-one years, nearly all of them had been used to describe her. In scrapbooks kept by Windjammer Barefoot Cruises at its Miami headquarters, countless travel stories were headlined "Ten Days Before the Mast" or some such, usually accompanied by a photograph of a sunburned tourist grasping the helm. A remarkable number of these accounts began with a captain shouting in a "thick Scottish brogue: Raise the jib, men!" The crew was invariably a "swarthy band," and the daily "ration of grog" spoke of Mike Burke's own pirate yearnings reworked into marketing lingo.

The *Fantome* was christened with similar nostalgia. In 1925 Britain's Duke of Westminster commissioned the Orlando Naval Shipyard in Livorno, Italy, to build a riveted steel hull and place inside it the decks, cabins, and furnishings of his wooden yacht *Flying Cloud*, which itself had been refashioned just four years earlier from an American schooner made to look like an eighteenth-century British frigate. The result was a cross between a dark buccaneer and the most sumptuous private yacht in the world. With a raised foredeck, a central "well deck," a raised quarterdeck at the rear, and six guest suites below, the *Flying Cloud* was rated 100A1 for seaworthiness by Lloyd's of London, though the duke only moored her at Monte Carlo and puttered up and down the French Riviera with a crew of eighty, including footmen and a gun bearer.

In the quarterdeck space later occupied by Windjammer's dining saloon, the duke and duchess kept separate, private quarters built of fumed oak from their Cheshire estate. Around the 30-foot stern sprawled a lounge with a fireplace and several sofas. Their quarters were entered from the well deck through a door guarded by huge oak columns and an arched shell "designed to resemble the front door of an old Cotswold house," the duchess recalled. "The cabins were furnished with small-scale Queen Anne furniture, perfectly proportioned to their size, which had been collected with some trouble. In my cabin was a four-poster bed with embroidered Florentine silk curtains, and, when stationary, one would almost believe that one was in a private house in England." Years later, when Mike Burke bridged over the well deck with the top, party deck, making the *Fantome's* "lobby," he retained the duke's original oak columns, the elaborately carved stairways to the poop deck above, and the carved shell over the dining room door.

In 1932 the duke sold *Flying Cloud* to Nelson Warden, scion of one of John D. Rockefeller's partners. Warden, then in his sixties, had married as his second wife a beautiful young Pennsylvania farm girl named Zoe Busler and kept her, in the manner of a trophy wife, on the ship. Her job, according to nephew Martin Busler, "was going to parties." She told her nephew that the duke sold the ship because the duchess was tired of entertaining his mistresses, among them Coco Chanel. Zoe Busler and her flapper friends were served by a staff of forty, and, legend has it, two dairy cows kept aboard for fresh milk. Warden, unfortunately, died two years after he bought the ship. Busler distributed some of the furniture and silver to her family and then let the yacht go for death taxes.

The *Flying Cloud* was acquired at auction by Arthur Ernest Guinness, second son of the Earl of Iveagh and an heir of the Irish family stout business. He renamed her *Fantome*, the French word for phantom or ghost, a name he'd used on three other yachts. In 1939 he ordered her to Vancouver, British Columbia, to rendezvous with King George VI, there to dedicate a bridge built by a Guinness syndicate. Under Captain Archibald Frogbrook and a crew of thirty-four, the *Fantome* arrived in San Francisco via the Panama Canal after a voyage of fifty-one days, averaging 10½ knots. "Full sail is used only in good weather. We use the forestays'ls, mains'l and jigger in rough weather to steady her. That [weather] makes her roll a lot. She's a beautiful sight under full sail," Frogbrook reported upon arrival. But when the crew hoisted and aired out the ship's large canvas sails in Puget Sound in July 1939, it was *Fantome's* last hurrah as a luxury yacht. The war in Europe broke out in September, Great Britain drafted all but three of the *Fantome's* crew, and U.S. Customs sealed its eighty cases of Scotch, champagne, and stout. A year after armistice, with the ship still anchored near the Seattle Yacht Club, King County's assessor slapped Guinness with a six-year, $17,591 property tax lien. Guinness sued and three years later, won relief for all but $2,324.

A.E. Guinness died forty-five days later, and his estate sold the "million-dollar" *Fantome* to Seattle brothers William and Joseph Jones for a reported $50,000. Operators of Alaska fish canneries, the Jones boys were astounded by the yacht's opulence, including Guinness' suits still hanging in closets. "I wish you could have seen the rich, soft blankets and the white linen, the heavy silverware," Joe Jones told a reporter in 1954. Three years later, stripped of more china and antiques, *Fantome* was sold to Sincennes-McNaughton Lines Ltd., a salvage firm in Montréal. The company had cut hundreds of ships into metal scrap and everyone thought *Fantome* was doomed. In a eulogy rich with metaphor, Harry Furniss wrote in *B.C. Magazine*, "While other great windjammers of a bygone era have ended their days in humility as grain carriers, or barges, or nobly splintered their aging planking on coasts the world over, *Fantome* came to grief on a legal reef." For the next three years, *Fantome* lay alongside the Richelieu River in Sorel, Québec, kept spotless by the Simard brothers, who often entertained VIPs aboard. They abandoned plans to tear out her engines, instead pressing her on a customer who had recycled a number of old Canadian ships into a shipping empire. In the first week of May 1956, the fabled

Fantome was towed out the St. Lawrence Seaway by a whaler. Befitting a ship with her name, the *Fantome*, already mothballed for seventeen years, disappeared from public view for another fifteen.

❦

As the sun crept up Monday morning and *Fantome*'s passengers emerged from their air-conditioned warrens, they followed their noses to coffee, the sharp tang of Bloody Marys, and sticky buns laid out in the breezeway. Most went topside and sat on the benches to warm and wake up. With sails down, the ship was approaching a small, flat island, motoring slowly through purple and brown patches of reef visible through the shallow water. The channel into Utila is narrow and winding, and the *Fantome*, with a draft of 19 feet, had to be guided at the speed of a canoe while curious, if hungover, passengers looked on. For a clear view, Captain March, who supervised every harbor entrance, strolled back and forth on the roof of the deckhouse, looking 30 feet down and periodically speaking to the crewman at the helm.

"Starboard ten. Midships. Port one-half."

"There was a very nasty reef, a tricky little spot," recalled Steve Hooper. "You could see him baby this 280-foot bloody tall ship through those reefs and drop the hook. It was a beautiful piece of seamanship."

March's ability to maneuver ships was Windjammer lore. "You could give him a bathtub and he could make it dance," said his younger brother, Paul March, who served under him on the *Fantome* when March was a relief skipper in 1996. "It didn't matter if it was 3 feet or 300 feet, he docked it calmly, no effort, no shouting or screaming. There were stories about him on the *Amazing Grace*, his first command. It was like you and I driving a car. It flowed with him. No matter what ship he drove, he made a point every week of sailing it off the dock with staysails. His record, on the *Yankee Clipper*, a good sailing ship, with different islands every day, was using the engines only fifty-five minutes in a whole week."

Guyan March was a natural sailor—gifted, many said—one of those occasional people who never struggle with tiller and wind. Born in Bristol, England, on May 1, 1966, he first tasted seawater as a boy in Cornwall—"I'm Cornish, not English," he often corrected, his "Cornwall" sounding to an American ear as "kewn wew"—Britain's narrow Land's End, when his engineer father opened a dive shop on St.

Austell Bay. For adult socials and for playmates for their three boys, Jenny and Reg March joined the Porthpean Sailing Club. Tony, Guyan, and Paul—ten, eight, and six—fell into sailing, first as crew on friends' yachts and then in Mirror dinghies, 10-foot sloops with a daggerboard and tiller. The boys built a couple in their basement and became part of the club's rabid competition on Wednesday evenings and Sundays. When Guyan manned the tiller, "we usually won," Paul said.

Tony went to university to study electrical engineering and Guyan followed, but not for long. He was not academically inclined and didn't do well, especially in mathematics. Instead, he enrolled in the Youth Training Scheme, a government-supported apprenticeship program that included a sector in sailing. In 1983, at age sixteen, Guyan March was accepted at the Island Cruising Club in Salcombe, and within six months was an assistant instructor on the club's one hundred Optimist dinghies, lasers, and Olympic-class Solings. In another year he was a full instructor.

"He was a lucky guy who stepped on a boat and felt the wind wherever it came from. He adjusted the boat and sheets, the angle of attack, before the wind got to him. Like a racing driver, he could spot things ahead. It's because he started so young," said Jeremy Linn, who ran the school. "On weekends in the evenings, the staff raced. He always won. Everybody was upset. It didn't matter what you put him in, the worst boat. He could make a boat go anywhere in any condition. Even if you penalized him, made him capsize, do a 360 turn in the water, empty the boat and carry on, he'd still bloody win."

The seventeen-year-old March also trained aboard the club's 34-foot yacht and in 1985 was chosen by Linn as first mate on *Hoshi*, the club's 72-foot schooner. They made overnight trips across the English Channel to the Channel and Brittany Islands. On several occasions March tried to sail the hefty schooner like a small and maneuverable dinghy.

"I remember the first time he was in charge of *Hoshi*. We were at sea at night. I went to my bunk and told him to look for a lighthouse. He popped into my cabin four hours later."

"We're there. We're at the lighthouse," March announced to Linn.

"I expected to see it four or five miles away," Linn said later. "Instead I was a half-mile off, looking up at it. We were too close for comfort in the middle of the night. We got canvas down and turned around."

Eventually, as March learned to translate charts and work through the math, Linn came to trust him completely. They sailed one tall-ships race, from London to Norway, and returned by way of Amsterdam. The tall ships enthralled him, liberal Amsterdam excited him, and Guyan March began to think beyond dinghies.

"I watched him grow from a shy, unassuming kid into an experienced, very young chap who could handle traditional boats. He came here because it was the only thing he knew how to do, knocking about in boats. He saw you could make a living at it. He was really happy he had found something, a sport, that he really loved doing." March also blossomed into an extremely handsome young man, chased, said Linn, by "a lot of girls. His social skills developed quite quickly. He had one party trick. He could get from the forward end of the 14-foot bowsprit to the back end of the ship—86 feet in all—without touching the deck. He climbed up the forestay, across the triatic, and down the topping lift. He could do it drunk or sober. He was basically a monkey. He never used ratlines. He'd climb up any rope he could find, hand over hand."

March took the Yacht Masters test of the Royal Yachting Association, a rigorous, overnight trial of sailing and theory granting a basic license to run a yacht with up to twelve passengers. It was the only formal license he ever earned from an established maritime administration. For a season, he skippered a charter yacht in the Mediterranean and the Canary Islands. But Linn suggested the West Indies: "Sunshine, money, hot, easy sailing. A vast selection of different crafts, big plastic fantastics or large traditional ships. If you're looking to go off sailing, go there." March's father, who by then was involved in tall ship renovations, knew Windjammer's chief engineer. In 1987 Guyan March joined Windjammer as a junior officer. He worked his way through the fleet and ten years later, after several relief stints on her, including time in the company's new cruising grounds of the western Caribbean, was named permanent captain of the *Fantome*, the company's flagship. At age thirty-two, Guyan March was Windjammer's golden boy.

🔊

After a breakfast of eggs, bacon, and fresh pastries, passengers gathered at the "horseshoe," a wooden buffet on the top deck, where the barefoot March greeted them for his first "story hour." Though boyish—when he began with Windjammer he looked like a twelve-year-old, with deep dimples, wavy blond hair, and a warm, open smile—March assumed a command pose, knees locked, hands clasped behind his back, chest out, rocking on his heels.

"Good morning," he shouted cheerily.

"Good morning," came a ragged reply.

"That's terrible. For those who haven't done a Windjammer before, the proper greeting is, 'Good morning, Captain, Sir.' Otherwise you don't get any rum in your swizzles at 5 o'clock."

That drew a laugh.

"So we'll just try that once more. Good morning, everybody."

"Good morning, Captain, Sir!" came a chorus.

"All right! We've got a bunch of alcoholics on board."

In his pinched West Country accent, March explained that the *Fantome* had sailed through the night to Utila, the first of the Bay Islands to be visited during the week. His "story hour" would be a daily routine to explain the ship's movements, cover a bit of history and ecology, and offer some advice on where to hike and get a cold one while ashore.

March then introduced the ship's crew of forty-two, identifying them affectionately by their nicknames in a review that had the feel of a curtain call. After First Mate Brasso, his officers—all of them in white shirts with the embroidered Windjammer emblem, a bare foot under sail, on the breast—included Second Mate Onassis Reyes from Panama, Dive Master Cathie de Koeyer, Activities Mate Laura-Jo Bleasdale, and Purser Laurie Fischer, whom Captain March dryly introduced with a practiced double entendre as keeper of the Sea Chest: "If you haven't seen her chest already, she gets it out on display later today.

"Then the actual deck crew that do all the real work. Heading up is the bosun, Cyrus—or Turtle." Cyrus Phillips, known for nicknaming his crew and changing the monikers daily, called out a line of West Indian men—"Chuckie, Francis, Jerry, Colin, P.P., Blinky, Jesús, and Jallim"—who passed with arms raised. The galley crew was headed by chef Eon Maxwell, natty in a starched white chef's shirt with gray neckerchief, "probably the only person we'll wait for if he misses the last launch." Eon brought out Kevin Logie, Patrick Bryan, Vanil Fender, Alvin George, and galley aide Pedro Prince.

Passengers recognized chief steward Chrispin Saunders by his height and smile and lilting tongue, a product of his native Grenada, at once pleasant and nearly incomprehensible to the northern ear. Holding hands up like a beanpole prize fighter, Chrispin introduced stewards Bobby, Alan, Enoch, "and the girls"—Jasmine, Daphne, Beverly

(Chrispin's sister), and Muriel. Sheldon Alexander, the laundryman, and two bartenders, C.J. and Castle, also received a round of applause. "And then we have the engineers. That's headed up by Pope, the chief engineer." Pope introduced a line of men dressed in blue T-shirts or overalls: "Ion, Django, Rhon, Morris, Brusch, Dode, Bara, and Roberts."

Passengers were put through a fire and life-jacket drill, whaleboats were lowered, and Francis Morain and the August brothers, Colin and Chuckie, began ferrying people ashore. This would be the routine for the next five days, a blur of drinks, dining, diving with dolphins, dancing on deck, midnight sails, and daytime stops on islands still safe from the mega–cruise ships that had begun to dominate the eastern Caribbean. Looking back on the week, an impromptu gang that coalesced around the gregarious Steve Hooper remembered only an idyllic haze.

"Roatán—that was Tuesday, right?"

"Was it Wednesday or Thursday we stopped at Guanaja?"

On Thursday at Cayos Cochinos, the galley crew hauled a barbecue to the beach. Hooper found a guitar with a missing string and led his new best friends into a howling version of "Cheeseburger in Paradise." Later, someone grabbed a snapshot of Hooper pulling a halyard behind a crewmember. The photo and caption, posted later on Hooper's personal Web site, captured the warming mood between guests and crew after only a few days together. "Usually everyone pitches in to hoist the sails after a few rum swizzles. 'Amazing Grace' blasts through the deck speakers—I'll never forget how Captain Guyan was such a stickler for tradition. Everyone would grab a rope and start hoisting and he'd be hollering from the bridge, 'Wait for the music! Wait for the music!' "

Rum and romance were the legacy of Windjammer founder Mike Burke, a man who, in 1948, turned the idea of "going to sea" into a bed and breakfast. As described in a company sales brochure:

World War II had ended and I had finished my hitch in the Navy. With $600 pay in my pocket, I went to Miami to "paint the town red." The next morning I awoke with a head-splitting hangover in a vaguely familiar 19-foot sloop. During the night I had purchased her with my $600. With a few swigs

of scotch left in the bottle I christened her "Hangover." Little did I realize
that she was to become the first vessel in the world's largest fleet of tall ships.

But like a good fish story, the origins of Windjammer Barefoot Cruises
depended on the telling. At one time, Windjammer's brochures re-
counted how "Cap'n Burke" won *Hangover* in a poker game. The boat
was 22 feet, then 27 feet. Once it was a ketch rig. In later interviews, he
said he didn't play cards and didn't wake up drunk on the boat but
rather found *Hangover* sunk off an island in the Abacos chain of the
Bahamas, paid $200 for it, and got local boys to help drag it ashore. "I
remember like it was yesterday. Living on the beach, trading food for
fish, cooking on a kerosene lamp. It was a great life. I was in great
shape. The island girls loved me." But that version wasn't quite true either. With Burke, one was never sure if he was trying out lines, quoting
a deeply held truth, or repeating stories told so many times that even
he had begun to believe them.

Windjammer's story really began in Lakewood, New Jersey, where
Mike Burke grew up as Nathan Mendelson, son of a kosher butcher. He
encountered the ocean on family vacations to the Jersey shore. As a
teenager he went to sea "baiting hooks and mopping up vomit" on a
tourist fishing boat. In 1942, at age eighteen, he joined the navy's submarine service, exiting as a quartermaster, although he claimed to have
capped his career by helping bring home one of Hitler's submarines
from Argentina. Discharged in 1946, Mendelson took the name "Mike
Burke" from a buddy he said was lost at sea. He told his son that a
Jewish name had a "stigma" that failed to fit the shipping magnate
image he wanted to create.

In Miami, in 1946, Burke met George "Harry" Reid, a merchant marine officer who had spent the war working on commercial ships. He invited Burke to join him on a boat-hunting trip to the Bahamas. Reid,
later a master seaman and author of several texts for professional
mariners, said he provided the $240 for the 25-foot *Hangover*, a wooden
sloop. Burke claimed he put up the money. Either way, the men spent
several months together, Reid teaching Burke to sail. "The boat was
loaded with cockroaches. To get rid of them, we sank it. It looked like
a friggin' swarm of bees out the mast," Reid said. "We had fun, knocking back," Burke added. "We were as close as two men can be without
being lovers."

Later that year, they sailed *Hangover* into the Miami River and Reid took off to pursue other interests. Burke ran an ad, looking for someone to share expenses on the boat. "The response was tremendous," Reid recalled, "mostly young ladies who included photographs of themselves in bathing suits. Initially it was the good old *cojones* thing, pursuing them for a little friendship. But Mike was enterprising. It occurred to him that there was a market. This is what started the idea."

Burke, who was painting buildings at the time, told *Newsday*: "I used to take girlfriends to Bimini for a weekend and gradually there were more and more girlfriends." He also told the *Miami Herald* that he set off to sail *Hangover* solo around the world. "It was tedious and he frequently put ashore in the Caribbean for cold beer and conversation, making it only as far as Puerto Rico," the *Herald* reported. So "going to sea" became a trip across the Gulf Stream to the Bahamas and back. Somewhere in the mid-1950s Burke started charging to cover the costs of food and booze. One of his first published fares was $59 for a long weekend. With that money he traded through a series of boats: a 32-foot sloop, a 48-footer for $800, then a 65-footer. His first big boat, the 134-foot schooner *Janeen* in the early 1960s, launched him into a bona fide business that came to be called Cap'n Burke's Windjammers. The boats had seen better days—*Janeen*, later renamed the *Polynesia*, was aground in the Bahamas when Burke paid her owner, Sir Oliver Simmons, $5,000 cash and a percentage of earnings. Burke struggled to make payments. But he proved a genius at spinning old boats into dream catchers.

"In the old days I did most of the cooking," said Burke. "I had a 20-pound turkey for 50 people. I'd slice the shit out of it, paper thin, and a lot of bread and gravy. I'd give them a reel and say, 'You want to eat? Fish!' We cleaned and cooked the catch right in front of them. They came back year after year."

He also gave free rides to travel writers, traded trips for magazine ads, made up blue-blood histories for each of the boats, encouraged his crew to dress and act like pirates, and sold cruises to singles and the occasional gay and nude group. Nude sunbathing was encouraged on the forecastle, known as the "sex deck," and a sign read "No friggin' in the riggin'." Windjammer soon gained a reputation as an offshore bacchanal. When twenty-five-year-old Coast Guard officer Harvey Schuster boarded one of Burke's boats in 1959 to check for safety equipment, he recalled, "Part of me wished I had been a passenger on it.

There was minimal clothing. The crew all talked about what a paradise it was. What you didn't get in safety and amenities you got in sex and free love. In a word, it was a floating whorehouse."

Miriam Otera, a single woman with IBM in Canada, began sailing with Burke in 1960. "You wouldn't take a boyfriend. That would be like taking a sandwich to a banquet. Every cruise there were some gorgeous men and gorgeous women. There was pairing up, playing in the sand. I used to sow wild oats and go home and forget who and why, and I did that for many years."

In a *Cosmopolitan* piece, entitled "A Single Girl on a Windjammer Cruise," writer Gail Sheehy, later Hillary Clinton's biographer, described Burke as the "first of many pleasant surprises, bulky shouldered, forty-two and weathered like good rope—He is in Bermudas, owns no socks. Smiles like an old friend . . ." He confided to her having twelve children with three wives and "nursing a poor boy's dream."

Burke's most notorious trip featured Marilyn Chambers, the pornography star. "You'll get a royal bang out of this princely voyage . . . see where Ernest Hemingway shacked up," blared an ad in *Genesis* magazine. When more men than women signed up, Burke gave away bunks to women, neglecting to tell them the trip's true nature. One of them happened to be a *Chicago Tribune* reporter, who later described Chambers as "one of the more sane people aboard, except for walking around with nothing on." One male passenger wore high leather boots and jacket in the tropics. Another, 4-foot-1, carried a whip. "I couldn't walk through the main saloon without someone grabbing at me," said the reporter. At the captain's dinner, "three guys thought it would be great to come up to each table and drop their pants. I mean, while you're eating your lettuce!"

With publicity like that, unerring marketing instincts, and liberal rum lubrication, Burke carved a niche in the conservative cruise business. He claimed in 1965 to be carrying 5,200 passengers a year and grossing $1 million. His formula would serve him and his heirs well for the rest of the twentieth century.

On Thursday night, October 8, *Fantome* hoisted sails and began a lazy downwind run from Cayos Cochinos back to Omoa. Passengers were told to dress up, either in togas, using sheets, or as something beginning with "P," as in prostitute, pirate, proctologist. During a scavenger "sea hunt," one woman remembered racing to the deckhouse, opening the door to the captain's cabin, and snatching a pair of his underwear from an outstretched hand. During the deck party that followed, every man's attention was diverted by a cute blonde in a white stretch dress and high heels. Her long, straight platinum hair hung to her chest, and her buns were every woman's envy. "She" turned out to be the captain in drag. It was the only night Guyan March was seen wearing shoes.

Afterward, a wild dance broke out on deck. Caribbean music boomed from the speakers. Chrispin Saunders, in what looked like a diaper, and his chief assistant, Bobby Pierre, gyrated crazily. Steve Hooper recalled: "Part of the song was, 'Who let the dogs out. Woof! Woof!' and everyone bellowed this line when it rolled around. The whole ship was laughing." The night reminded Hooper of summer camp, after a week with new friends who would last forever. "I'm a diehard now," he blurted. "Jammer for life."

As the *Fantome* motor-sailed under the stars, its decks ablaze with costumes and tunes, a dark squall line half a world away thundered across West Africa. Its origin, like those of similar, brief furies of wind and rain that passed every four or five days each summer and fall, was unclear. Half a dozen meteorological theories offer competing, equally plausible explanations. These "perturbations" might be stirred by a belt of disturbances that circle the equator. They might start as an eddy of wind in the Himalayas or as a more conventional rising-heat cumulonimbus cloud in Chad's Tibesti Mountains. They have in common low atmospheric pressure and a slow, counterclockwise rotational wind flow more than 50 miles in diameter. These lazy-Susan cyclones, embedded in the atmosphere at 10,000 feet, blow west with the continent's prevailing winds. As they move between the hot, dry Sahara desert to the north and the warm, moist Gulf of Guinea to the south, they also develop a line of thunderstorms. Often fearsomely black with lightning and rain, they bring moisture to the Sehel grasslands and whip up sand, tingeing the atmosphere red. At night, the thunderstorms often dissipate. But the perturbation continues to move stealthily westward at 20 to 30 knots.

This particular wave might have gone unnoticed except for the daily routine of a small government meteorological office in Abidjan, Côte d'Ivoire—Ivory Coast—the impoverished former French colony on the

Gulf of Guinea. On Thursday, October 8, staffer Ohoua Akou and an assistant launched a 12-foot hydrogen balloon tethered to a small plastic box. Before the balloon burst and the fifty dollar box fell to earth on a parachute, its instruments detected and transmitted southwest winds at 10 knots, a temperature of 77 degrees, and humidity of 94 percent. At noon Greenwich Mean Time, these data were transmitted to Senegal and from there to the World Weather Center near Washington, D.C. Crunching its numbers with data from five hundred other balloons around the world, an IBM supercomputer spit out a world map covered with "feather" symbols, indicating wind speed and direction. The one over Côte d'Ivoire looked a little frazzled, and by itself it meant nothing. But twelve hours later, another balloon with another box sent new data. Twice the next day the staff repeated this routine. Overnight, the feather on Côte d'Ivoire shifted a bit, not dramatically—the weather station was on the southern edge of this perturbation—but enough to catch the practiced eye of meteorologist Lixion Avila at the National Hurricane Center in Miami, who then looked at a satellite view of the Atlantic Ocean. Skies were largely clear of clouds except for Hurricane Lisa, with a telltale swirl in midocean between Florida and France. But over Côte d'Ivoire he did notice a couple of large, white cloud clusters, a sign of thunderstorms.

One of Avila's jobs at the center was tracking African tropical waves. He counted about sixty a year. Ten percent of them became hurricanes. Described by his boss as the "Will Rogers of tropical waves—he never met one he didn't like," Avila gave each wave a number, marked its location on a photo strip with a red grease pencil, and followed it west, penciling notes in the margin: "#25—Great wave, spinning like a top" and "#31—This system is good." On October 8, his photo strip displayed five vertical grease lines at various points. Number 41 was in the Pacific, west of Honduras. Number 42 was over Mexico. Number 43 was causing squalls over Panama, and Numbers 44 and 45 were in the middle of the Atlantic.

Thirty-six hours later, on Saturday morning, October 10, as *Fantome's* guests rose for one last Bloody Mary and sticky buns breakfast and Avila ended his overnight shift, he stared a long moment at the broad cloud system now trailing southwest-to-northeast off the African coast. In the last day, another set of balloon data over Dakar, Senegal, had shown a definite wind shift and drop in barometric pressure associated with this system. The perturbation had moved 500 miles. Holding his red grease pencil, Avila made a vertical slash at longitude 17° W, just on the edge of West Africa. He labeled it "#46." "This," Avila penciled in the margin, "is another impressive system."

🐚

"What would you do in the event of a hurricane?" a *Fantome* passenger had asked Captain March just a week before. The question, chewed on by all Caribbean sailors until they were toothless, was always on March's mind during hurricane season, June to December. He listened to weather forecasts religiously and required his watch officers to log Caribbean weather every six hours. On Saturday evening, October 10, as he took his 4 P.M. to 8 P.M. watch at anchor in Omoa, he would have known that the Caribbean was blessedly clear of storms.

Drawn on a single map, the tracks of all 970 Atlantic tropical storms between 1871 and 1998 look like a black writhing mass of destruction, a Rorschach that screams to the cautious: "Get out during hurricane season." Many yachters do. Yet across the Caribbean every summer and fall, life goes on. Sailors sail. Bananas grow and are shipped. Lovers honeymoon. And Windjammer ships kept operating, running or hiding from an average of two or three tropical storms every year. In Guyan March's eleven years in the eastern Caribbean, 126 tropical storms or hurricanes had developed in the Atlantic, with 21 blowing through or brushing by the West Indies close enough to require evasive action or serious hurricane preparation on the ships he served. Both he and the *Fantome* had encountered heavy weather on the edges of several hurricanes.

The geography of the eastern Caribbean offers several choices in the event of a tropical storm. Though appearing like fragile dots on a vast sea, dwarfed by a hurricane's size, many West Indian islands provide shelter, harbors, and even a few hurricane holes, anchorages with such good holding ground and surrounding topography that they are sanctuaries when storms approach. There are also hundreds of miles of running room—sea in every direction. A typical hurricane track through the eastern Caribbean often threatened two or three Windjammer ships as it moved north. The company's ships ran north from Hurricane Marilyn in 1995 and south from Hurricane Georges in September 1998. Running and hiding was Windjammer's standard hurricane strategy, one that had always worked.

The Gulf of Honduras is another story. The map of historic hurricane tracks shows a mere scribble—one storm, on average, every ten years—crossing near the Bay Islands. The problems are shelter and sea room, for the gulf is a textbook example of what sailors call being "embayed." A 90-degree crotch of Central America—Belize to the west, Honduras to the south, and Guatemala in the corner—the entire coast is a "lee shore" where prevailing winds blow toward shifting shoals, reefs, and barely visible islands. No less a mariner than Columbus cursed the northern coast of Honduras during his final voyage to the New World in 1502. After sailing past the island of Guanaja on July 30 and anchoring near Puerto Castilla, where his son said the first Catholic mass on the American mainland, Columbus ordered his square riggers to beat east against wind and current. For twenty-eight days he fought "continual rain, thunder and lightning . . . the ship lay exposed to the weather, with sails torn, and anchors, rigging, cables, boats and many of the stores lost; the people exhausted and so down in the mouth that they were all the time making vows to be good, to go on pilgrimages and all that; yea, even hearing one another's confessions. Other tempests I have seen, but none that lasted so long or so grim as this. Many old hands whom we looked on as stout fellows lost their courage. I was sick and many times at death's door." According to biographer Samuel Eliot Morison, "Nobody without Columbus' perseverance would have kept it up. Every morning the caravels had to heave up anchors and claw offshore on the starboard tack, stood inshore again, and at sundown anchored off a sodden coast in an open roadstead, the caravels pitching and tossing all night, and the crew fighting mosquitoes from the swamps. Some days they gained a few miles; on others they fetched up opposite the same grove of obscene mangroves off which they had spent the previous night. The average distance made good was only six miles a day." When Columbus finally turned the corner and headed south along the Mosquito Coast toward modern-day Nicaragua on September 14, he called the point "Cabo Gracias a Dios"—Thank God Cape.

Windjammer was aware of these problems when it moved the *Fantome* to the western Caribbean in the summer of 1997 to find new cruising grounds away from the cruise ship–crowded Antilles. Captain March, who didn't like having his back in a corner, went along with misgivings. "We talked about the possibility of hurricanes a great deal and options that were open to us if we were caught up in one—the locals talked about a big one being due," said Annie Bleasdale, the purser at the time. On a trip home to England two months earlier, March had discussed the issue with his brother Paul. The Gulf of Honduras "wouldn't be a place you'd want to be if a hurricane came," Paul said. "Guyan was well aware that if something came through, which was highly unlikely, you were not in the same position as in the eastern Caribbean. You are kinda trapped. Having said that, he was happy to go out there to run the ship."

In his answer October 2 to passenger Victor Lohman's question— "What would you do?"—March said the *Fantome's* location made it nearly impossible to outrun a storm. The Yucatán Peninsula is 360 miles to the north and Cabo Gracias a Dios is 330 miles to the east, both land-forms surrounded by treacherous shallow banks. To find real sea room, the *Fantome* needed two and a half days' notice to get out of the gulf, he said. Since that much lead time was highly unlikely, there was little to do but "hide in the lee of one of the Bay Islands," he told Lohman. Lohman later recalled, "He did console me with the fact that very few hurricanes had ever traveled that far west at such a low latitude, and as such we had little to fear."

As it happens, Windjammer planned to leave the western Caribbean November 1 and not return. Passenger response for two summers had been fairly good, but logistics had been a nightmare. First Mexican officials required bribes, and then the *Fantome* ran aground on the Yucatán's windblown lee shore. The company also feared bandits enough to hire armed escorts when transporting passengers to and from the airport at Belize City. "We were hoping never to have to return to Central America," said Annie Bleasdale. "As it was, bookings had already been taken for the next summer, and we returned in June 1998." Omoa, a remote fishing village, chosen as base, was central enough to offer alternating weekly trips to the Bay Islands and Belize, but its only "attractions" were its beach and a massive, brooding fort left over from Spanish exploitation and known as "the graveyard of Honduras." Carlos Arita, a local restaurateur, built a café on Omoa Bay expressly to serve waiting guests, and he bent over backward for March, running errands, and allowing the crew to use his phone to call family and a VHF radio to call the ship. He also rounded up local workers to help clean and polish the ship on weekends for ten dollars a day plus meals. MC Tours, an established Honduran tourist company, purchased a new forty-one-passenger bus to carry Windjammer's guests back and forth from the airport in San Pedro Sula. MC's manager arranged a twenty-four-hour phone line for Windjammer requests that ranged from plantains and curry for the crew, batteries for watches, and, once, Pampers for an incontinent guest.

Still, passengers complained about the expensive airline fares to San Pedro Sula—often requiring two days of flights—and the ninety-minute bus ride to Omoa, especially the last twenty jarring, pothole-swerving miles punctuated by military-style bridges of wood beams and clattering steel plates. Along this road, vast plantations of banana, pineapple, and coconut-oil palms covered a 50-mile swath of alluvial plains. The most common vehicle on the highway, aside from the ubiquitous, gaudily painted buses named "Dios es mi camino" or "Yellow Thunder," was the fruit truck barreling to the coast to meet a Dole or Chiquita freighter. Anything grew there—oranges, lemons, exotic fruits, and coconuts—and a comparison to Eden would not have been far off were it not for the shacks along the road. Honduras had rich agricultural resources, but half its people lived on less than one dollar per day. So the first impression of Omoa on arriving guests was a medley of banana trees, wild chickens, backyards strewn with drying laundry, and a beach lined with a row of homemade *pulperías*, open-air restaurants with the decor of a Pepsi-Cola can. According to Laura-Jo Bleasdale, Annie Bleasdale's sister and the *Fantome*'s activities mate, passengers fretted about the lack of shopping.

Fantome's crew didn't like Omoa, either. They couldn't see their families in the eastern Caribbean. Officers missed fleet meetings. Supplies were hard to get. Late summer was humid and hot—the rainy season began in October. The mosquitoes were bad and sand fleas a menace. And on weekends between cruises, there was really not much to do. On Saturdays most of the crew went ashore to hang out at Carlos' bar or next door at Champa Virginia, a rustic beach place whose owner rented massive loudspeakers and hung a rotating disco ball. The crew entered through a side door, grabbed beers from the family's refrigerator, and boogied until 1 A.M. They called it the "Fantome Disco."

On the evening of October 10, Guyan March remained in his small deckhouse cabin, adding to a "chain letter" that he worked on all week and mailed to Annie Bleasdale from port. March had known Annie since 1993, when the petite dark-haired twenty-three-year-old from Liverpool hired on at Windjammer "looking for adventure and travel." On her second cruise, aboard the fleet's supply ship, *Amazing Grace*, an elderly couple insisted she meet "the young, fresh, smiley face of Captain Guyan. . . . As soon as I met him, I knew that I was going to fall in love with him," she wrote later. "He had a typical British manner of politeness, joined with the confidence and experience of greeting a million people and situations before. Besides that, he was 26 years old and very lovely."

In May 1997 March arranged for Bleasdale to be his purser aboard *Fantome*. "From that day forward, we ate, slept, played, worked, breathed everything together, all without one bad word said," she wrote. "He was so loving, so warm and soft natured. At night, besides other things, we'd just hold each other so close that you couldn't get any closer. We'd fall asleep hugging and holding hands and wake up in the morning in exactly the same position. He'd wake me up at 0600 with coffee and sticky buns. After I finished my daily duties, I'd sit on the bridge top while he was on watch. Many times, I'd just study him— he had beautiful hands—I'd watch him write his bridge night orders for the crew. Maybe somehow I knew that he was going to be taken away from me and that I had to memorize every detail and feature of him. I used to tell him he was my angel because he was too good to be true."

In August, when March and Bleasdale went back to England to meet their families, Annie decided to stay and take the four-month Offshore Yacht Masters course, the license March held. Although March loved tall ships and had a picture book of famous yachts in his cabin, Bleasdale said they planned to quit Windjammer "when the time was right and get into private yachting, buy our own boat and sail off into the sunset, him as captain, me as mate." When she kissed him good-bye August 8 she cried in front of her parents, which embarrassed her. "I had always told them that I'd never cry over a man. If only I knew just how much he would make me cry."

By October, with the weather in England raw and Annie tiring of extreme sailing, Guyan's once-a-week chain letters kept her going. "He told me that he'd never loved anyone else in his life the way he loved me. He said he loved talking about me to Laura-Jo, and was playfully upset when I sent her a letter also. My highlight of the day was going to the card shop to choose another one to send. I kept every single one of his letters and read them over and over again. He was due home December 5 after repositioning the ship. He was counting down the days. That's all I could think about. What I'd wear to go and meet him at the airport, where we'd go and what we would do."

As Guyan March added to his love letter Saturday night, Annie Bleasdale, in England, awoke with a nightmare—her third in a row. The first awoke her on October 8, the night Tropical Wave 46 was detected in Africa. "I was standing on the dock in Roatán and watching the ship roll over on its side. All the crew was trapped. . . . The next night I dreamt that the *Fantome* was in a really rough bay, the anchor was down, a huge wave came from behind and totally engulfed the ship. It was like the anchor stopped them from rising over the wave." On the third night, "I was dreaming that I was kissing him, but when I opened my eyes, it wasn't Guyan." The following night, "I was wearing a wedding dress, I was walking down the aisle of a big church. When I reached the altar, Guyan turned around but it wasn't him. It wasn't anybody I knew, but I knew I didn't want to be there with this stranger and where was Guyan? These dreams were all very unsettling and upsetting. I put them down to lack of good sleep, worrying about the exam, and missing Guyan terribly."

At midnight on Saturday, Second Mate Onassis Reyes handed the anchor watch to First Mate Brasso Frederick. It was a lovely night on Omoa Bay. The temperature was 78 degrees, the barometer 1009.1 millibars of mercury and rising. A whisper of easterly trades blew across the point of land that deflected the waves rolling in from the Gulf of Honduras, just enough to swing *Fantome* toward the east-northeast. Brasso gazed at a sky he'd seen many times. Orion, the hunter constellation, was overhead. Pegasus was falling into Belize. The North Star was low to his left, the Southern Cross on his right.

Somewhere up there in the sky also was GOES-8, a weather satellite in geostationary orbit with a photographic view of half the globe. Every eight minutes it snapped a picture of the earth's midsection from longitude 10° W, near Africa, to 140° W in the mid-Pacific, and transmitted it to the earth. After dark, the satellite snapped infrared images. GOES-8 had been a godsend for the National Hurricane Center during the 1998 season, with twelve tropical storms—eight of them hurricanes. During one thirty-five-day span, from August 19 to September 23, ten tropical storms had erupted. At one point in September, the satellite showed four hurricanes spinning at the same time, a first since 1893. The worst was Hurricane Georges, which bore like a freight train through Antigua, Puerto Rico, the Dominican Republic, Cuba, Key West, and Mobile, Alabama. Georges, which died on October 1, was the strongest and deadliest hurricane of the year, with 602 fatalities and $6 billion in property damage. As Brasso scanned the starlit sky, GOES-8 watched the newest tropical wave cross the meridian at 20° W longitude. Although 4,080 miles away, Tropical Wave 46 was moving toward the *Fantome* at the speed of a school bus.

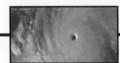

BELIZE

October 11–17, 1998

🌀

"D O I HAVE ANY VIRGIN WINDJAMMERS?"
Laurie Fischer, the *Fantome's* purser, walked through the dining saloon Sunday evening, refilling cups with rum swizzle while ignoring the chorus of rude rejoinders. A stocky woman in dress-white shorts and shirt, Fischer held up a Windjammer "doubloon," a gold-colored paper punch card.

"This is a ten-dollar card. You can buy them at the bar. They are charged to your room. Each punch is worth forty cents," she shouted above the hubbub. "So, for example, if one beer is five punches, how much have you paid for a beer?"

"Too much!" hooted one man. The crowd of fifty-some recently arrived guests, about half the ship's capacity, cheered. They were in good spirits despite the heavy rain that had greeted them in Honduras and left the air a steam bath. On the way to Omoa from the airport, they'd seen rivers brimming with turgid runoff. Where each emptied into the Caribbean, a large, balloon-shaped chocolate plume formed in the blue. The water in Omoa Bay was "filthy dirty. Everything had washed down from the hills—plastic containers, trees," one guest remembered. Sunday's rain, associated with Tropical Wave 43, paused long enough for a top deck buffet and barefoot dance under the bright mastlights. But as the ship took off at midnight toward Belize, the low-pressure stew of winds and lightning buffeted their northbound passage. At dawn, the decks were wet and the sky had a low, sullen feel to it.

"I'm sure you're thinking about the weather forecast," Guyan March said at his story hour Monday morning, October 12. "All they're saying now is unsettled weather. Which basically means a few showers." He looked across the deck. "I see there's a couple more on their way in." He hustled through a life-jacket drill: how to tie the bulky orange jackets, how to find an attached whistle and a squeeze-on light, and when to muster on the top deck to board the life rafts—white, barrel-shaped contraptions bolted along the deck edges just outside the rails. *Fantome* had eleven of these "hydrostatic" rafts designed to inflate automatically when immersed in water. Each raft held twenty-five people. "They really think of everything inside," March said. "They've got basic survival equipment, fishing kits to keep you entertained—all sorts of good things in there."

March then introduced the crew. His affection for them was obvious, as was theirs for a boss who never seemed to "order" them. Isolation in the western Caribbean had enhanced their sense of family. Rather than scattering to homes and hangouts on weekends, as they did in the Antilles, the crew, black and white, hung out together. An easy camaraderie pervaded the ship, as when Eon Maxwell once again would have to chase Cathie de Koeyer and Laura-Jo Bleasdale out of his refrigerator, where they liked to go for illicit bread rolls and lime for ceviche. They'd squeal good-naturedly and run away. Some of the men who didn't read well would ask the female officers to read them their mail when it arrived in weekly pouches from Miami. After one crewman failed a drug test and Guyan March fired him, March took the bewildered St. Vincent native in tow, flew with him to Miami—it was the man's first plane ride—bought him dinner, and took him back to the airport to board his homebound flight. "I'll never forget the look of thanks and admiration on his face when we left him at his gate," recalled Annie Bleasdale.

The ship's intimacy and casual atmosphere also fostered a sense of familiarity between crew and passengers that was unusual on cruise lines. When first introduced to guests on Monday mornings, crewmembers' nicknames and faces blurred. But as days went by, as Brasso held a midnight star navigation show, as Onassis Reyes gave an impromptu sailing lesson at the bar, as Chrispin made the preparation of salads and desserts a performance art, as Cyrus Phillips knotted a Turk's head bracelet, and as crew shined brass and served soup and rum swizzles, their personalities and family histories emerged. Guest feedback invariably praised the *Fantome*'s crew for making the trip memorable, and repeat Jammers routinely asked reservation clerks: "Who's going to be on board? Is Brasso on this trip? Chrispin?" Rarely did a guest forget a first conversation with Carl James, a slim engineer from Guyana. When asked "How are ya?" his standard comeback, delivered with a grin sparkling with one gold tooth and a Caribbean rhythm that made him sound like a West Indian James Bond, was, "Cool and deadly. Green, fresh, and young."

Yet, in many respects, the *Fantome* mirrored the divide between the Third World and the First. Like all cruise lines, Windjammer counted on a low-wage labor pool to maintain its profit margins, and the Caribbean Basin provided an abundance of cheap, often skilled labor. The thirty-four West Indian crewmembers aboard the *Fantome*, some of them physically imposing and deeply colored, disarmed American passengers with brilliant smiles, laconic deference, humor, and the good manners learned at home. Their mothers, whom most still called "Mommy," had taught them to say "good morning" and "good afternoon" to people they met and to welcome guests into their homes. Almost all had been brought up as regular Sunday churchgoers, raising the roof with gospel music sung to the beat of a steel-drum band. But behind their cheery exteriors, they worked for indentured wages. They came to Windjammer from subsistence economies. Once hired, they consented to a complicated labor transaction that was in turn exploitative and filled with opportunity.

A full *Fantome* grossed more than $400,000 per month for the Mike Burke family. The captain—who had always been white and Western—was paid $4,100 per month. The chief engineer earned $2,800 per month, and the mates and department heads earned between $1,000 and $2,200. Windjammer paid the rest of the crew a few hundred dollars per month—the range was $125 to $750—plus room and board. There was no insurance of any kind. Popular steward Chrispin Saunders made $300 per month; Colin August, $175; Alan George, $150; Alvin George, $330; and Cyrus Phillips, the bosun, $600. Put another way, a typical weekly passenger fare of $1,000 paid two to five months of one deckhand's salary.

Unlike the officers, the crew received tips. Windjammer encouraged each guest to tip $50, and in a good week with a full ship, the crew divide would be somewhere between $80 and $120 apiece. Thus, tips, which came not from company coffers but from passengers' pockets, equaled or exceeded many base salaries. Chrispin, for example, earned more than $350 in tips per month on top of his $300 salary. "They lived for tips," said Melody Filarey, a regular passenger who knew many of the crew. In sharp contrast to the officers, who were assembling marine résumés, and the white female crew, who often were enjoying career sabbaticals, the men and women of the Caribbean viewed the *Fantome* as a job that was better than anything they could find at home. By and large, they boarded *Fantome* for economic reasons: to support families, to gain experience for better jobs elsewhere, and to lay the groundwork for that most elusive of grails, a U.S. visa for travel and work.

Chrispin Saunders, twenty-six, trained in electrical wiring and moonlighting as a security guard in Grenada, found a way of life aboard ship that would have been impossible at home. His showmanship belied a quiet upbringing in a tight-knit, strict, religious family surrounded by "God Bless Our Happy Home" knickknacks. After surprising his mother, Shirlan Saunders, by jumping aboard the *Fantome* in 1995, he phoned her from different ports of call—"I'm in Trinidad. I'm in Carriacou"—excited by the novelty. "He was always bringing me something I liked," she said: clothes and shoes, white teddy bears, china fish and dolphins, a new hi-fi system. When the ship docked in Grenada, Chrispin strutted like a peacock, telling a passenger: "My dad will walk by on his way to work. He'll be so excited."

Cook Kevin Logie, twenty-four, followed his brother Neville to Windjammer after both turned their backs on the oil fields of Trinidad. Neville began as a deckhand and ended up mate on Captain Burke's private yacht in Miami. Kevin, the artistic one, needed seed money to open a combination hair salon and tailoring shop. "I told him the most he could make was five hundred dollars. Multiply that by five for the exchange rate in Trinidad, and he could save two thousand Trinidad dollars. He had no kids. You live on a boat. You don't have to pay to eat or sleep. Drink a beer once in a while. So that's how we calculated it. He could spend three years and save money and go back," said Neville. "Windjammer offered West Indians a fair chance to do something with themselves if they wanted to. The opportunity is there. The pay is not great. It will never get great. The opportunity is great."

No one aboard knew that better than Brasso Frederick, the thirty-six-year-old first mate. Born to a poor family on Antigua, Brasso followed his father and older brother, Clive, to Windjammer, first by polishing brass and washing dishes as a seventeen-year-old galley aide. He learned to sail tall ships on the job. "He wouldn't have gotten to where he was unless he had jumped on the boat," said Louise Reece, a Windjammer activities manager who was Brasso's lover when they worked together on the *Fantome*. Brasso's rank and salary of $2,200 a month were rare and phenomenal achievements for a black islander in the cruise industry, and he encouraged others while teaching them the ropes. They, in turn, told Brasso stories, like the time the *Yankee Clipper* was laid over—"knocked down," sailors call it—by a squall off Dominica. Brasso took the helm from the apparently immobilized captain, turned the ship into the wind, released the sheets, and dumped the wind from the sails, saving them from a possible foundering. When asked about his feats, Brasso would chuckle and say, "We did it together," or, "Just luck, mon," in a harsh West Indian accent that the American ear found hard to make out. A stone-faced 6-foot-3, described by one passenger as "a presence" with the strength of three, he wore a gold necklace that carried a chunk of black coral embedded with gold. "He was the tallest man you'd ever meet. He was the blackest man I ever saw. You were intimidated by his looks," said Rhonda Epperson, Windjammer's onetime personnel chief. "And then he talked to you, and you felt he was a soft teddy bear."

In a joint dream intending to make him the fleet's first black captain, Windjammer paid half of Brasso's maritime school tuition in Jamaica. But something went awry with the sequence of course work, and he didn't sit for exams. His brother Clive, who spent twelve years with Windjammer, noted that despite his nineteen years of experience, Brasso was passed over several times for promotions that went to white men. Still, he plastered the walls of his deckhouse bunk with favorite photos of yachts and tall ships, including those in the Windjammer fleet, that he dreamed of one day commanding.

Fantome owed one-quarter of its staff—eleven men—to the long, troubled history of Guyana, the former British colony on the northeast coast of South America known as the gruesome home of the late cult leader Jim Jones. A member of the Caribbean Community, Guyana had no particular maritime heritage other than being the first stop in slavery's Middle Passage during the sugarcane trade. Independence from England in 1966 was followed by a socialist, pro-Castro regime shunned by the West. In 1998 Guyana's economy was at its low point, the exchange rate 180 Guyanese dollars to one U.S. dollar. A trained nurse in Guyana made 25,000 Guyanese dollars a month, the equivalent of $138 U.S. A retired schoolmaster limped along on a government pension so puny that, given the exchange rate, his entire pension would have been depleted with one vacation to Disney World. A local gallows joke claimed that if the United States were to open its doors to unlimited immigration, Guyana would empty by nightfall. So Guyana's brainpower fled: nurses to England, teachers to Africa, and young men to the cruise industry. Lured by rumors that bartenders on Carnival ships made $1,000 a month in tips, thousands applied. Unscrupulous "agents" claiming they could find jobs on cruise ships charged up to $1,000 for nothing more than filling out a pilfered application form. Most men worked for far less than advertised, but still made far more than they could earn with their educations at home.

Electrician Vernon Brusch, twenty-six, for example, whose father worked for the "sugar estate," packed his bags full of electrical test tools in 1997 and left his parents' simple, sturdy wood house raised on stilts, telling Athelene Brusch: "Mommy, if I get work I won't be back." Brusch began with Windjammer at $125 a month, and after his promotion to ship's electrician he was earning $500 plus tips of $350. He sent most of it home as cash with shipmates to divide between his parents and the mother of his four-year-old daughter, Otaphia. On his first break, he'd given his daughter a CD storybook of Cinderella and Little Red Riding Hood. He also took his mother tablecloths, a TV, a CD player, and CDs of Ray Parker, Sheryl Crow, Mahalia Jackson, and a Windjammer collection of various renditions of "Amazing Grace." "When he sent it I played it steady," said Mrs. Brusch. "He told me they played it in the morning, this barefoot cruise, when they are raising the flag or something."

When Jerry King left New Amsterdam, Guyana, for Windjammer in 1995 at age thirty-seven, he experienced his first trip abroad, his first airplane ride, his first passport, his first foreign port, and his first significant contact with North Americans. "I hope you won't forget us," his sister, Dawn, wailed at the airport. He never did. He sent money home. He remembered birthdays. He sent large towels with "Windjammer" written on them. "Everyone wanted a piece of his clothing," said Dawn. "I got a T-shirt with stripes on it." A strapping, tall, natural athlete prone to hitting his head on the *Fantome*'s doorways, King rose rapidly to bosun's mate, the busiest man on deck. He led the deck crew in mending lines, varnishing wood, polishing brass, raising anchors, lowering the launches, caulking seams, painting the hull. King was "part of an oiled machine," said Marc Burton, a Windjammer manager who was married to one of Mike Burke's daughters. "The captain never had to tell him when or how or what to do." After three years, Windjammer paid King $275 a month. "Regardless of the salary, he knew that if he got experience, he could move on to a better job," said sister Dawn. "And he planned to move on."

Across New Amsterdam, the close-knit family of deckhands Colin and Chuckie August also lived vicariously through their travels. The men told of their sails to the French islands. They brought home photos of various ports of call and crewmates. "If they needed a hundred dollars, one of their shipmates loaned it, no questions asked," said Suzette August, their sister. Colin, known as "Coffee" on the *Fantome* but "Dovey" at birth because of his sweet and peaceful disposition, was the third of ten children. Growing up, each of the boys adopted one of their sisters to protect. "Colin was my boy," said Suzette, a nurse-midwife. "He would hide me from any whipping. He was for me, before anyone else." Colin was homesick for his wife and daughter, she said. "But he needed to make a sacrifice for his family. After three years he was making three hundred dollars a month. With tips, sometimes he sent five hundred home. 'The money's nothing much,' he told me. 'If I can find another ship, I will.'"

Deonauth Ramsudh, the rough-looking sweetheart who kept air cool and beer cold as *Fantome's* refrigeration repairman, was another New Amsterdam native. Born to a large and discordant family and nicknamed "Django," he joined Windjammer in 1995 after self-employment in refrigeration. He openly complained of the lack of insurance and benefits with Windjammer, and he hated being away from his family. He repeatedly vowed to quit and told his brother he really wanted to move to the United States. In January 1998, while gambling in an Antigua casino, Django won $69,000. He flew home immediately and established an education trust fund for his girls, who were seven, twelve, and thirteen, the oldest having just won admission to Guyana's most prestigious private school. He then returned to the ship, telling passenger Melody Filarey: "I might as well do this until I get something better. At least it enables me to send money home to my family to keep a roof over their heads and food on the table. Understand, Melody, this job is far better than anything I could get at home." Windjammer paid Django $650 per month.

With twelve-hour workdays nonstop for months, crew turnover was high. In 1996 the *Fantome's* entire "hotel" staff—cooks and stewards— quit when they were ordered to pay $75, half a month's pay, for a new Seaman's Book, a log of their hours at sea. "Most of the guys were very hardworking," said Fedor Steer, a Canadian first mate who served on the *Fantome* for six months ending in April 1998. "I made sure they got at least their one afternoon per week off because I was very sympathetic to the fact that these guys worked pretty much seven days per week for twelve months straight before they got a month's vacation. We often had brand-new guys who couldn't read or write, didn't have any experience at all, and were often not particularly bright or hardworking. They usually didn't last too long. Guyan had no problems firing people who didn't work out, but often they'd get replaced by someone else who wasn't experienced either."

Three of the men aboard were "dock hires," temporary help from Omoa who had cleaned the ship on weekends. Carlos Arita, who had recommended them, said they were paid $125 per month. Pedro Prince, thirty-three, a galley aide, had a wife and several children in Omoa. Prince told his mother that Captain March had promised him a letter of recommendation, which he hoped to parlay into a full-time job in the cruise industry. Aníbal Olivas, a quiet Nicaraguan in his early twenties who worked as a local waiter, had befriended Chrispin Saunders and had come aboard as temporary steward.

The third man, Jesús Hernández, one of eight children who had grown up on a subsistence farm outside Omoa, had a wife and two little boys of his own. Trained as a welder, he desperately wanted a visa to the United States, where his mother and brother lived in Miami. "He was proud of going to sea and excited by the prospect of meeting people from all over the world," said passenger Don Conyngham. "We talked for an hour one starlit night about how little Americans appreciate how much they have compared to others, and how much they would learn to appreciate it if it was lost. He gave me some Honduran money with maps of his country printed on it. He showed me his home area on the bill. I attempted to swap him some bills but he wouldn't accept. He joked that since one of mine was worth so many of his it wouldn't be fair." When Carlos Arita warned Hernández in October that the job was temporary and that the *Fantome* would leave for the eastern Caribbean at the end of the month, the twenty-four-year-old Jesús said, "No problem. I would like." None of the three dock hires had visas to enter another country. Still, when they looked out from Omoa at the American company's flagship anchored near the old fort, they hoped that the *Fantome* would sail them to a new world.

The tropical wave that showered the *Fantome* every few hours on Monday and Tuesday forced Captain March to create itineraries on the fly. Large clumps of fast-moving, gloomy clouds swept over the ship. Winds reached 20 knots, kicking up gray, breaking seas outside the barrier reef. If the ship had ventured out, the *Fantome*'s famous roll would have sickened passengers while washing Deck A with sheets of water. A launch, attempting to pick up mooring lines, rocked like a toy. March announced on both days that the day's "activity" would involve taking the whaleboats to a tiny island, 100 yards long and 20 yards wide, and swimming and snorkeling around it. Weather permitting, he said, the crew would serve lunch under the island's six palm trees. "Oh well," one passenger said to him after a wet day, "it wasn't bad if you were snorkeling or diving."

In contrast to Carnival Line cruise ships—"Foo Foo ships," Windjammer Barefoot Cruise passengers called them—it was a point of pride to have tasted a squall or run aground. Even breakdowns became part of the "adventure" under Mike Burke's faux pirate banner, yarns to be spun before home fires. One client offered this description of his honeymoon trip in the 1960s: "No hot water, the bunks were way small, the best time we ever had. . . . Campin' on the water with a bartender." In the 1970s, when Burke advertised for "passenger-crew" to pay for the privilege of working on his ships, Mike Alford signed up. "We had numerous mishaps and breakdowns, most of which were not too serious—failed generators, seawater backing up into the lavatories, problems with the anchor, deteriorated rigging and sails, and a general atmosphere of buccaneerism among the officers and crew. The cabins below were not well ventilated. It really stank. Most of us slept on deck. But I don't mean to complain. The trip was billed as an adventure and most of us were young and adventuresome." Kathe Swales, the *Fantome*'s first chief stewardess, remembered flushing toilets by hand with buckets of seawater. "That was wonderful. And we ran out of food, we ran out of ice, no this, no that. You just learned to live with it. You learned to lie. . . . It was the best two and a half years of my life." George Braun, a *Fantome* bosun in 1977, called his time aboard "Hard work in paradise. The things I remember: the nights we sailed with schools of dolphin escorting us under a full moon; the wave that came over the bow, carried away the wheel, and filled Captain Wynn's cabin with water; diving off the mast from 80 feet up and hitting bottom almost 30 feet down; five passengers and three crew trying to get a 350-pound grouper into the whaleboat after being foolish enough to spear it (rum swizzle didn't help)."

Even professional mariners who worked for Burke in the 1970s and 1980s laughed later at the travails they faced with the old sailing fleet. Laurie MacLeod, retired from twenty-five years with the British Royal Navy, described how the bowsprit of Burke's *Yankee Clipper* repeatedly knocked down light poles at the Nassau dock, once even tipping over a bus. He also witnessed another captain, attempting to sail the *Fantome* out of Nassau harbor, sweep the lower deck of a passing cruise liner, the majestic *Rotterdam*, shattering $30,000 in lights with its bowsprit. Credited with introducing the "Amazing Grace" bagpipe tradition to Windjammer, MacLeod was captain when the *Fantome* broke both anchors and went aground in the Bahamas during a storm in 1987. The ship tossed so badly that the galley stove overturned, requiring him to fire up barbecues for hot dogs on deck for 126 passengers. Another time his first mate, Sam Bass, another Royal Navy retiree, drank himself into a stupor over a spurned love affair with a stewardess, climbed into the rigging, and before gathered guests at "snacks and swizzles" jumped to his death in the water. "He left a letter and empty bottles," MacLeod said. "It was ruled a suicide. We wrapped him in old engine parts and buried him at sea.

"After 25 years in the Royal Navy, it was a completely different experience—playing the pirate. You had to be inventive to keep people entertained. In rough weather I used to put on my life jacket and lead the Lord's Prayer."

In sharp contrast, other professional mariners came to regard Mike Burke and the Windjammer company as amateurs in a rogue industry. This reputation arose largely from a series of disasters and deaths in the 1960s and early 1970s when Burke was expanding rapidly, hiring crew who were often inexperienced and cutting corners while operating on tight cash flow rather than credit.

In 1962 Chris Lundahl, the British captain of Burke's *Cutty Sark*, was taking his passengers for a day of snorkeling in the Bahamas when he disappeared overboard at 1:55 A.M. Lundahl, a sailor for twenty-seven years, could not swim and was not wearing a life jacket, the Coast Guard was told. Burke later claimed that Lundahl was despondent and jumped to his death, but friends, including sailing author Don Street, said an incompetent crew couldn't turn the ship around in time to save him. During a 1964 world cruise of the brigantine *Yankee*, one of seven circumnavigations Burke offered, seventy-four-year-old passenger Sarah Reiser disappeared in the Galápagos. Burke intimated to the *Miami Herald* that she committed suicide, too, even though a shipmate said she was having the time of her life. The *Yankee* eventually sailed on but was shipwrecked four months later on a reef near Rarotonga. J.D. Jones, the ship's cook, blamed the accident on a freak tidal wave that broke anchor lines and beached the ship. But before a Cook Islands board of inquiry, other crewmen and passengers said generators failed, batteries were dead, and the engines couldn't be started in time. Irving Johnson, a famous sailor who had made seven circumnavigations with student sailors aboard *Yankee* years before, wrote a letter to his alumnae describing the finale: "Windjammer Cruises made several rather half-hearted efforts to refloat her. . . . Less than a fortnight ago a hurricane swept through. . . . She lost both her masts and was severely pounded on the bottom. . . . The hull will probably stay there for many years, not a pleasant sight or even romantic anymore."

In other mishaps of those years, two divers died in accidents on Windjammer cruises and a third man disappeared off the *Yankee Clipper* near Puerto Rico. In February 1968 the chief engineer of the *Polynesia*, twenty-five-year-old John Blackman, was killed in a compressor explosion while at sea near the Bahamas. The ship, on a ten-day cruise from Freeport, ran out of fuel, then blew its sails out in a 60-knot storm and drifted for five days with thirty-seven passengers and fifteen crewmen aboard. J.D. Jones said Blackman's body was stored in the freezer until they were rescued.

Burke's crews later lost the 128-foot *Mandalay* on Triumph Reef, 20 miles south of Miami. After rescuing twenty-three passengers and a crew of twelve, the U.S. Coast Guard blamed an inexperienced crew for being 20 miles off course in a well-marked area. The "captain," as the Coast Guard punctuated the word, had no license of any kind. "The mate," according to the Coast Guard report, "had only been aboard the *Mandalay* for two days and his prior sailing experience was on his 17-foot catamaran."

These accidents earned Mike Burke the reputation among East Coast mariners as a man "who sank more schooners than any pirate."

Reminded of this history years later, Burke argued that with five trips a week, "sooner or later you are going to run into something, aren't you? We make a thousand cruises with no problem, and we travel those waters in deep-keeled schooners, not going from A to B in blue water like those Fontainebleus with a keel." Increasing his fleet required him to hand the helms to other men. "The only times my ships got in trouble were with captains with proper licenses. These proper guys take shifts every four hours. I never went below. I slept on the bridge. I'd rather have a guy with lots of balls who came up on little boats." Burke, who called himself "Captain" but never had a "proper license," lashed out at his critics. "New England yachtsmen—I call them WASPs—of course they are going to frown on me. I do more sailing in a week than they do in a year. They take good ships and put them in a morgue. They look at them. I use them. Hitherto, sailing was the sport of kings. These boats were being scrapped. Everyone thought I was crazy. 'Who's going to pay good money to go on an old boat?' they said. I started buying them up. I hurt them by buying their fancy yachts and putting firemen and nurses—poor people—on board. I pulled into Cat Cay [in the Bahamas] where they all lived and they were upset. When I first sailed into English Harbor [Antigua], it was an affront. A buddy, a magazine editor, took me to lunch at the New York Yacht Club one time. I had myself paged. 'Captain Mike Burke. Captain Mike Burke.' And there were a lot of dirty looks when I walked out. I could feel the animosity. I was in their sacred haunt. It felt good."

The story of the *Fantome*'s resurrection, near the end of this troubled period in Windjammer's history, was classic Mike Burke: a tall measure of bravado, adventure and fun, nickel and diming, a few mishaps, and success in spite of it all. In 1969, during Burke's search for larger sailing ships, a broker led him to Aristotle Onassis, another self-made man who had begun his Greek shipping empire at the abandoned Nazi shipyard in Kiel, Germany. Along with several surplus freighters, Onassis had purchased the *Fantome* in Canada in 1956 and towed her to Kiel. According to Burke, the broker said that Onassis intended to give her to "Grace Kelly as a wedding present. But something went wrong. He wasn't welcome in Monaco, so the ship went nowhere." That little embellishment became part of the ship's romantic past, published countless times in stories about the *Fantome*. However, Onassis didn't buy the ship until after the gala April 18, 1956, wedding, and he was very much in attendance, throwing the couple a party that cost him 22 million francs, complete with the biggest fireworks Monaco had ever seen. Whatever Onassis' intentions, *Fantome* remained in the Kiel Canal, rusting, freezing, peeling, and forgotten.

"She was laying on the bottom. Her deck was awash, the masts were askew, the standing rigging was rotten, the teak was peeling away from the deck," said Burke, who flew to Hamburg in 1969. "I first saw her at dawn, in a heavy fog. It was a cold and bleak day. I was quite discouraged. But I saw the beauty of her, what she could be, what she had been. I cut a deal. Onassis was stuck with it. I had no money. I did it on shoestrings." In 1972 Burke told the *Miami Herald* he paid $100,000 for the *Fantome*. In 1999 Burke said he traded two AP2 surplus freighters and $60,000.

"I cleaned her up, pumped her dry, got some generators going. I got a couple of men—I couldn't afford to pay. I couldn't get a cruising permit to take her out under her own power. So I had her towed away from the shore, out of sight. Then I took her to Skagen, Denmark. I heard they had cheaper labor than in Germany. I got her rerigged, her masts straightened. Quite a feat. Just a handful of men. No money. Everything was done piecemeal. Got her engines cleaned up and got a life in her."

"Life" for Mike Burke was a relative term, according to Terry Bewley, a British captain working with Burke's nascent fleet who was ordered to sail her to Spain for remodeling. "I remember the grass growing around the waterline. She had two propellers, but they were both like cheeses. You couldn't tell if they were left-handed or right-handed. Everything was just covered in moss, a green-gray moss." An item in a Skagen newspaper, showing a hull streaming with rust, was headlined: "The *Fantome* is not a proud swan, but she is very solid."

After shoveling snow off her deck and replacing burst pipes, American engineer Larry Otera rebuilt the huge, seized pistons, each as large as a man, and the generators. Bewley collected a ragtag crew, some Danes and several Spanish fishermen who'd been left in Denmark. "Just before I left, I got a call to phone Captain Burke. He used to always call with the most outrageous ideas. He said, 'Terry, I want you to bring the ship straight to Miami and not go to Spain. I know what you're going to say. You are going to say I need more charts.'" Bewley persuaded him to stop in Spain first. As he cast off the 282-foot ship, he learned that "the ropes holding her alongside were not the ship's. They were the dock's. I had to let them go." Bewley, a master mariner who'd navigated the *Windsor Castle*, the fifth-largest liner for the Union Castle Line in Britain, steered *Fantome* through fog and leftover World War II mines in the North Sea. "I had a little wireless. I used to key that to my ear and turn around so I could get one of the transmitters from a lighthouse. It was radio direction finding, but every mast acted like a secondary transmitter. I couldn't get a fair signal. So I had to walk up and down, turning as I went, to know where to alter course in a very shallow area of the North Sea, before heading down to the Dover Strait. A ferry came very close. We must have looked like something in the fog. A weird color—the bottom of the sea. No sails. Going very slowly."

Engineer Otera remembered stretches of bad weather when "we like to lost her." The square port windows on B Deck, designed to open on tracks, were not sealed properly and leaked. The ship rolled so far in heavy seas off Cape Finisterre that 2 feet of water washed the well deck. At one point, "the ship rolled so badly that water came into a generator exhaust port and blew a head off a cooling water pump." As they motored along, the crew began tearing the wood cabins apart and throwing the trash into the sea. After stopping briefly in Spain, the *Fantome* was sailed to Miami by a new motley crew under Windjammer captain Peter Newe. As they crossed the Atlantic, the crew scrawled notes to each other on the embossed stationery left aboard:

Swimming Ev. Day at 1600 ST if weather permits. Rum punch 16–1700

The *Fantome* got to Miami in the spring of 1971. With what became known as "Burke's Navy"—a crew of hippies, Vietnam draft dodgers, and deserters—Mike Burke remodeled the *Fantome*. "They were smoking a lot of grass. They were trying to grow grass on the stern," Burke said years later. "I would get frequent visits from the FBI. I'd get the word to the boat, 'Hide the men.' I had a Grumman Goose [sea plane]. The next day they were in the West Indies. I felt good about it. I had three sons and I would never let my sons go [to the war]."

Burke's refit didn't qualify *Fantome* for a spot on an historic ship registry. "He wanted all the cabins replaced with smaller ones," said Bewley. "I said to him, 'Why not leave the duke's study? It's so interesting. Americans love old things. We could leave it fitted out with his books and telescope, which is how Guinness left it, and use it as a quiet room away from the hurly-burly.' And he said, 'Frankly, I can get six people in there, and they pay your wages.' It all had to go. They'd nail up any old bit of wood, plywood, to make up three double cabins. It made me sick. There were so many amazing things on board. There was a catalog from a local chandler. In those days, a catalog given to a captain was leather bound and gold embossed. It must have been 4 inches thick, and everything was included, from shackles to oil-fired ranges. The captain's name was embossed on this book. All the prices were there from the duke's day. And some hippie took it away with all sorts of other stuff. I have a key tag, 'Oak Dresser Duke's Cabin.' Everything was left like that."

Before the refit was completed, Burke sold a maiden voyage. His wife, June, rechristened her, and the *Fantome* left Miami in Christmas week of 1971, packed with 130 guests, reporters, the hippie carpenters, and 40 crew—far more than he had bunks for. Picking up more passengers in Bimini, in the Bahamas, Burke ordered the ship back to sea in a norther. " 'These people are expecting a cruise. You have to go,' " stewardess Miriam Otera remembered Burke saying. "Two hours out of the channel we had at least 150 people sick and puking all over. I was sick but on my feet, and I spent the next three days cleaning up puke and laundry, doing what I could for the passengers."

And that's how the *Fantome* assumed its place as the "pride of the Windjammer fleet."

For a while in the 1970s, Burke sold penny stock in his growing empire and used the money to invest in a shrimp fleet, a seafood restaurant chain, and three cargo ships with hopes of carrying supplies to the Vietnam War. He failed completely and returned to the cruise business. As the company grew and he entered his 60s, Burke in 1986 handed day-to-day management of Windjammer to six children, who began incremental upgrades to Windjammer's fleet, reputation, and family appeal. Still, Burke's legacy cast a long shadow. He retained sole ownership, with veto power over major investments. He went into the offices every afternoon, where he retreated to a warren behind a door that was opened with a wheel, as if on a submarine hatch, and sporting a brass plaque that said, "Cap'n Burke's word is law." His portrait looked down from several walls, a striking painting of a younger, bearded Burke with a full head of hair, a wrinkled brow in a knowing scowl, gold chain showing under an open shirt, beer in hand—a man larger than life, larger even than the tall ship behind him.

In the Caribbean, his aging fleet and intimate sailing "adventures" retained their drawing power, even as mainstream cruise ships grew into behemoth, floating cocoons with climbing walls and nightclubs. For every passenger turned off by the hijinks of a Captain Paddy Shrimpton, fired in 1989 for urinating on a female guest's feet, there were ten others ready to join in the mooning of a passing Foo Foo ship. When one captain ran the *Fantome* aground off Mexico in October 1996 and was fired for it, passenger Tony Sibol reported: "The seas were washing onto the lower deck, and the pounding on the sand bar became unrelenting. I went to the cabin and got my wallet. A number of things might have happened, and most of them were bad. Looking back over this report, it sounds like a disaster. . . . Why did I have such a good time? The answer is, the people you meet on a WJ'er are the kind who just know how to have fun. We went ashore at Isla Mujeres not knowing what the rest of the cruise would be like or if we would ever get away from this island. But we had a great day and no one seemed to care if we were stuck there for three hours or three days." Melody Filarey, booked for the next week, managed to find a launch ride to the ship for what she later called the "Cruise to Nowhere." With seas of 12 to 15 feet, no one could leave. A launch took garbage ashore every day but returned with it even riper. The cooks ran out of meat. "We made jokes about the 'wet look' as we sat on the floors of our cabins drying our underwear with our blow dryers. I took great pride in leading our group in a rendition of 'There's Got to Be a Morning After' from *The Poseidon Adventure*." An undaunted Filarey sailed twenty-eight weeks on the *Fantome* in three years. Another Jammer racked up forty-six trips, and another, more than fifty. The faithful met for "Jammerfests" back in the States, get-togethers filled with insider jokes and gossip. A couple of dozen personal Web sites contained photos and trip reports, chat rooms, and memories of such events as "battles" with another Windjammer ship, complete with pirate flags and cannons firing blanks. The "Burke and Ellen" Web site included an audio version of "Amazing Grace" with this invitation: "Relax, open those photo albums, have a rum swizzle (with recipe link) and think about raising the sails."

At age seventy-five, Burke spent most of his time at home—a brooding homemade castle on Miami Beach's Back Bay. Guarded by an iron gate, turrets, and an elaborate moat with live sharks, the castle was sculpted of dark gray mud, the walls an endless revelation of gargoyles, mermaids, sea creatures, and oblong faces emerging from bas relief as if from nightmares. Inside he displayed masculine icons: a pool hall, knight's armor, guns in a case, an Arthurian sword in a stone, and a pool on the bay with a concrete dolphin sculpted in mid-jump. Prominent in the kitchen was a soliloquy attributed to Teddy Roosevelt:

> Far better it is to dare mighty things
> To win glorious triumphs, even though checkered with failure
> Than to take rank with those poor spirits
> Who neither enjoy much nor suffer much
> Because they live in the gray twilight
> That knows not victory nor defeat.

"I've lived that," said Burke, who sipped Absolut vodka while taking a regular sunset swim with *Madame Butterfly* blasting from speakers. He admitted to drugs, alcohol—"alcohol sharpens my mind"—and two palimony suits. He professed his admiration for actor Lee Marvin, "his independence, of not caring. . . . Heroes live their dreams and achieve self esteem." Burke hadn't lived with his wife, June, for twenty-two years— "It's cheaper than divorce"—though she came and went with grandchildren on whom he doted. He liked taking them sailing Sunday afternoons on his steel yacht, *Tondeleyo*, docked with its live-in crew of four in downtown Miami. Barrel-chested with thinning hair and a sideways grin, Mike Burke was a gregarious, self-made curmudgeon, at once his own best and worst public relations agent. Prone to outrageous macho epithets, he could charm a feminist. Full of boast and conceit, he was also an endearing raconteur with an endless store of self-deprecating sea tales. He could be crude. He had hardened, perhaps scabbed over, after fifty years of dealing with ships and sailors, regulations and regulators, successes and failures. But there remained a little boy inside, the one who looked out from the Jersey shore and dreamed of sailing. "My only regret," he avowed with characteristic bluntness, "is things I haven't done—the women I haven't fucked, the boats I haven't sailed."

In 1998, designated as the company's fiftieth anniversary, Windjammer Barefoot Cruises, Ltd., with six ships and five hundred employees, was grossing $25 million. Returning guests accounted for 40 percent of the business, said to be the highest return rate in the cruise industry.

The reason clearly was that a Windjammer cruise still had the feel of a private sailing party with Cap'n Burke. In the company's new brochure, he mused:

> By all that's glamorous, it is the seas. The deep and dark blue sea that can also knock the tar out of me. The sea that asks nothing and gives nothing except, sometimes, a chance to prove your strength. Mine has been a covenant with the sea. In her honor, I have built a fleet of tall ships which roam from the Bahamas to the Grenadines with mates who share my yearning. . . . I taste the salt upon my lips. I feel the scented violence of the wind. . . . The crew gives back yell for yell to a westerly gale, or tempts the sun-flecked dolphins teasing the bow, and then furls sail from topmast to boom as we make safe harbor.

The *Fantome* sailed in this bubble, a *Flying Dutchman* of rum and romance. Floating in this sparkle, there was no need to question Mike Burke's castle in the sky, until a real wind, unscented and with untold violence, blew through his life.

On Wednesday, October 14, the bad weather canceled several side excursions in Belize City, and passengers spent the day in windbreakers. Chrispin Saunders went ashore to see Faith Herrera, a cocktail waitress whom he'd met the summer before. Herrera had suffered a miscarriage earlier in the year but was again pregnant by him. She was resigned to the visitation habits of a sailor, the night here and there, a week here and there. Occasionally she would come aboard and sail a day with him to Placencia, south of Belize City. Bosun's mate Jerry King also stopped to see his Belizean girlfriend, Teresa Au Gustus, and their baby, Princess Marissa King. Ashore, he mailed a letter to his mother with photos of Princess. But he also enclosed a photo of a woman he'd met in Maryland in September. On the back of the snapshot he wrote: "This is why I miss my flight . . . the girl soon to be my wife." King also had a Guyanese wife with whom he had fathered three children.

Fantome's oral history was steamy with gossip of liaisons on and off the ship. Mike Burke had set the tone, and the close quarters of a ship in romantic settings fueled the fire. The crew and passengers were far from their homes and normal standards of propriety. Plus, the men "all had something the girls saw, whether it was the whole sailor thing, the uniform, or just that they all were gentlemen," said Laura-Jo Bleasdale. Some female guests, called "black widows," made a point of bedding West Indian crewmen while on vacation. First Mate Brasso was a "semi-legend" with women. Alvin George, a twenty-eight-year-old cook nick-named "Spice" for his native Grenada, had a smile his shipmates called a "girl trap." Engineer Rhon Austin's "baby face" had a similar effect. Wilbert Morris, a welder with a lean boxer's physique, turned eyes just by standing against a wall—arms crossed, head shaved. O'Ryan Hardware, a twenty-year-old Jamaican engineer, was regarded as the best-looking crewman and the best dancer in the Windjammer fleet. When he went ashore, "all the girls would follow," said Laura-Jo.

Fearing sexual harassment claims in the 1990s, Windjammer officially banned intimate relations with guests and discouraged fraternizing be-tween crewmembers, especially between white women and black men. The company sometimes transferred personnel to cool off emotions. Onassis Reyes, for example, was aboard in October 1998 because a rela-tionship between a mate and one of the women officers had fallen apart, according to Rhonda Epperson, the personnel chief at the time. Epperson knew only too well that close proximity and crew ratios fa-vored the heart. In 1993, newly separated and shipping with Wind-jammer as a purser to "escape from reality," Epperson began an affair with engineer Canute "Pope" Layne. A former car mechanic from St. Vincent, Layne could fix anything with a coat hanger and file and was largely credited with keeping the *Fantome* running. He'd been with Windjammer for nine years. "He was 5-foot-11, very black. He had these little skinny legs. He had wonderful muscles, and beautiful dark brown eyes, almost black," said Epperson. "We had a lot of personality conflicts. He didn't party. He rarely drank. I was loud, obnoxious, al-ways partying." Yet in November 1993 Epperson discovered she was pregnant, and she gave birth to Dannielle on July 31, 1994. "I thought we would get married and live happily ever after. Pope was chicken. He came back for the birth. I still remember his face. He gave me virtually every penny he earned to pay the bills. He always used to say, 'Yo, Yo, Yo.' He'd leave a message on the phone, 'Yo Yo Yo, Rhonda it's me. How are you? How's my baby girl?' "

Epperson, who later married Windjammer captain Pete Hall, hosted

Pope on his visit to the States in September, when he entertained her with stories about a girlfriend from Canada, a woman "down island, and some girl from Ft. Myers." He was also sleeping with nineteen-year-old Laura-Jo Bleasdale on the *Fantome*.

"We were best friends—and a little extra on the side," Laura-Jo said. "I appeared very outgoing, but inside I didn't have self-confidence. Pope helped me come out of my shell." Curled up with him in an engineer's bunk deep in the ship, "he taught me what life could be. I wanted to go and do things. He said, 'Go and do them.' The relationship we had—it would never go any further. It's hard to have a relationship on a ship. When all is said and done, it's for the company. You become so close that it's going to happen."

As the *Fantome* headed south on Wednesday evening with her sails and white masts lit up by floodlights, lightning filled the sky, but the water inside the barrier reef stayed relatively calm. Second Mate Onassis Reyes, having handed the watch to Brasso, joined the hard-core revelers at the bar and, using props and his hands to point things out above them, described how the *Fantome* sailed. A dark, handsome man with a cropped black beard, Onassis was the third son of a middle-income Panamanian family surrounded by marine potential. His father, Gilberto, ran a maritime school and recruited for shipping firms. His older sister was a maritime attorney, and his older brother was a shipping pilot. Onassis had gone through four years of State University of New York Maritime College, one of the toughest merchant marine schools in the United States, with a 60 percent dropout rate. He'd passed navigation but flunked the business side and gone off for a couple of years to log hours on a cargo ship. Signing on with Windjammer in 1997, he was a favorite relief mate, sought out by all the Windjammer captains. He had talked with his father about becoming a pilot on the Panama Canal, a prestigious and lucrative job paying up to $100,000 a year, but he loved sailing and savored the rare occasions when the *Fantome*'s twin diesels were turned off and she became a pure sailboat, with the sounds of the eternal wind on cloth, a soft purr in the shrouds, the groan and squeak of blocks and lines under tension, and the solid splash of the hull through water.

By definition both a "tall ship" and a "schooner," with a theoretical maximum hull speed of 17 knots, the *Fantome* had never carried the acres of canvas customary on historic clippers with their scores of crewmen swarming up the ratlines and out the yardarms to manhandle sails. Mike Burke had replaced the original gaff-rigged sails, with their heavy spars top and bottom, with staysails, large Dacron triangles that, when flown, were sheeted tight along the centerline of the ship. Except for the rare publicity photo, the crew didn't raise the topsails, which required risky climbing up the rigging and an effort wasted on short trips between islands. Rigged as she was, for looks and sail handling ease, the *Fantome* could not sail anywhere close to the wind. "With all sails up and a very good wind, she could probably do about 5 or 6 knots, mostly sideways. With an average wind, maybe 3 knots," said former first mate Fedor Steer. "During any kind of rough weather, we would rely on the engines and keep up maybe a couple of sails pulled in tight for appearance and to help dampen the rolling a bit." *Fantome*'s quick roll left the decks wet and passengers sick. To a man, Windjammer captains said *Fantome* "sailed like a pig."

At 2 A.M. Reyes headed for his bunk, but first he offered to show a passenger the inside of the deckhouse. Stepping down into the chart room, he pointed out the two radars and a GPS (global positioning system) navigation system. Pointing to a door on the right, he put a finger on his lips. "Ssshhh. Skip's in there. He'll kill me." Down a narrow passageway to the left were a small office with a PC, a head, and two tiny quarters for himself and Brasso Frederick. As he bade goodnight, Reyes whispered, "It's kinda like being on vacation and getting paid for it."

As Onassis crawled into the bunk of his coffinlike quarters, 6 by 9 feet and tucked back under the bridge, he could gaze up at photographs of his American girlfriend, Glenn Parkinson, taped to the ceiling over his pillow. He had met Parkinson the previous Christmas on a Windjammer cruise in Grenada. Parkinson had been with her mother. "We annoyed each other," she recalled. "But on the last night we exchanged phone numbers. Three weeks later he came to New York. We got together and fell in love." Parkinson, a social worker who specialized in trauma survivors, called Reyes "an extraordinarily attractive man." He was six-foot-one with dark hazel eyes, lean and strong and "the most alive person I've ever known," she said. On later cruises, in their nights together in his bunk, he talked to her of becoming a captain of a tugboat. "He loved tugboats," she said. Reyes was planning to join her at Christmas in New York and re-enroll in school in January.

Passengers awoke Thursday morning in the bathlike waters of Placencia, behind a Belizean barrier peninsula. It was another quiet day for activities, the most exciting of them a walk along the "world's narrowest Main Street." As they departed that afternoon, another fierce lightning storm struck. The *Fantome* rocked as she left the protection of the reef and headed southeast toward Omoa.

On Friday night, anchored off Omoa, Eon Maxwell's "Captain's Dinner" looked good enough to be an advertisement. Renowned for beautiful presentations, even of leftovers, Maxwell always wore a meat thermometer and pen in his pocket, an affectation picked up at the Johnson & Wales University's College of Culinary Arts in Florida. After seven years of catering for cruise lines, including Carnival, he went back home to Guyana to marry Alisa, a school sweetheart. But he couldn't find good work there. Three months after his marriage, in August 1995, he joined Windjammer and began to spread his ideas of style among the company's cooks, which included wearing a double-breasted chef's jacket with meat thermometer in its pocket. He always wore his collar tight, even soaking wet in the galley heat. In a food article, one writer said of Maxwell that he "looks as though he should be working in a health club instead of slicing plantains for an afternoon snack." Maxwell, in fact, was a martial arts devotee, pumping iron on the foredeck gym. "He was the Steven Segal of the *Fantome*," said Laura-Jo Bleasdale. In April 1997, when he went home for two weeks' vacation, his wife became pregnant with their first child. The boy would be one year old in December, and Maxwell planned to be there for the baby's birthday. "I wouldn't say I like living on a ship. It's tough," he told a culinary writer. "I'll work seven days a week for nine months and then take four weeks off."

At the end of the Captain's Dinner with its seafood soup, prime rib, twice-baked potatoes, and fresh bread, Captain March introduced Maxwell, who bounded up the wooden steps from the galley to the dining room like a movie star, waving and walking around. For dessert, Chrispin Saunders turned out the lights and prepared a flambé. Holding the rum bottle high, he poured it onto the hot platter.

"More?" he egged.

"More!" the Jammers shouted.

That evening, as the music cranked up at the Fantome Disco, Guyan

March received a fax reading, "I passed!" Annie Bleasdale had taken the eighteen-hour Yacht Masters exam on Thursday in heavy seas. March called to congratulate her and urged her to fly to Omoa for the last two weeks of scheduled cruises plus the two-week repositioning trip to Trinidad. She agreed, but after realizing that it would use up vacation time saved for Christmas, she called him back. "We should stay with our original plan," she said. "I'll call you next Saturday."

Halfway around the world, in Romania, another *Fantome* couple was wrestling with the same sailors' dilemma. Heila Bucur, wife of the ship's chief engineer, Constantin Bucur, was trying to persuade him to extend his month-long vacation by one week. She didn't tell him why. Bucur, forty-six, a veteran merchant mariner, had been with Windjammer less than a year. He'd worked for years on refrigerated fishing boats and all over the world on various cargo ships. But now he was torn between his love for the sea, his wife (an economist with the largest bank in Romania), and their two young children. After their second child, a boy named Vlad, was born, Heila Bucur had prevailed upon her husband to stay home. "And because he is a fantastic man—I think it is very hard to find a man like him, a father and a husband and all things—he leave the sea, and he remained home with us. He never told me, 'You are a bad wife, you oblige me to stay near my children, I want to go to the sea.' He never said something like this. But sometimes, you know, sometimes I see, looking in his eyes, and sometimes when he was speaking about the years when he was sailing, I feel he was maybe a little sad. And one day I tell him, OK, I'm thinking it is better to go back to your life." At first Bucur protested, but then "it happened someone called him and told him about this company, Windjammer."

During the night of October 16, Bucur awoke to his wife's cries of, "No, No. No. I don't want you to leave."

"What's wrong?" he said.

"Never mind. A bad dream."

In her nightmare, Constantin was "very deep into the water. I wake up crying. I try to see again this dream and I cannot tell that he was dead, but he was very deep into the water. So, you know, when I wake up, it was in my mind that he will have some problem. I have never told to somebody I dreamed something bad, because I was afraid that it would happen," said Mrs. Bucur later. "I don't tell my husband. But all this time, before he leave the house, it was in my mind to tell him,

'Please, stay. Please, call them. Please stay for one week, just one week stay more home.' So he didn't. He is a very serious person." Bucur packed his bags to return to the *Fantome* in Omoa.

🐚

On Saturday night, October 17, 1998, Tropical Wave 46 passed Barbados in the Windward Islands of the eastern Caribbean. It had been a slow ocean passage, buffeted by west-southwesterly upper-level winds that threatened to blow the wave apart. For all their nastiness, tropical waves and their bigger offspring—depressions, tropical storms, and even hurricanes—can also be fragile and sensitive beasts. Westerly winds can knock their tops off. Large, bulbous high-pressure systems can nudge them around like soccer balls. Cold fronts can drag them into the harmless chill of the Atlantic. But not Tropical Wave 46, which kept its low-pressure profile and plodded westward in a ragged and changing array of clouds stretching over several hundred miles. On one of the last daylight views from GOES-8, the clouds in the wave looked like a witch on a broom, her cape flying.

Thunderstorms were at the heart of Tropical Wave 46. They formed, like any thunderstorm, when warm, moist air rose, carrying water vapor aloft to expand, cool, and condense into clouds. When a molecule of water condenses from gas to water or ice, it releases to the atmosphere the heat of the sun that it absorbed during evaporation. Each pound of water vapor contains enough heat to boil a pint of water. This heating raised the height of the cumulonimbus clouds in Tropical Wave 46 and further disturbed the atmosphere around it, leading eventually to rain, hail, and lightning. To a mariner in front of it, the wave would have looked like a dark line of thunderstorms mixed with periods of scudding gray clouds and cells of torrential rain. Caught in one of its squalls, a yacht sailor would have reefed or lowered sails to avoid being knocked down by wind bursts of 50 knots on the advancing line. The rains would often have been strong enough to flatten 6-foot breaking waves, providing an eerie, almost peaceful interlude amidst the downpour. Typically, rain and hail cool a thunderstorm, killing it in less than an hour. Cool night air, with the sun turned off, has the same effect.

But something unusual was occurring with Tropical Wave 46. Its thunderstorms didn't stop at night. They were visible on GOES-8's infrared shots, the high, cold tops of cumulonimbus clouds showing as red splotches. The wave had become what meteorologists call a "convective engine." The "gas tank" was ocean water of 85 degrees, which evaporated into vapor and was pulled into the bases of the thunderstorms. As temperatures rose high in their columns, the atmospheric pressure was lowered at sea level. Air then flowed in from miles away in an attempt to balance the pressure. This wind, blowing across the warm ocean, evaporated more molecules of vapor, which, one by one, rose in the vertical shafts of the thunderstorms and released more packets of heat. Because of the spinning of the earth and the Coriolis effect, the wind rushing in curved to the right of the low-pressure center, establishing a counterclockwise flow near the ocean surface.

Late Saturday night, Tropical Wave 46 passed Grenada in the West Indies. It raised humidity, lowered the barometer to 1010 millibars—3 below normal—and dropped rain. In his logbook at the National Hurricane Center in Miami, forecaster Lixion Avila, a native of Cuba, made another grease-pencil slash at 62° W. He penciled beside it: "Vortmax moved over islands and produced SW winds as it went by!" Using the Spanish way of punctuating with two exclamation points, the first one upside down, he added: "¡beautiful!" "¡dream!"

In Georgetown, Grenada, high on a volcanic shelf, in a house sheltered by topography, neighbors, and vegetation, the sound of a huge tree landing on the roof awoke Shirlan and Clarence Saunders. It sounded as if it had fallen on the corner over Chrispin's empty room. When Clarence looked out, there was nothing on the roof. The tree closest to the house, a tamarind, was untouched and still. At daybreak, he could find no marks and no debris. A neighbor woman told Shirlan it was a "sign." Tropical Wave 46 was 1,680 miles from the *Fantome*.

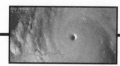

BAY ISLANDS, HONDURAS
October 18–24, 1998

🍥

U NDER NEAR-PERFECT SKIES, *Fantome* sailed again Sunday for the Bay Islands: Utila, Roatán, Guanaja, and Cayos Cochinos. The ship carried ninety-four passengers, half of whom were veterinarians and their partners attending on-board classes on dog and cat cancer. The cruise had an unusual, tempered air, perhaps because the ship's season in the Gulf of Honduras was drawing to a close. When not involved in their four daily hours of pet oncology, the vets did their share of swizzling rum and diving in warm water that teemed with life. While they studied the latest techniques for diagnosing and treating tumors, Captain March maneuvered the 1,200-ton *Fantome* into and out of islands the old-fashioned way—by eye.

Though surrounded by velvety blue and mauve waters, the Bay Islands are a navigational challenge for mariners. The few nautical charts of the area are of such gross scale and age as to be virtually unusable. Forty known islands are charted, but there are scores of half-submerged banks, cays, and coral columns that go unnoticed on a calm day. They only show their rocklike faces when winds pick up, terrifying sailors as seas break over them. The coral reef, said to contain 95 percent of all known Caribbean coral species, grows at the rate of one foot every five years, a kind of creeping underwater ledge that constantly creates new hazards to the bottom of a boat. The marshy, foul coastline of Honduras to the south also changes constantly as rivers wash soil into the sea. Navigating in the Bay Islands requires what sailors call "local knowledge." Even the U.S. National Imagery and Mapping Agency's *Sailing Directions* describes the approach to Utila like this: "The entrance must be navigated by eye . . . a church steeple, in line bearing 20 degrees with a prominent tree, is the leading mark used by local pilots." In 1998 a stake in the coral reef was the only "navigation aid." Roatán was better but still tricky; the *Sailing Directions* recommended that when approaching Coxen Hole, the main harbor, ships line up a "conspicuous white church, with a red roof and a square bell tower." On Tuesday, October 20, padding barefoot around the bridge and the deckhouse roof, calling directions to the helmsman and radioing twin-prop commands to the engine room, Captain March guided *Fantome* toward the bell tower and against a T-shaped concrete dock built for cruise ships. The dock touched *Fantome* 3 feet below the B-deck portlights.

Long and skinny, 28 miles by 2 miles, Roatán looks like a section of the Continental Divide in the Rocky Mountains, except that the crevasses and ridges that fall away from the spine disappear into water. Roatán is, in fact, the top of a mountain, an extension of the Omoa range, and the "canyon" between the island and mainland is 4,000 feet deep, a crevasse that runs east past Guanaja and that may be the source of the name Honduras, which in Spanish means "depths." Roatán's south side is scalloped into a dozen deep bays and bights guarded by treacherous coral heads, sand shoals, and shipwrecks. Though deep, the bays must be entered through openings fifty to two hundred yards wide. In a space no longer than a whaleboat, the water depth changes from five feet to seven hundred. Anchoring is impossible where the bottom drops off like a cliff. But since buccaneer days, boats have tucked into the deep inlets to escape storm or discovery. A trace of pirate blood from English sailors and runaway slaves still runs through the shrimpers who, with local knowledge, move in and out of Dixon Cove, French Harbor, Oak Ridge, Calabash Bight, Jonesville, Port Royal, and Old Port Royal. The *Sailing Directions* gives this outdated, homespun advice for entering Port Royal, on Roatán's eastern end: "In 1938, the 0.1 mile wide channel between the reefs had reported depths of 5.5 to 8.2 meters. The eye is sufficient guide as the reefs are steep-to and easily seen. A good landmark is the 224-meter peak that stands west of the harbor."

The north side of Roatán is one long coral reef with bountiful diving and snorkeling. Scuba divers have their pick of walls, caverns, tunnels, wrecks, and the rare pillar coral. Anthony's Key Resort, built around a heavily wooded cove and mangrove island on the northwest coast, arranged a day dive for twenty *Fantome* guests on Tuesday. A classy hotel, Anthony's offered several dive boats, a decompression chamber, and a pod of wild dolphins conditioned with food to come when signaled for videotaped encounters with divers.

As *Fantome* passengers frolicked with dolphins, a roomful of forecasters at the National Hurricane Center in Miami was watching Tropical Wave 46. In the previous two days, its cluster of thunderstorms had moved 600 miles westward to longitude 71° W and latitude 12° N, just off the northern Venezuela–Colombia border. From the GOES-8 satellite, the wave now appeared as a large white clot two hundred miles across, barreling west at 21 knots. What caught the forecasters' eyes was a telltale movement, apparent on large computer screens that captured the last eight photographs from GOES-8, shot over four hours and strung together in a constantly repeating loop. Over and over this jerky, four-second video showed clumps and gauzy strips of clouds beginning to curl around a point, as if sucked in by a magnet.

To tropical storm analysts this was a sign of "organization," a profane and inadequate word to describe one of nature's most beautiful mysteries, the transformation of chaos into order, of perturbation into cyclone. Atop the counterclockwise whirling of thunderstorms at the ocean surface, they detected high cirrus clouds turning clockwise. This "anti-cyclone" vented the air stripped of vapor and heat to the outer perimeter of the storms below. From there, the cooler, relatively dense air could fall back to the ocean and rush back in over the sea surface to replace the rising air at the center of the cell, gathering more moisture along the way. The mechanics of this rare alignment were not well understood, nor did "organization" adequately describe what, from GOES-8, resembled a star forming in space. Out of wild and random weather—warm water, low pressure, a lazily spinning tropical wave— molecules of air began arranging themselves around a central, organizing force. There was an ignition, and a vortex roared to life. It was a birth, really, and a thrill to watch. Hurricane experts live for it.

Several of the center's computer models already were predicting a full-scale hurricane from the cluster. Sorting data from weather balloons around the world, sniffing wisps and puffs and troughs sampled from the infinity of the globe's atmosphere, the models sensed rapid intensification. By late morning on Tuesday, Jerry Jarrell, the craggy director of the National Hurricane Center, thought it was time for an investigative flight. As helpful as the models and satellite pictures were, they could not measure barometric pressure or wind speeds near the ocean. That still took a human hand, and it was the policy of the National Oceanic and Atmospheric Administration (NOAA), parent organization of the National Hurricane Center and all U.S. government weather agencies, to fly into all potential hurricanes west of longitude 55° W. The planes and crews were furnished by the Air Force Reserve at Keesler Air Force Base in Biloxi, Mississippi. John Pavone, the Hurricane Center's flight coordinator, asked the on-call crew to prepare a flight for the following afternoon. That would give forecasters time to look at Wednesday morning's satellite pictures and call off the flight if the wave dissipated.

At 10:53 A.M. Tuesday, John Hope, a retired National Hurricane Center hurricane specialist working at the Weather Channel, went on the air for his regular tropical update to show the world what his former colleagues in Miami were watching. Pointing to the clouds just north of Colombia, Hope said, "There is pretty good evidence of organization. . . . This does have the potential to become a tropical depression."

After leaving Roatán near midnight, the *Fantome* arrived at the island of Guanaja, shortly after first light on Wednesday, October 21. Captain Guyan March anchored in a quiet bay a quarter mile from shore. The route in, between two small cays covered with palm trees and private homes, caught the attention of even the landlubbers on board. The unmarked "channel" was barely wide enough for the 40-foot-wide hull, and passengers looking down from the deck could see the dark brown stain of reefs on either side. At his morning story hour, March adopted his command stance and began: "Here's what there is to do on Guanaja." In the silence that followed, guests finally realized he was making a joke.

Guanaja is another Honduran mountaintop surrounded by ocean. From its rugged central peak jutting 1,400 feet above the harbor, the land descends 8 miles northeast and southwest over lumpy slopes. Columbus called the island "Isla de los Pinos" after a thick cover of evergreens. Timbering and periodic fires, usually caused by trash burning, had denuded and blackened large tracts of land. One fire, fanned by the trade winds, had swept through a stand of trees only a week before. A physically difficult, steep-sided landscape, the island did not have a single motor vehicle. The only way to travel was by boat or by puddle-jumper plane to the Honduran mainland.

Guanaja's population was an isolated, fractious cultural gumbo of German millionaires, Honduran laborers, Seventh-Day Adventists, Baptists, and shrimpers and lobstermen descended from English pirates. Along the rocky shoreline, shacks and estates faced the same water and shared the same vistas. The descendants of white settlers speak English and an English-derived patois and have more in common, historically, with the British Caymans than with Spanish Honduras. In 1998 most of the islanders lived in one of four jumbled clusters of stilt houses erected over the water to avoid the dreaded sand fleas and to take advantage of sea breezes and tidal waste disposal. Houses were reached by boat or by way of swaying, rickety docks. Three of the clusters were on the south side of the island: Bonacca, Savannah Bight, and East End Village. On the northeast side, reachable through a canal that slices the island in half, was the stilt settlement of Mangrove Bight.

Guanaja also had a handful of resorts and expatriate compounds that fit everyone's vision of "Fantasy Island." On the western tip, for example, David Greatorex, a British transplant, had carved West Peak Inn, a kayaking resort, out of 30 palmed, beachfront acres. Over twenty years he had built a thatched-roof bar and restaurant, six guest cabins, a greenhouse, and an employee cabin. He stayed in this paradise while his wife, Jean, took reservations in California. Halfway up the island's north coast, the Bayman Bay Club, a diving resort, looked like a Malibu Beach house. Its gorgeous cabins with their louvered wood windows clung to a pitch flowing with vines and flowering broad-leafed plants. Manager Don Pearly and his staff descended a three-story ladder-stairway to reach their dock.

Farther east, on the island's northernmost point, Doug and Mary Solomon had built an elegant family compound at Black Point, an area named for a huge boulder that rose from the sea 100 yards from the Solomon property. Their side of the island was much more beautiful and varied than the south, with mangroves, soft folds of pastures, and granite cliffs, broken here and there by native pine and the occasional palm. The reef was close to the land, about 400 yards out, and the fishing made starving an impossibility. The Solomons, both in their late fifties, had set off from South Africa in 1978 with their two children in a 30-foot sailboat, the *Sundance Kid*, to roam the world. They landed on Guanaja in 1996, sold the boat and settled. Because sea level was only a foot below their sandy spit of ground, they erected telephone-pole-sized posts and built an elevated, 60-foot-long, air- and light-filled house. Surrounded by mahogany furnishings covered in Guatemalan fabric, gray-haired Mary Solomon arranged her earthly possessions, including all the journals and photos of their world cruise. Doug, a sturdy 5-foot-8 with dimpled, handsome face, fashioned a self-sustaining universe with a diesel generator, photovoltaic electrical panels, and rain catchers. They planted the property with bougainvilleas and bananas. In two years it had grown into a tropical garden. In keeping with her seafaring ways, Mary Solomon each day turned on a single sideband radio and called sailing friends around the world. On Columbus Day 1998, she hosted her first real party to show off their new home and garden. Their vista was enduringly, almost achingly beautiful. After twenty years of roaming, they felt, finally, they had a home for life.

Across Guanaja, on the south side, *Fantome* was anchored directly in front of the island's classiest diving resort, Posada del Sol. The resort offered reef trips, a small sandy beach, and a lovely deck around a pool adjacent to a bar. Built in heavy-beamed Spanish hacienda style with an orange tile roof, it was the kind of place that made barefoot passengers in T-shirts feel elegant. Before the passengers headed to the bar, though, Guyan March challenged them to a "No Excuses" hike, a race against him and the crew up a steep streambed to a ridge above the resort. For those who huffed and puffed up, the view was spectacular. The bay below them was framed by an archipelago of small, coral islands that arced from Black Rock Point on the left to the stilt community of Bonacca on the right. Each island resembled a private estate jammed with jungle vegetation and palm trees. Past the arc of islands, clearly visible 25 miles away, lay the north coast of Honduras, with Trujillo, a major banana port, and Santa Rosa de Aguán, a Garifuna Indian village built on the sandy delta where the Río Aguán meets the Caribbean.

The day at Guanaja was idyllic. Snorkelers near the seawall were treated to rays, barracuda, a big, shy eel, and other tropical fish. The water was unusually warm, 82 degrees Fahrenheit at 80 feet down. Veterinarian Alex Patterson hired a water taxi and took the oncology instructor, Dennis Macy, to see Patterson's new beach house next to Savannah Bight. It was built on pilings off the sand beach, with an airy dayroom and front porch over the water. Two hundred yards behind, nestled up into the hillside, Patterson's sister had a house, complete with a concrete cistern designed to catch rainwater. Macy asked Patterson about adjoining lots for sale, and they hiked along a jungled path under palm trees and past envy-inspiring retreats built by Americans in recent years. "Oohh, this is not too bad," Macy remarked.

As lunch was served aboard the *Fantome*, Hurricane Hunter Teal-43, a lumbering four-engine C-130, left its Mississippi base to take a look at the swirl of clouds 600 to 700 miles southeast of Guanaja in the great cavity of the Caribbean north of Panama. Lixion Avila, the hurricane forecaster, had taken a look at the satellite photos and penciled beside Tropical Wave 46: "Exploded on the 21, looks like a TD [Tropical Depression]. We will see!" The swirl's image from GOES-8 looked remarkably like a small nuclear bomb.

Sometime that afternoon, *Fantome* passenger Ron Hale and his wife were walking along Guanaja's shoreline and happened upon a group of men gathered around a shortwave radio. A tinny voice from far away was discussing a storm. The consensus was that it posed no threat to Guanaja, but Hale rushed back to the bar at Posada del Sol like a man with gold nuggets.

"I've got news on Mitch," he said to someone.

The response was, "Who's Mitch?"

In the parlance of tropical weather, a tropical "wave" graduates to a tropical "depression" when wind begins to circle around a low-pressure center. If sustained wind speeds reach 34 knots, it becomes a tropical "storm" and is given a name. If rotary winds reach 64 knots, the storm becomes a baby hurricane. Naming storms was first widely practiced in World War II when military meteorologists, trying to keep multiple typhoons separate in the minds of commanders, began using the names of their girlfriends and wives. Caribbean forecasters followed suit in 1953. In 1970 hurricane forecaster Gil Clark was asked to draw up ten-year revolving lists of women's names. He consulted baby books and eliminated any name that would be a double entendre in French or Spanish, languages spoken in the Caribbean. He also used every woman's name in his own family, assuring his daughter Roxanne that she was too far down the alphabet to be embarrassed. In 1978, under pressure from the women's movement, the World Meteorological Organization added male names, alternating gender storm by storm. Bob became the first memorable "male" hurricane a year later. Clark's own name, Gilbert, used in 1988, still held the record for the most intense Atlantic storm in history, barometrically speaking, with a low pressure measured off Jamaica of 888 millibars. Roxanne also became a hurricane in 1995. If there was to be a Tropical Storm 13 in 1998, after christenings of Alex, Bonnie, Charley, Danielle, Earl, Frances, Georges, Hermine, Ivan, Jeanne, Karl, and Lisa, it would be called Mitch.

As word of the developing depression spread, people called it Mitch for convenience' sake. Ham networks used its handle and location. Belizean and Honduran broadcast stations buzzed with its possible threat, and local mariners on VHF bands gossiped about a disturbance named Mitch. The Internet carried reports to Central America, where many dockside bars had a satellite dish tuned to the Weather Channel or its local equivalent, the Caribbean Weather Channel, which aired classical music with photos from GOES-8. These reports touched off warnings, discussions, regurgitation, speculation, and sometimes exaggeration. The effect, by midweek, was that the possibility of a tropical storm named Mitch was no secret.

Captain March would have known it at 4 P.M. on Wednesday, when he eyeballed *Fantome* back through the Guanaja reef, hoisted sails to the strains of "Amazing Grace," and set a course of 240 degrees, southwest toward Cayos Cochinos, the Pig Islands, 20 miles south of Roatán. It was a beautiful evening. Fibrous "mare's tail" clouds curled into the sky from the east. For once the trade winds were not bucking the current, which often causes boisterous seas and a 10-degree roll across the strait even in fair weather. As if to signal a pleasant trip, a school of dolphins leaped in play as the ship sailed toward the sunset.

The *Fantome* was reasonably equipped to receive timely weather forecasts and storm warnings. The bridge had a two-way single side-band radio for long-distance communications and weather broadcasts, a VHF radio for line-of-sight transmission and reception (up to 30 miles or so), AM-FM receivers, cell phones, and a satellite telephone that allowed both voice and e-mail transmissions. The *Fantome* also carried a weather facsimile receiver—commonly known as a weather fax and designed to receive and print out weather maps and satellite photos from broadcast stations around the world—but it was not operating. According to Guyan March's brother, Paul, the ship was in a poor reception area. But he said March tuned to the shortwave forecasts on the single sideband radio every six hours and directed his mates to do likewise and record the data in *Fantome*'s log. "When he came out of his cabin, he would look at the book," said Paul. The basic forecasts from the National Hurricane Center were widely available over shortwave and commercial radio frequencies. Shortwave broadcasts from the United States gave the location of a storm and its forecast positions for 12, 24, and 36 hours ahead. March was a particular fan of David Jones, a British accountant turned "Caribbean Weather Man" who created the Caribbean Weather Net for yachters in 1993. Based in Tortola in the British Virgin Islands, he transmitted on single sideband twice a day, at 7:30 A.M. and 5:30 P.M., the official forecasts for the entire Caribbean plus his interpretation of a U.S. Navy forecasting model available on the Internet. "He is forty-eight hours ahead [of the National Hurricane Center]," said Paul March. "This guy will go back across the Atlantic and tell what's coming in a week's time and what might develop." After Jones broadcast his synopsis, listening yachts from around the Caribbean would call in their weather and ask his opinion about their travel plans. For five days, Jones had been talking to a woman aboard *Dreamcatcher*, a sailing yacht in San Andrés, an island off Nicaragua, 180 miles southeast of Cabo Gracias a Dios. The woman was looking for a "weather window" in which to sail to Roatán, a passage of some 400 miles, to meet a group of friends for a Bay Islands cruise. On Tuesday, October 20, "she became quite agitated when I advised her not to make the passage," Jones said later. "Although the current weather conditions were favorable, I did not like the look of the concentrated core of convection activity near 70° W. I remember saying that of course it was their decision to make, but if they were to ask me if I would make the passage, I would not!" On Wednesday, a yachter named Jack on *Velella* called Jones from the Río Dulce, a popular cruising river in the corner of Guatemala emptying into the Gulf of Honduras. Jack, too, wanted to head to Roatán. "Jack was doing a circumnavigation of the Caribbean and had been checking with me fairly regularly." He advised Jack to stay put.

As dark fell on the Caribbean Wednesday evening, there was still enough light to illuminate the tops of the stark white cumulonimbus anvil heads that the C-130 Hurricane Hunter plowed into 200 miles off the Colombian coast. Flying a cross-shaped pattern 1,500 feet above the ocean, the Hurricane Hunter found a "tight center" of low pressure at 12.8° N, 77.9° W, measuring 1001 millibars, about 9 millibars below average for that area. Steady winds of 30 knots were punctuated by higher gusts. Clearly the disturbance had become a tropical depression and was approaching the strength of a tropical storm. At 7:15 P.M. the crew e-mailed the data to the National Hurricane Center in Miami.

Forecaster Lixion Avila read the dispatch and rolled his chair to a screen that displayed the forecast tracks of a dozen computer models. Each track was a different color. Together, they resembled a bundle of colorful straws blown and bent by a breeze. Streaks of rose, yellow, green, and blue pointed generally west toward Cabo Gracias a Dios. A couple of the models sent the storm right through Nicaragua and Honduras, but most bent their straws in a gradual ninety-degree turn north on a track between the Cayman Islands and Honduras' Swan Island. Moving a cursor mouse on a pad, Avila drew a white line roughly through the middle of the bundle. He placed square dots where he estimated the disturbance would be in 12, 24, 36, 48, and 72 hours. He then rolled his chair to a blank screen and began to type:

BULLETIN
TROPICAL DEPRESSION THIRTEEN ADVISORY NUMBER 1
HURRICANE HUNTER PLANE FINDS THE THIRTEENTH TROPICAL
DEPRESSION OF THE SEASON . . .

Transmitted a little before 11 P.M. Miami time on Wednesday, October 21, the advisory predicted that Tropical Depression 13 would strengthen quickly into a tropical storm and become a hurricane in 48 hours. By that time, Avila predicted, TD-13 would be only 60 miles from Cabo Gracias a Dios, but turning northward. In his written analysis, available on the Internet but not broadcast to ships at sea, Avila admitted difficulty in determining the storm's direction. He estimated it at 290 degrees (or northwest) at 8 knots. He said the depression could fall apart from high-level wind blasts, but "most of the models are forming a large upper-level anticyclone over the western Caribbean in about 36 hours, a pattern which is more conducive for strengthening. The official forecast places a hurricane between Swan Island and Grand Cayman by 72 hours, a potentially dangerous situation for the northwestern Caribbean." The center of Tropical Depression 13 was 650 miles from the *Fantome*.

"Red sky in the morning—sailors take warning." The old mariner's adage drifted through the mind of more than one passenger as they climbed the stairs to the *Fantome's* party deck on Thursday, October 22. The morning was warm, but a veil of high, thin clouds was moving in from the east and Captain March mentioned Tropical Depression 13 at his story hour. He had marked its center on a large laminated map of the Caribbean. It appeared to be stalling and "shouldn't bring us any bad weather," he announced.

But throughout the Caribbean, TD-13 was putting people on edge. A developing storm is the dark cloud in this tropical paradise, tending to dominate thoughts and moods, daily steps and future plans. For mariners and their families, particularly, hurricane season is punctuated with tense days of worry intensified by separation. Guyan March made sure the crew knew about every storm and its possible threats to home islands. That week, too, the pending return of the *Fantome* to the eastern Caribbean was in the thoughts of forty-odd households. In Grenada, Margaite George, mother of crewmembers Alvin and Alan, dreamed that she'd lost two pairs of shoes. The next night, the *Fantome* came to her in another dream. She watched the boat catch fire and go down. And in Guyana, Sherry Jallim, wife of carpenter Deodatt Jallim, awoke sobbing from a dream in which her husband was dead. "My mother-in-law said I was just thinking about him," she said later.

As the *Fantome* anchored inside the coral reef of Cayos Cochinos and the deckhands lowered the launches for another fine day ashore, the crew seemed preoccupied, almost weary. For the first time, on the grease-pencil storyboard mounted on its easel near the Sea Chest, the activities mate mentioned Tropical Depression 13 along with "BBQ on the beach."

A few hours later, as the galley crew packed up lunch and returned to the boat, a second Hurricane Hunter plane flew into TD-13 and found wind gusts of up to 51 knots at 1,500 feet, or an estimated 40 knots at sea level. The barometric pressure was down another millibar, to 1000. That afternoon, John Hope of the Weather Channel announced, "We expect that at 5 P.M. it will be a tropical storm. If so, it will be tropical storm Mitch."

Watching TV at home in West Chester, Pennsylvania, Karyn Rutledge blurted, "Oh my God!" and called her boyfriend. They were booked on the *Fantome* in three days. She braced herself for a call from Windjammer canceling the trip.

The National Hurricane Center's 5 P.M. bulletin not only announced the birth of Tropical Storm Mitch but warned that it would soon strengthen into a hurricane. The center backtracked on its initial forecasts of rapid movement west and north. Instead, Mitch was nearly stationary, turning in a "cyclonic loop" much like the bottom of a child's spinning top, and in fact it appeared to be south of the first estimates based on an indistinct eye. Still, nearly all the computer models showed Mitch eventually moving northwest and then north. At 11.5° N, 77.6° W, Mitch was 670 miles from the *Fantome* in a straight line across the Mosquito Coast.

🦜

Before leaving Cayos Cochinos on Thursday, Guyan March offered a tour of the *Fantome*'s deckhouse and engine room, parts of the ship passengers didn't normally see. Veterinarian David Horne, a nonsailor, was surprised at what he saw—a deckhouse of angelique tongue-and-groove over plywood, attached to an angle iron frame that was bolted to the deck. In heavy seas, it seemed, this structure, containing the ship's vital electronics, would be vulnerable to boarding seas. The outside helm, of course, was entirely exposed. "It didn't make any sense," Horne said later. "I asked the captain, 'So, let's say you're in a big storm, and you've got waves breaking over the bow. Obviously your electronics room is going to take a direct hit. Where is your alternate wheelhouse?'" Captain March's response, Horne said, was nervous laughter. "We just strap Brasso on and he can steer it."

That evening, a downpour forced the dress-up party into the dining saloon below. "The ship was really rolling," said one passenger. "It would roll to one side, and a whole river of rainwater would pour off the top deck. It was pretty impressive." The rain also leaked through the deck into one of the Admiralty suites, staining clothes in its closet with a varnish-colored water.

Guyan March wore his usual sleeveless number to the party, with vast amounts of rouge. Melissa Fryback, who won the costume contest for her portrayal of a pregnant sailor about to give birth, and her husband, Chad, dressed as an "ignorant slut," led a group of people up to the party deck to dance in the warm, windy downpour that was pooling 4 to 5 inches deep. "We were kicking water up on each other. Chrispin, in an iridescent bra, danced wildly, a kind of punta, a rhythmic shimmy. We were all screaming, 'Can it rain any harder? Harder! Harder!' We were taunting Mother Nature."

Later that evening, during a break in the weather, Second Mate Onassis Reyes led a knot-tying class at the bar and smoked a fat Honduran cigar offered him by a group of women. At some point Captain March walked by and chatted to someone about the storm. "We're keeping our eye on it. We're not worried about it," he said. "It barely registered," one of the women said later. "I got the feeling, how he said it, it must have been off in the distance."

As the *Fantome* slipped westward toward Omoa, Tropical Storm Mitch began moving north at 5 knots. Puzzling over the suite of computer models, Lixion Avila forecast a Category 1 hurricane within 24 hours but noted in his written discussion that "the [track] models disagree beyond 48 hours." Two of his favorites now turned the cyclone sharply westward toward Cabo Gracias a Dios, while all the others showed a north, then northwest track. Nearly all of them predicted that Mitch would be near the Yucatán Channel off Mexico in five days. "It appears that we are going to be busy for several days. Interests in the western Caribbean should closely monitor the progress of this system, which could become a potentially dangerous hurricane."

Friday morning in Omoa dawned beautifully clear. A handful of *Fantome*'s guests visited local waterfalls with MC Tours. Others walked around town. Eight passengers had signed up for a second week to see Belize, and others were considering it, including the mother and niece of Purser Laurie Fischer. Her mother was ailing, and the niece was supposed to return to school classes. When they asked Captain March about the weather, he "didn't appear concerned about Mitch and its impact on the next sailing," recalled one guest who was there. In fact, there was speculation from the National Hurricane Center by late Friday morning that Tropical Storm Mitch might break up, though the official forecast still called for a Category 1 hurricane by Saturday night.

That evening in Omoa a group of local children, dressed in pink and orange costumes, came aboard to dance barefoot on the top deck. At the Captain's Dinner, Steward Chrispin Saunders made a Caesar salad to begin the meal. The making of the dressing was a standup act.

"You want garlic? More? More? Yeah. A little dark pepper. Mustard. Lemon juice. Egg."

His whole body wiggled as he stirred the eggs.

"Vinegar. Worcestershire sauce. Anchovies? No? Yeah."

The passengers were rowdy now, bellowing their answers as he played their appetites.

"Olive oil. A leeetel ahliv oyle. A little Parmesan cheese."

Using two salad plates he scooped up bowlsful. People were clapping. Captain March stood up and lifted a champagne glass.

"First of all, I'd like to propose a toast to the four things in life: lying, cheating, stealing, and drinking. If you lie, be it to save a friend. If you cheat, cheat death. If you steal, be it to steal the heart of a loved one. And if you drink, be it to toast long life, health, and happiness. Cheers."

He introduced all the crew again. Forty-two men and women paraded through the saloon, waving and bowing to applause. Chef Eon said, "Those of you leaving tomorrow, God bless you all. Later."

"Hope you enjoyed the cruise," said March. "Hope we'll see you back again with Windjammer in the near future. Thank you for staying with us."

The night ended in the dark with Chrispin's flaming Cherry Jubilee. Holding a bottle of rum high overhead, he kept asking, "More? More?"

The crowd was with him.

As another Hurricane Hunter plane droned south to rendezvous with Mitch Friday evening, weather officer John Talbot and veteran technician Mike Scaffidi expected a routine, even boring night. Their colleagues' last flight had spent hours nosing through Mitch at an altitude of 1,000 feet and found nothing higher than 40-knot winds. Talbot had programmed into the plane's GPS the target coordinates for the storm's last fix. "We were going to fly around down low during the night, 1,000 feet above the water. It wasn't doing anything. It wasn't strengthening."

Scaffidi, a stocky chief master sergeant with twenty years of hurricane flying, had made some coffee in the back bay to wash down the junk food he usually carried, Dunkin Donuts and deli snacks from a 7-11. Nicknamed "Drop" for his job—shoving weather-data "dropsondes" out a tube in the floor—Scaffidi was part of that swashbuckling fraternity descended from an army flight instructor named Joe Duckworth, who, on a dare from fellow pilots, flew an AT-6 trainer into a hurricane near Galveston, Texas, in July 1943—becoming the first human to fly into a hurricane eye. Hurricane Hunters remained volunteers in 1998. They described their jobs as mostly a grind, a dozen wearying hours of noise and vibration to fly into the unthinkable heart of a storm. But those cowboy moments were the source of their unique identities forged of equal parts meteorologist and the "right stuff." They reveled in both the rock 'n' roll flights and the dramatic retelling back home.

"After twelve hours, when you walk off the airplane and turn on the TV and there's the Weather Channel and it's a major storm and there's your sea level pressure, there's your data, they've just moved a warning or watch, there's nothing like it in the world. That was mine!" said Scaffidi.

An hour away from their rendezvous with Mitch, the National Hurricane Center radioed Talbot of a dramatic increase in heavy thunderstorms in the system that could make it dangerous to fly in low. Downdrafts could put them into the water. "Something didn't feel right," said Talbot. "So we made the decision to go in at 5,000 feet, just to be on the safe side." With the targeted fix still 60 miles ahead, Talbot noticed with alarm that winds were increasing, and a dark large cell had blossomed on his radar, right beside the plane. "That's where the center is," he told the crew. They banked hard. Winds were 65 knots on the first pass. Ninety minutes later, they were 97 knots on the southern, supposedly weaker side. "Here it had been just a weak tropical disturbance for several days," said Talbot. "All of a sudden it just took off."

> *BULLETIN*
> *5 AM EDT SAT OCT 24 1998*
> *MITCH STRENGTHENS RAPIDLY INTO A HURRICANE . . .*

The computer models had been right on one count. In 53 hours, Mitch had exploded from a tropical wave to a hurricane. Infrared cameras on GOES-8 now showed a "ragged eye." Mitch was moving north-northeast, 015 degrees, away from Central America, in the general direction of Jamaica. But the computer models showed "a rather sharp bend in the track toward the left after about 24 hours. In fact, none of the dynamic models have Mitch north of 17N by 36 hours," the analysis reported. The ninth hurricane of 1998 was centered at 14.3° N, 77.7° W. If this forecast was correct, in 48 hours, Mitch would be 500 miles from the *Fantome* and moving toward the Yucatán.

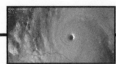

OMOA AND MIAMI
October 24–25, 1998

❦

D EEP IN A CONCRETE BUNKER bristling with antennas, the world's weather, including Miami's, appeared only as an abstraction. So secure was the National Hurricane Center that forecasters were sometimes surprised, upon leaving their shifts and swinging open the heavy steel and glass front doors, to find an overhead thunderstorm booming and pelting rain. The beamed portal resembled that of a subway station, and inside, the impression of industrial strength was reinforced by hallways of rough concrete, exposed pipe, and stainless steel pillars, interrupted only by framed front pages of newspapers with headlines like

"The Big One"
"An Awful Howl"
"Destruction at Dawn"
"Hundreds of Bodies Found in Wreckage on Florida Keys"

Half-page aerial photographs showed flattened neighborhoods. Columns of type described the horrors of storms past. Interspersed were large blowups of beautiful, perfect, terrifying hurricanes. In nearly every concrete office, favorite pinups adorned surfaces: a particularly nice tornado, a symmetrical Category 5 eye, a bright red infrared image of an eye wall, and many shots of Hurricane Andrew, which blew through Miami in 1992, terrorizing the staff's families even as they tracked it. The photos and pages served both as combat nostalgia and sober warning.

In the middle of the building sat the center's "war room," an expansive rectangle bright with artificial light. On one long wall was a 20-foot map of the cyclone world, the North Atlantic and the Pacific. The water areas were powder blue, and the margins were lined with brown, movable magnetic type. Down one side were the chosen names of storms yet to come. And across the map, mostly in the Caribbean and

North Atlantic, were the wild, curving tracks of 1998 storms, each one beginning with a green trail for its tropical depression stage, followed by a yellow segment for tropical storm, leading to red for a hurricane stage. On Saturday, October 24, the map displayed nine red lines. Mitch, the shortest, had moved only 40 nautical miles.

The room was surrounded by banks of computer screens—eleven on one side, eight on the other—with scattered keyboards, mice, printers, and the occasional Doppler radar. In the center of the room was an island desk, surrounded with clipboards in slots and covered with a melange of maps, papers, and telephones. From there it was a short, clattering roll in a purple office chair across beige tiles to any workstation, and that's how the forecasters spent hurricane season, from June to December, rolling back and forth.

Into this box poured the world's weather, raw data from weather balloons; sea buoys; satellites, including cloud-penetrating rain estimations; sweeps of coastal radar; and reports from ships, planes, and ham radios. Through a thicket of satellite dishes and antennas on the roof and buried T1 high-speed lines came data analyzed at eight other national weather centers. A "family of services" streamed in from domestic and international satellites, including forecasts from French, English, and Japanese meteorological offices. From the National Center for Environmental Protection in Camp Springs, Maryland, came the best number crunching money could buy, the output of IBM and Cray supercomputers predicting what hurricanes would do.

At the center of this deluge at any given time sat one or two hurricane specialists. They were, in the estimation of Dr. Peter Black, "the great synthesizers," mathematicians who divined the forces of nature every six hours. They matched the raw data against an array of computer models that sifted the same data into forecasts of strength and direction. They calculated which of the models had performed best under similar circumstances in the past and mentally weighed which ones to lean on now. "Then they figure out, is it going to weaken or intensify, is it going to spread out or shrink. They are very right brain. Their brains are really good at being able to create images as to what this storm is developing into," said Black, a leading researcher of hurricane behavior who watched their work from another NOAA office across Miami. "On top of that they are very good communicators. Then they have to sit down and tell the story to emergency management people, to give them guidance in their decisions, which is the most crucial step. They have to be able to think fast on their feet and not get rattled by pressure. They have to be real easygoing guys, cool under pressure. It's like writing an article and having a million people depend on what you say. And all this has to take place in about an hour."

The man in the box Saturday morning, October 24, was Miles Lawrence, trim, concentrated, given to wearing starched shirts and bearing a resemblance to actor Charles Bronson. He sometimes called himself "The Mechanic" after a 1972 Bronson movie character, a meticulous hit man without feelings of remorse who got the job done. After thirty years in the hot seat, Lawrence was unflappably analytic. "I turn the crank," he said, which vastly deprecated his mathematical, musical mind. His was the one private office without a storm pinup. He had a Dilbert motto, "Trust Only The Lazy," an Arbin's book of classical tunes for cornet in B flat, and a framed copy of the navy hymn: "Eternal Father, strong to save, Whose arm doth bind the restless wave, . . . O, hear us when we cry to thee, For those in peril on the sea. . . ."

When Lawrence arrived for work at 7 A.M., Mitch's appearance had changed dramatically. It now looked like a classic hurricane, a swirling circle of clouds 300 miles across doing a jerky Saint Vitus' dance on the war room's screens. The satellite loop showed an "impressive central dense overcast," jargon to describe a thickened middle, almost like stirred pudding. Its color in GOES-8's sunrise shots was like a golden flan. There was also just the hint of a dimple—an eye—in the pudding's center.

Lawrence rolled his chair to the track and intensity models. In his years as a forecaster, prediction methodology had dramatically improved. When he began, forecasters had looked at wind and barometric readings from planes and ships, historical tracks, and, most important, the storm's existing track extrapolated forward. "You made your own forecasts," said Lawrence. Once a day he would get a satellite photo to double-check his estimate. As a result, in the old days, the center's 72-hour forecasts were wrong, on average, by more than 400 miles. Computer models had cut that error in half.

Lawrence surveyed twenty models. They ranged from the simplest track model, CLIPER, which was essentially an archive of 970 past storms that looked at Mitch's location, then searched the database for one or more historic storms that had been in the same spot and drew a path based on what the old storms had done. The most complex model, GFDL, from the Geofluid Dynamics Laboratory at Princeton University, used motion equations to analyze atmospheric flow around the world. Fed the data from weather balloons, buoys, and airplanes four times a day, the models spit out the hurricane's future track and, in some cases, an animation of large-scale weather patterns familiar to anyone who watches TV weather. The GFDL was the forecasters' favorite because of its ever-improving track record. But even its predictions only made sense of the data available at the time of its calculus. As such, GFDL and all the other models were idiot savants, often brilliantly prescient, their screens projecting a cyclone and spinning it across the ocean as if it were real, days in advance. Sometimes, however, their drawings were a figment of a machine brain that could be off by 700 miles. Rarely did the models agree with one another, and half the job of the hurricane specialists was mediating the models.

"The best model forecast is my first guess now," said Lawrence. "For the most part, unless I have some additional information, it is my final forecast. I rarely deviate from the best models. You have to have a good reason to deviate, and it's hard to find good reasons."

Tasked with drawing Mitch's future track and writing the 11 A.M. advisory, Lawrence conferred with other meteorologists looking at the same data, satellite shots, and models. In the war room itself, he was accompanied by one or two colleagues, including the man who had just signed his name to the last forecast and was leaving after an eight-hour shift. It was the center's practice not to change the track dramatically, to avoid whipsawing the public. The specialists worked by consensus, debating, sometimes arguing, over factors they felt strongly about. An outsider might be startled to watch these weather masters mutter, argue, bitch, laugh, dismiss a cyclone as a "fish storm"—important to fish but no danger to land—or admit their uncertainty with the announcement, to no one in particular, "I hope nobody takes this forecast seriously." Because the world's weather data were gathered only three hours before a forecast was due, the final, "happy medium" forecast and accompanying analysis were written about an hour before the deadline.

At 11 A.M., Lawrence centered Mitch at 14.9° N, 77.9° W, an estimate that, using the jerky satellite loop, could have been off by 30 miles. He estimated its track direction at 5 degrees, just east of north (10 degrees to the left of its heading six hours earlier), moving at 6 knots. Using a mouse to control a cursor, Lawrence drew a white official forecast track through the ensemble of colored model tracks, stopping to mark where he expected the storm to be in 12, 24, 36, 48, and 72 hours. Following the colored strands, he bent the white line gradually west. Then he typed: "The forecast track is for a gradual turn toward the West over the next 72 hours at about the same forward speed." His forecast put Mitch in the open sea halfway between Honduras and Cuba—a slightly more northerly trajectory than that of the 5 A.M. forecast. Mitch had sustained winds of 85 knots, a Category 2 storm, and Lawrence predicted 100 knots, Category 3, within a day. Because his forecast track came close to Jamaica, he recommended a hurricane watch there, making it the first country to officially warn against the storm. A watch indicates that storm conditions are possible in 36 hours.

※

After sticky buns and a last Bloody Mary Saturday morning, passengers bid good-bye to Guyan March and the *Fantome*. Several "stowaways"— passengers staying for a second week—left the ship for an overnight trip to the Mayan ruins at Copán. Veterinarian Alex Patterson and his wife, Monique, caught a plane to Guanaja for a few more days' vacation at their new cottage. Just about the time they landed, Don Pearly, manager of the island's Bayman Bay Club, took a look at the Weather Channel on his Direct TV dish, watched Mitch's forecast track, and "quit worrying about it. I literally said a prayer for the Caymans and Cuba," he said later. His last guests flew off for the mainland, and he and his staff cleaned up for another crew due on Sunday.

In Miami, Windjammer's marine superintendent, Paul Maskell, stopped in the office and checked the weather. The office was equipped to receive the entire suite of "products" from the National Hurricane Center, including 48- and 72-hour outlooks, the strike probabilities used by emergency managers, the propagating radii of high winds and waves, and the often candid discussions of models and their conflicts. If it chose, Windjammer could relay this information to its fleet by satellite telephone. British-born Maskell, who kept day-to-day contact with the Windjammer fleet captains, had no formal marine schooling, but he had skippered two of Mike Burke's ships on circumnavigations of the globe. He also had more than twenty years' experience with

Windjammer in the Caribbean and was considered a conservative, thoughtful mariner. At the time, he said, Mitch posed no threat to the *Fantome*, nor was there any hurricane in the eastern Caribbean to bother Windjammer's five ships there. He didn't talk with Captain March Saturday, saying later, "We didn't think at that time that there was any real need for concern."

But across town, forecasters at the National Hurricane Center weren't so sure. Nothing about Mitch seemed certain. The storm's rapid intensification had caught them by surprise. It had started west, stopped, backtracked, and headed east of north, then north, when they had expected it to go northwest. Some of the more reliable models were acting squirrelly. On Friday, for example, the GFDL model had Mitch plowing into the Mosquito Coast; twelve hours later it moved the track north over Swan Island, and by Saturday it had darted south again toward Cabo Gracias a Dios. A government aviation model called AVNI first headed Mitch toward Cuba, then later decided on Belize. The Navy's NOGAPS, another data-hungry state-of-the-art model and the one used by short-wave broadcaster David Jones, had favored a Honduran landfall for two days before turning toward Mexico, then retreating a bit and skimming the Bay Islands. Complicating matters, the top quantitative models, including GFDL and NOGAPS, took so long to crunch data that they ran hours behind the simpler models. Still, the forecasters had to publish an advisory every six hours. Drawn on a map, broadcast to the world, the advisory took on the certainty of a road cut through a dense forest. Most people, including sailors, took it as gospel. In reality, no one really knew what the atmosphere in the western Caribbean was doing.

Even in good times, Central America had only nine weather stations capable of launching balloons to collect wind, humidity, and barometric readings. But in October 1998, six of them were inoperable and the others were sending data only every three or four days. Costa Rica had run out of balloons. The weather station at Honduras' capital, Tegucigalpa, hadn't sent in a report for a month. Belize City's weather station had been struck by lightning the week before. Mérida, Mexico, usually the most reliable station in Central America, was inexplicably silent. Nor were there balloon launches from Cuba, Nicaragua, Guatemala, or El Salvador. "When you stop getting data, the model is sort of living on itself. It's not reality anymore," said Jerry Jarrell, the center's director. "In the absence of data, you have no idea."

With models wavering, and at least two predicting an eventual U.S. landfall, Jarrell dispatched a NOAA Gulfstream jet to sample the atmosphere at high altitudes throughout the Caribbean, hundreds of miles from the storm. Unlike the Hurricane Hunter planes, the fragile jet couldn't fly into the hurricane, but would sample conditions from the Bahamas, the Gulf of Mexico, and the Central American coastline. Based on past flights, it could improve modeling by 30 percent. The plane sampled the air with the same GPS dropsondes used by Hurricane Hunters—$500 tubes that measure and transmit pressure, temperature, humidity, and wind, much like balloon sondes except that they fall on little drogue parachutes. First used in 1996, dropsondes revolutionized hurricane forecasting by gathering data from the airplane down to the sea surface, or until the sonde stopped working.

By midday Saturday, Mitch was clearly growing and showing no sign of turning westward. Based on the satellite image, Lixion Avila, who had joined Miles Lawrence on duty, issued an intermediate advisory at 2 P.M., warning that if Mitch did not turn northwest soon it would strike Jamaica in a day and his homeland of Cuba soon after. Some 350 miles east of Cabo Gracias a Dios, the storm had crossed the latitude of the Honduran-Nicaraguan border on the Mosquito Coast. Jamaica raised hurricane warning flags, an indication that hurricane conditions were expected within twenty-four hours.

Just as Avila's advisory moved out, another Hurricane Hunter crew shoved a dropsonde into Mitch's eye wall. As it fell, transmitting a pressure of 976 millibars, it was blown sideways at 93 knots. Reading the data, Avila began to fidget.

"It's beautiful. I'm scared!" he muttered aloud, rolling his chair across the tiles. The excitement showed in his body. "I never keep my mouth shut."

Avila was eight years old and already a weather nut when Castro stormed to power. As a boy he used to pester farmers and sailors, "Is it going to rain?" He remembered waiting for afternoon showers and watching the runoff drain from Havana streets. At age seventeen he began to study hurricanes—Cuba invented hurricane advisories, issuing the first in 1876—becoming a top student at university. But because he wouldn't join the Communist Party, Avila was blackballed and not even allowed to attend graduation. "All I wanted to do was forecast hurricanes," he recalled.

Emigrating during President Carter's détente with Castro, Avila boldly went to see Dr. Neil Frank, then the director of the National Hurricane Center. "I introduced myself with my two words of English. Frank wrote a letter of introduction and said I should find a job in radio, broadcasting hurricanes. He invited me to visit anytime. That was in my first week in the U.S." After enrolling in the doctoral program at the University of Miami, Avila used to stop by the hurricane center for maps. One day someone said, "Hey, you want to help us translate into Spanish?" When he became a citizen with a doctorate in meteorology, he was hired in the center's satellite division. "It was July 4, 1986. I treated myself after by flying to the fireworks at the Washington Monument. I became a person in the U.S."

As the afternoon passed and the computer models absorbed incoming data from the Gulfstream flight, Avila said to the screen: "Ooooh. It's ugly." Typing in two fingers in his second language, occasionally asking how to spell a word, he tapped out:

BULLETIN
5 PM EDT SAT OCT 24 1998
MITCH BECOMING A POTENTIALLY DANGEROUS HURRICANE

Centered at 15.3° N, 78.2° W, Mitch's winds were 91 knots at sea level, a Category 2 hurricane. It was moving nearly north, 355 degrees, at 5 knots. But conditions were ripe for serious strengthening and a turn to the northwest and west, Avila wrote in his discussion. In the next 36 hours Mitch would become a Category 4 storm with winds of 120 knots. "The latest GFDL moves Mitch toward the west and westsouthwest and keeps it meandering near the northeastern tip of Honduras. Only CLIPER continues to show a northward track. I would rather follow state of the art dynamical and global models and forecast the westward turn." Avila bent his cursor through the pack, placing the storm halfway between Honduras' Swan Island and the Cayman Islands in seventy-two hours. By Tuesday, October 27, the center's computers estimated, there was a 12 percent chance of striking Guanaja and a 10 percent chance of striking Key West. "This is a potentially dangerous hurricane which is forecast to move very slowly through the western Caribbean during the next several days," Avila wrote in his discussion. "This would allow some time for the long-range pattern to change and consequently a future change in the track. Interests in the entire western Caribbean should be prepared for this hurricane."

On his afternoon shortwave broadcast, David Jones of the Caribbean Weather Net repeated the warning of the western turn. The Navy NOGAPS model showed Mitch heading directly toward the Bay Islands. Afterward, sailing yacht *Departure II* called from Belize. "I advised them to head southward ASAP towards the Río Dulce, a hurricane hole for small yachts in Guatemala. I told them they had only some thirty-six hours before a northeast swell generated by Mitch would reach them."

Throughout the northwest Caribbean, the forecast of a Category 4 hurricane turning to the west got people's attention. On the island of Guanaja, a local doctor received a call from a friend in the States: "This thing is serious. Buy plywood." Boat owners began to sink their open boats in the mangroves. Across the strait in Trujillo, wind from the storm's outer edge—it was more than 450 nautical miles away—was already driving water from the north onto a low-lying area occupied by the city's airstrip, the Gringo Bar, and an orphanage. As the water rose, Americans Jim Davis and Mike DeLury drove their Jeeps into the water and evacuated the orphanage.

Aboard the *Fantome*, Guyan March did not appear at ease, either. "There's a hurricane out there," he told Annie Bleasdale in a call to North Wales sometime Saturday. The weather already was turning bad, overcast with squalls. "He sounded very concerned and serious," she said later. "He was awaiting an update and info from the head office. He said he didn't want to sit around and wait as they usually did. He didn't want to pick up passengers. He wanted to get out of there then."

Aboard ship, March talked to his department heads about who should stay aboard if the *Fantome* were to run. Laura-Jo, Annie's sister, had told him she wasn't getting off. He discussed her insistence with Annie, who told him to let her sister stay. "He halfheartedly joked that Laura could have his four stripes in exchange for her airline ticket out of there."

That evening around 7 P.M., March invited restaurateur Carlos Arita and another Omoan aboard for a drink with him and a few other officers. The talk naturally turned to *"la tormenta"* Mitch.

"Don't leave Omoa," said Carlos. "It's a safe area. If you'll drop two anchors and lots of chain, you'll hold."

"It's not my decision," he later remembered March telling him. "I would like to find a safe place for the boat and crew. This is a $20 million ship."

Arita, who had worked twelve years on petroleum tankers, told of a storm he had weathered at sea. In big waves, he noted, "nothing is left on the deck."

"Yeah, I know. I've had experience with that," March said. "We lost stuff in another storm." The horseshoe buffet on *Fantome's* top deck, filled with life preservers, had broken apart during Hurricane Bertha, a Category 3 storm that battered the Leeward Islands in July 1996, while March was aboard.

March and Arita discussed anchorage options—places where March might secure the ship and ride out a major storm. The few ports on Honduras' northern shore are sheltered from the gulf's easterly trade winds by west-hooking, thumb-shaped capes, but they are exposed to the northwest winds that would be generated in advance of a hurricane passing to the north. The coastline toward Guatemala, which borders Honduras 12 miles to the west of Omoa, is labeled "unsurveyed" on nautical charts. In the corner of the Gulf of Honduras, another thumb-shaped peninsula called Cabo Tres Puntas partially protects Puerto Barrios, Guatemala's only deepwater Atlantic port. Recalling the conversation later, Arita said, "He was sure he was going to find a safe place."

Laura-Jo Bleasdale, who was at the table with purser Laurie Fischer, said the discussion turned to Fischer's ailing mother, who had signed on for another week's cruise. "There is a possibility of stopping the cruise," Laura-Jo remembered Captain March saying. Mitch was forecast to pass north of them, he said. "But it could come closer. And we'd have to run, and your mom, Laurie, would have to be put off. It's your call."

As March and his guests drank white wine, Hurricane Mitch edged westward by 15 degrees. At 8 o'clock, and again at 11 P.M., the National Hurricane Center estimated its direction and speed at 340 degrees (north is 360 degrees, west is 270) and 4 knots. It was nearly upon the tiny island of Baja Nuevo and the 16th parallel, the latitude of Omoa. The barometric pressure in the eye had slipped 3 millibars to 973. Core winds were 95 knots and covered a donut-shaped area 110 miles wide, with tropical storm winds filling a circle 280 miles in diameter. The center of Mitch was 550 nautical miles from the *Fantome*.

March's worst fear was now a possibility. Whether he articulated them or not, he had three options Saturday night: sail north to find sea room in the Gulf of Mexico, find shelter somewhere between the Bay Islands and Guatemala, or wait in Omoa and see what the storm would do. Annie Bleasdale said later she was under the impression that March "was already talking to the office," but there was no evidence that weekend or later of any conversation Saturday.

Assuming he plotted the National Hurricane Center's forecast before going to bed, March would have known that Mitch was forecast to be a Category 4 storm by Sunday night, but moving northwest, away from the Honduran coast. The nearest storm winds Monday morning were forecast to be 220 miles northeast of Guanaja. If the forecast was accurate, staying put in Omoa might allow a cruise to continue.

❧

At 2 A.M. Sunday, October 25, when the United States shifted to standard time, Hurricane Hunter Teal-02 flew into Mitch's eye, finding it open at the top with a view of the stars. The pressure inside had dropped to 949 millibars—"a significant pressure drop of 27 millibars over thirteen hours." Mitch was now a bona fide Category 3 storm with winds over 100 knots. An infrared image from GOES-8 showed a near-perfect red and blue circle with an eye 20 miles across.

Max Mayfield, the courtly deputy director of the National Hurricane Center, who was on duty at the time, wrote a new forecast, the first to greet the Sunday dawn. The storm had turned 45 degrees to the west in the night and was moving west-northwest, 295 degrees, at 6 knots. He placed Mitch nearly atop Swan Island in 72 hours—70 miles south of the track Avila had forecast the previous afternoon. Swan Island is 120 miles northeast of Guanaja. Given the size of the storm, tropical storm winds of at least 33 knots would arrive on Guanaja early Wednesday morning. In his 4 A.M. discussion Mayfield warned that the lack of good data was confusing the computer models. "The GFDL and UKME models both practically stall the hurricane after 36 hours . . . while the Navy NOGAPS continues a slow westward motion toward the north coast of Honduras."

In West Chester, Pennsylvania, Sunday morning, Anthony Moffa and Karyn Rutledge dropped their dog at her parents' house and headed for the airport and Honduras. It was almost a relief after three days of the Weather Channel, staring at the crimson and blue irregular glob spinning in jerks near Honduras. Hour by hour the storm had grown, and still no call had come from the cruise line. "If there were a problem, Windjammer would let us know," Rutledge told herself. When they landed in Miami, the sun and puffy white clouds outside cheered them. Moffa remembered news of Jamaica evacuations. "I never really gave it much thought after that."

At 10 A.M., Miles Lawrence announced to the world that Mitch had become a Category 4 storm. Winds were 115 knots, pressure 942 millibars, and movement 295 degrees at 6 knots. "All the guidance models show a slow west-northwest to westward motion for 72 hours," he wrote, again placing the storm directly over Swan Island on Wednesday morning. "The GFDL and NOGAPS are the southernmost models, showing a possible threat to Honduras in 72 hours." Lawrence told Jamaican authorities that they were probably out of danger and said intensity models indicated that the storm was near its peak strength.

After watching the Weather Channel at her home in New York, Glenn Parkinson dialed the satellite phone on the bridge of the *Fantome* to talk to Onassis Reyes.

"What's going on?"

"We don't know yet if we are taking on passengers."

"What? I can't imagine you're taking on passengers!"

"I really don't know yet," he said. "We're just waiting for the company to decide."

A few minutes later, Guyan March called Ed Snowdon, a friend and former Windjammer captain in Fort Lauderdale. "We were making plans for the Christmas holidays," Snowdon said later. "We were going to rent a house, either in Bequia or the Florida Keys. I asked Guyan, 'What are your intentions?' If memory serves, he told me was going to take passengers to Belize City, and then turn and go back to Puerto Barrios."

At 11 A.M., Captain March held his weekly meeting of department heads. Omoa's weather was getting worse. The ship's barometer had dropped 2 millibars to 1009. The wind was blowing from the north-northwest directly into the open bay, and short bursts of hard rain beat on the deck. The horizon to the east was black.

"We didn't know whether passengers were coming in, whether the cruise would be canceled. We didn't know," said Laura-Jo Bleasdale. "Canceling the trip wouldn't have been Guyan's call. He was waiting to hear. There was talk about continuing the cruise and staying in the Bay Islands."

Chef Eon Maxwell called his wife to say he would call again from Belize. "I miss you. I'll call you next week." Alvin George called his mother. "I'll see you in November," he said.

At around noon, the first passengers arrived at San Pedro Sula along with the *Fantome's* engineer, Constantin Bucur, from Romania. But two replacement crewmen were missing. Oxford Tuissant was stuck in Grenada because the FedEx package containing his airline tickets hadn't arrived. Chuckie August, due back after two weeks off in the States, had called Captain March from the United States and been told not to bother coming because of the hurricane. As incoming passengers de-planed, Laurie Fischer's mother and niece, having decided against another cruise, joined veterinarian David Horne on one of the flights back to the States. As the jet roared out of the valley, Horne couldn't believe the sight to the east. "I live on the ocean. I've been in the tropics. I've seen storm clouds. But boy, the sky—it was not like it was part of the sky. It was like all the sky was being approached by this big, giant, purple-black cloud. It was very ominous."

At Restaurante Río Coto in Omoa, waves were curling gray on the beach, and the sky was low and menacing. Carlos Arita warned Pedro Prince and Jesús Hernández, two of the temporary dock hires from Omoa, not to get back on the ship. Prince couldn't be dissuaded. He said Captain March had promised him a reference letter so he could get work on another cruise line. Jesús declined, as well. "The captain gave me the opportunity to work as a sailor," he told Arita. "I will go with the captain to the end."

※

At 1 P.M., Miles Lawrence issued an intermediate bulletin from the National Hurricane Center. Hurricane Mitch's winds had reached 126 knots. The pressure had fallen dramatically to 929 millibars. Jamaica was experiencing heavy rain, wind, and flooding, and Lawrence was expecting hurricane warnings in the Cayman Islands later in the day.

The storm was at 16.4° N, 80.3° W, moving west-northwest, 290 to 295 degrees, at 7 knots.

Though Lawrence did not say so, Mitch was exposing the greatest single weakness in hurricane forecasting—the inability to predict rapid intensification of a cyclone. As he and his colleagues watched dumbfounded, Mitch had exploded in 24 hours from a "garden-variety" hurricane with winds under 100 knots to a Category 4 storm. "Some additional strengthening is possible during the next 24 hours," Lawrence wrote.

As Lawrence puzzled in the war room, a crosstown colleague in the hurricane business smelled opportunity. Peter Black, the hurricane researcher at NOAA's Hurricane Research Division, was watching Mitch with mounting excitement. Black, a tall, lanky Massachusetts native who sounded remarkably like the late Bobby Kennedy, was the on-call duty officer on Sunday morning. He had been fascinated by storms since childhood, when his mother had to pull him from a window during Hurricane Carol. Watching Mitch on TV at his home, Black felt an old stirring. The satellite photos were sensational: a beautifully creamy circle of clouds, a classic eye, and a width that was breathtaking. Black could picture Mitch's eye wall—a dark gray whirlwind embedded with tornadoes. He'd seen the equivalent in Hurricane Hugo in 1989, when he'd flown a research plane, similar to a Hurricane Hunter C-130, into the eye. "At our briefings all the information we had indicated peak winds of 100 knots, and when we got there they were over 200 knots and we just about lost the airplane. It was a really rough ride. An engine caught fire. I have a vivid recollection of seeing the flames shooting by my window. The turbulence was so severe that the fuel regulator had malfunctioned. They were able to douse the fire right away and feather the engine, but that meant we were in the worst part of the storm with only three engines. This turned out, in retrospect, to be a really unique set of data. They showed for the first time what these smaller-scale meso-vortices look like at the edge of the eye wall that were actually contributing to that deepening. We still don't know what role they play exactly. But we were able to identify that as a new entity, a new scale of motion in a hurricane vortex that we had never really documented before." The existence of these meso-vortices, or little tornadoes drifting around the spinning eye wall, was demonstrated emphatically in Hurricane Andrew, which destroyed the homes of several hurricane researchers in Miami in 1992. Amid the chaos left behind were short, straight strips of destruction that looked as if they had been flattened by floods.

Peter Black picked up the phone. Researchers had rarely flown in a Category 5 hurricane, and Mitch could become one. He dialed a colleague with the same last name, Mike Black, who had just returned that morning from a vacation in the Alps. "Mitch is out there," Pete Black said. "And we're considering flying in."

✖

By midafternoon Sunday, the Bay Islands of Honduras were a madhouse. A ham radio "hurricane net" had warned of a 40- to 50-foot storm surge on Roatán. Shrimp and lobster boats were running into Jonesville's deep, crenulated harbor like chickens chased by a fox. Four sailboats took shelter in the mangroves there. They ran a line all the way around and tied a knife at every boat in case they needed to escape quickly. At Anthony's Key Resort, diving guests were called together at 4 o'clock and told to pack for a flight out first thing Monday.

On Guanaja, Don Pearly of the Bayman Bay Club called company founder Tom Fouke in Fort Lauderdale. "It's starting to come," Fouke warned him. Based on their conversation, Pearly thought he might have one day to secure the resort and his boats, two big 35-foot dive boats and three smaller craft. He sent them to the canal that bisected the island with instructions to anchor them and tie them into the mangroves in 3 feet of water. He then urged his thirty-eight employees to gather their families and take shelter in one of two concrete basements cut into the hillside. Across the island, Posada del Sol manager Buddy Thompson ordered all the deck furniture put away, windows and doors boarded up, and his dive boats sheltered in the mangroves near Savannah Bight. A new set of twenty-two guests had arrived on Saturday for a week's stay, and he moved them all into rooms in the main building off the pool. After watching Mitch on a neighbor's satellite TV, veterinarian Alex Patterson began tying down his beachfront cottage—literally. Copying an old local trick, he looped rope over the roof and under the pilings, like a bow on a Christmas gift.

The wisdom in the Bay Islands regarding hurricanes is anecdotal and borders on the superstitious. One obscure study of the ten Bay Island hurricanes from the past one hundred years showed that October storms that crossed the 83rd meridian between 16.5° and 17° N curved southwest and frequently hit the islands. Mitch was predicted to cross the 83rd at 17.3° N.

"You could already see the sea kicking up," said Patterson. Even if the storm struck Swan Island at 17.5° N and didn't turn south, "we were going to get some of it."

At 3 P.M., three hours before the scheduled boarding of passengers, Captain March called his boss, Michael D. Burke, son of the founder and president of Marine Resources, the fleet operations arm of Windjammer. Burke was at home in Miami. This, according to Burke, was his first conversation with March about Mitch.

"When Guyan called it wasn't to discuss whether or not we were going to cancel the trip. It was whether to alter our itinerary. He said he preferred not to go to Belize, but to repeat Roatán," Burke said months later.

"The storm is tracking north. Let's stay in the Bay Islands," Burke recalled March saying.

"I said that sounded reasonable, and we would discuss it after the next update. There was no particular alarm." Burke said he then began following the storm closely on the Weather Channel. "Frankly, it has always been the best source. It provides the visuals, as well as the raw data. You could see the color red. It added another level of intensity about the ferocity of the storm. That day, the storm dropped in barometric pressure more than any storm. It had grown into a huge monster that caused both Guyan and myself to pay extra attention. What gave me the most comfort level, it was already on the same latitude, or north of the latitude of the ship." March and Burke both knew that hurricanes in the Caribbean usually recurve north.

☙

In 1961, five years before Guyan March was born, Hurricane Anna struck Belize as the world watched from space. That first satellite photo of a hurricane revolutionized forecasting and changed the perception of tropical storms as mysterious forces that appeared unannounced from the dark edge of the earth. Though rural, isolated Hondurans still could be surprised by *la tormenta*, it was unheard of for someone with access to First World news sources not to know of a storm's approach. If they were caught, it was usually because of bad luck or bad judgment.

By Sunday afternoon, Guyan March should have known a lot about Hurricane Mitch: the location of its center, its strength, speed, and predicted track. Given his characteristic thoroughness, he no doubt plotted the storm's fix at 16.5° N and somewhere between 80.4° and 80.7° W, less than 400 miles east of the Bay Islands. He no doubt plotted Miles Lawrence's prediction that Mitch would move west-northwest, 290 to 295 degrees, almost parallel to the Honduran coast, at 7 knots. If he received the long-term information from the home office, he could have marked its expected Tuesday evening fix just off Swan Island, 150 miles from Roatán. But whether he pictured the sprawl of Mitch centered over Swan Island was unknown. If he had, he could clearly have seen the Bay Islands in its thrall. Miles Lawrence's wind radii calculations, available at Windjammer's headquarters, flatly predicted that by Monday night the Bay Islands would be awash in 12-foot seas, and by Wednesday morning they would be lashed with bona fide tropical storm winds of at least 34 knots.

According to people who talked to him, Guyan March wanted to cancel the cruise Saturday, when Mitch was growing, and again on Sunday morning when it became a Category 4 storm and turned west. By then, even booked passengers casually watching TV at home suspected that Mitch could be trouble. But on Sunday afternoon, with conditions worsening in Omoa and seas kicking up in Guanaja, he suggested continuing the cruise in the Bay Islands, more than 100 miles closer to the storm.

While waiting for a storm to reveal its intentions—in essence, doing nothing—is sometimes the right decision, waiting for passengers in Omoa only complicated March's choices. Laura-Jo Bleasdale's memory of an anxious March captured his dilemma: "His view of boarding the passengers was, 'I don't think they should. If the storm is heading my way, let's just go.' But if they were coming, we bring them to the ship. He didn't like leaving the passengers to fend for themselves in Omoa. On such short notice, there was nowhere else for the passengers to go." By the time March called his boss, guests were gathering at Carlos Arita's bar.

Between his calls to Annie Bleasdale on Saturday and his Sunday afternoon call to Michael D. Burke, a day passed in which the *Fantome* could safely have moved 150 miles. He could have reached Puerto Barrios by heading west into Guatemala, with time to reconnoiter the harbor and seek a secure berth or anchorage. He could have gone north toward Belize and been nearly halfway up the Yucatán Peninsula. Though that coastline offers no hurricane havens for a ship as large as the *Fantome*, he might have gained sea room in the Gulf of Mexico. Or he could have gone toward Roatán, as he had discussed with a passenger twenty-three days earlier. This would have given him all day Sunday to poke around the island's fjords for a sheltered anchorage.

In that critical twenty-four hours, apparently neither March nor his boss in Miami brought up a discussion of options. There also appeared to be no discussion that Mitch could turn closer or do anything other than what was forecast. Burke's recollection was that March used the word "north" to describe the storm's forecast track. The storm, in fact, was moving more westerly, and by Sunday afternoon was scheduled to go over Swan Island on Tuesday night. The 72-hour forecast bent the storm more northwesterly by Wednesday morning, but still just 100 miles from Guanaja. Mitch was already radiating gale-force winds of 34 knots for 125 miles in all directions. Its 12-foot seas reached 200 miles toward the Bay Islands.

Though captain of his ship, assigned to the company flagship because of his skill at running a large vessel carrying as many as 170 people through foreign waters, Guyan March did not command alone. The decision to make a dramatic move, to run from a hurricane or, especially, to cancel a cruise, involved his bosses at Windjammer. In a sense, the *Fantome* was steered by three men: Guyan March, thirty-two; Michael D. Burke, forty-two; and the ship's owner, Mike Burke, seventy-four, Michael's father. The younger men's professional lives were intertwined. Michael D. Burke had apprenticed under and learned the cruise business from Mike Burke, from whom he had assumed day-to-day management of fleet operations twelve years before, at the age of thirty. A year later, March had joined Windjammer, finding a company and fleet stamped in the senior Burke's image. Michael D. Burke had been March's boss from the beginning of his professional career.

Michael D. Burke, or MDB, as he was called inside Windjammer, looked a bit like his father, although smaller in stature. At Windjammer headquarters, with his father's portraits staring down, a visitor could not escape the impression that MDB was boss in his father's shadow. He had grown up sailing with Mike Burke, had crewed with several captains, and, at age twenty, had become the youngest captain of the fleet, master of *Amazing Grace*, the 257-foot supply ship. Terry Bewley, one of Captain Burke's first professional mariners, said he had tutored the teenaged Burke aboard the *Rogue*, a fishing boat purchased in England to supply the fleet. "The first voyage, I was to take the ship and Michael was sent. I didn't know he was supposed to be the captain. I remember messages were going to him. This was supposedly the trip he was in command, to take over from his father. He said he didn't want to be overshadowed by his father. He's a good lad, basically. Trustworthy. He's not a showman. He's sensible. He learns to do things properly, despite a rather unorganized upbringing." After deciding to make Windjammer his career, MDB declined the recommendation of older captains to attend merchant marine school, though his father had offered to put him through. He also turned down their recommendations that he get experience in the shipping world outside of Windjammer, a decision he later regretted.

Like Captain March, Michael D. Burke understood the risks of operating in the western Caribbean during hurricane season. "There is a potential for a bad setup," he said later. According to his staff, MDB had, in fact, resisted moving the ship to the western Caribbean the year before but had consented because of the passenger potential. "The fact that we do this annually doesn't desensitize us to the danger. But when you have fifty years of experience taking evasive action and you've been successful, you don't run with fear every day. It's very rare that Honduras is hit. The other consideration is, we're running a business. The eastern Caribbean is becoming more popular. We advertise we go to out-of-the-way locations. The reefs of Roatán and Belize are ideal. My dad has always been somewhat of a risk taker. . . . It is part of the business. You have to accept it."

By all accounts, Guyan March and Michael D. Burke had a collegial, respectful relationship. "I've been on the ship when we had to run from a hurricane," said Paul March, the captain's brother. "Michael gives you what they think, and then sends it over to you and says, 'It's your decision.'" Those who knew him said that Captain March made his own decisions and had, on occasion, rejected orders from Miami. Aboard the *Yankee Clipper*, he had even stood up to owner Mike Burke after March

built an enclosure on the aft deck to stow garbage, Ed Snowdon recalled. "In Windjammer circles, when Mike Burke speaks you've got to
listen. He comes to the ship and tells Guyan, 'Get that thing off my ship.
I don't like it.' Guyan says, 'What would you like to do with the
garbage?' Burke says, 'I don't care, Captain. Put it in your cabin.' Guyan
stood up to the man—resigned his job, basically. He was no pushover."
Jeremy Linn, March's first sailing instructor, who saw him once a year
and watched him progress through Windjammer's fleet, said, "I don't
think Guyan would be pigheaded about it, but I don't think he would
take orders from anybody who couldn't appreciate his situation. He
would go into the middle ground. Here's what's happening here. Here's
why I'm doing it. There would be a compromise in there somewhere. I
suspect Guyan would have the last word. He was captain of his vessel,
and that decision should have been his."

But Guyan March's entire career as a professional captain had been
spent at the helm of Windjammer's big, slow-moving party boats ply-
ing between Caribbean islands, and it was the combination of his sailing and public relations skills that put him on the bridge of the flagship.
He kept the crew happy and the ship off reefs while peddling rum and
fun to the guests.

In his conversations, March appeared more worried to his colleagues
than he let on to his boss. And MDB, for his part, did not seem to grasp
the pressures squeezing his captain—passengers arriving by road from
an airport to the south, and the harbinger gusts of a hurricane already
blowing in from the north. Given their mutual respect, either man could
have suggested canceling, but neither man did Sunday afternoon.

Michael D. Burke said later that the $100,000 cost of canceling the
cruise would not have been a factor. "Every year we cancel one or two
or three cruises. It's not financially significant for us to have to reim-
burse passengers or give cruise credits for a future trip. Even if we had
canceled on Saturday, people are still going to be arriving. There wasn't
time to call people at home and say, please don't come."

As the sun sank on a menacing sea, the need for both clear thinking
and a clear view of Hurricane Mitch went unanswered. March's real
blind spot, perhaps, was that he never saw a satellite photo of Mitch.
Isolated on a distant coastline, anchored next to a remote village, he
didn't have the advantage of his boss, who had access to the Weather
Channel, the Internet, and any number of news broadcasts. Had he been

able to catch just one glimpse of Mitch, he might never have suggested to MDB that he load passengers and take them to the Bay Islands.

Viewed from GOES-8 on Sunday afternoon, Mitch was a beautiful, savage sight. The misty nebula of Friday had condensed into a thick, white, revolving core, punctured by a perfect eye. A pinwheel effect showed clouds being sucked in from Mexico, Central America, Colombia, and Cuba—up to 800 miles away—toward a "black hole" that sparkled Caribbean blue at its bottom. A solid cloud cover stretched 500 miles from the interior mountains of Honduras to the south coast of Cuba. The storm's outer bands, with gusty winds and heavy rain, battered Jamaica, Cuba, parts of Colombia, the Costa Rica–Panama border, and, to the west, Omoa, Honduras, and Belize. Set against the deep blue sea, the stark-white "cold central dense overcast" with trailing globs and wisps was stunning. A thin, gauzy layer of cirrus clouds spun clockwise high above the storm, while the main body, with its eye, rotated the other way at the speed of an Indy 500 race car.

BULLETIN
4 PM EST SUN OCT 25 1998
POWERFUL MITCH CONTINUES TO STRENGTHEN

Miles Lawrence reported that Mitch was nearing the threshold of a Category 5 storm of 133 knots. Teal-14, the most recent Hurricane Hunter flight, had found 155 knots at 10,000 feet. Based on a standard reduction formula, sea-level winds were estimated at 130 knots with higher gusts. Pressure had fallen to 924 millibars. Miles Lawrence estimated that hurricane winds covered 140 miles of ocean, with tropical storm force winds sprawling across nearly 300 miles. Twelve-foot seas generated by the storm covered 550 miles of ocean. Jamaica dropped its hurricane warning, but a watch continued for the Cayman Islands. Lawrence forecast the storm to reach 135 knots, Category 5, by Monday morning. By Tuesday morning, the center of Mitch would be 165 miles from Guanaja. "The hurricane is now close enough to Honduras so that a hurricane watch and tropical storm warning would soon be appropriate." The GFDL model, his personal favorite, had flip-flopped in the last six hours, from turning south into the Bay Islands, to turning north. "The motion is so slow that the GFDL turn toward the north is considered to be in the noise level," he wrote. The other guidance models indicated a slow, mostly westward motion for 72 hours. Lawrence's forecast, 290 degrees at 7 knots, now put Mitch over Swan Island on Tuesday, but then slowed the storm to a near standstill.

In satellite shots from space at sunset, Mitch's clouds were gorgeous against the Caribbean blue, its soundless image floating free of the turmoil below. As it spun counterclockwise, Mitch appeared to be turning the corner of Cabo Gracias a Dios and heading west, which in fact it was.

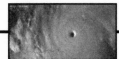

OMOA

October 25, 1998

EVENING

🐚

IT WAS GROWING DARK and pouring rain as the white mini-bus jarred through craters that pocked the dirt road to the sea. Each jolt tossed a slurry that, with the rain and breath on the windows, obscured the jungled and palmed coastline. The driver wrestled the steering wheel through each pothole, now and again braking the minibus to five miles an hour to rattle across steel plates on wood beams that spanned a dark, violent current. The clatter mercifully muffled the guide who'd been droning on for ninety minutes about tourism and its importance to the Honduran economy. From their seats in back, Karyn Rutledge and Anthony Moffa strained for a view of the ocean or a tall ship—something portending their first Caribbean cruise.

"What are we doing here?" Rutledge asked.

"Hey," said Moffa, seeing snippets of stars overhead, "maybe it's just a bad downpour and we're not in the situation, after all, of having to deal with a hurricane."

Ten miles ahead, in Carlos Arita's café, the palms hissed, rain blew sideways across the bar stools, and waves washed onto the tiled floor. Waitress Damares Madrid noticed a strange orange color in the sunset: "The noise of the sea was scary. It was *tremendo*," she recalled. Arita said to a dozen waiting *Fantome* passengers, sitting with their feet curled up, "You are a little bit crazy." By then, two feet of water surrounded the café's beach side. A Windjammer crewman said to repeating passenger Ron Hale, "Have another beer, mon. The launch is coming." But when the whaleboat arrived it was dark, and Hale and others had to wade thigh deep to the dock. Deanna Ramsey, who did not swim, was petrified. "They gave us garbage bags, cut holes to put our arms and head through, and got us in the launches," said her husband, Jack. "It was rougher than hell getting out there, up and down, up and down. When we finally got there, I said to Guyan, 'What is this?' He said, 'It's nothing to worry about. It's a tropical storm.'"

At 7 P.M., the National Hurricane Center's bulletin read: "Extremely dangerous Hurricane Mitch moving westward." Mitch, a Category 4 hurricane with core winds of 130 knots, now was bearing due west at 7 knots along the 16.5° N parallel. On that latitude, it was aimed at Guanaja, 250 miles ahead. The storm was expected to slow but continue westerly, with additional strengthening into Monday. "A hurricane warning may be required for portions of Honduras tonight." By Tuesday, 50-knot winds would be lashing the Bay Islands.

Less than an hour later, the lights of the Toyota minibus swept across Río Coto, and the bus stopped by the thrashing bay. It was raining harder than ever. The doors swung open and four crewmen thrust black garbage bags at Rutledge and Moffa, wrapped more bags around their luggage, and led them down to the stubby pier illuminated by a harsh security light. Waves were crashing against pilings, rain was lashing, the wind flogged their plastic-bag ponchos. Two of the *Fantome*'s three whaleboats were rafted together alongside the pier, hobbyhorsing in the waves. Moffa and Rutledge had to step across one boat to reach the outer one. One of the crew, most likely Colin August, shouted his mantra: "Step on the blue and grab the crew." Fifteen people crowded in, holding on to each other, the second crewman, and the metal frame that held a useless blue tarp overhead. No one wanted to sit down. The driver yelled for them to move right and left, to watch their balance. Then he pushed off into the waves.

In brochure weather the launch ride out took less than five minutes. In the pitch dark, in a rocking whaleboat, it seemed like thirty. Salt water splashed from the bow as it struck choppy two-foot rollers. Sheets of warm rain poured over them. Despite garbage bags, everyone was soaked to the skin. Anthony Moffa began singing the theme to *Gilligan's Island.*

"Just sit right back and you'll hear a tale, a tale of a fateful trip, that started in this tropic port, aboard this tiny ship. . . .The weather started getting rough, the tiny ship was tossed. If not for the courage of the fearless crew, the *Minnow* would be lost." Even the grim-faced among them tried to chorus: "The *Minnow* would be lost!"

Just then, Rutledge caught sight of the *Fantome*. She was floating like a castle in the gloom. "It was just beautiful. It was lit up, even with the rain." Light oozed from a row of portholes and spilled out of her waist—the "lobby" on A deck. A row of globes along her length appeared to mark a boardwalk. The bowsprit splayed spotlights on her massive prow. Blinding spotlights on the four white masts beamed down on the deck, lifting her out of the dark. Looking back, said Rutledge, "it's a haunting vision."

As the launch approached the boarding stairs, the waves and wind subsided in the hull's lee. At the head of the stairs, just under cover of the top deck, Brasso Frederick and Onassis Reyes stood in their bright yellow slickers. Their hands were out, and they were grinning.

"Welcome to the *Fantome*."

Instantly the storm receded. There was something steadying about the ship. People were laughing, sharing stories, and calling the launch ride "The Crossing." The big wood doors to the saloon stood open, and inside, rum swizzles and a buffet were laid out. People joked that they looked like drowned rats. The ship's aged and varnished wood interior glowed in the soft electric lights. The room was full of steel band music. Chrispin Saunders brought Ron and Rose Hale extra towels. They took a hot shower, dug out dry shorts, and joined the party. In the cover of the lobby, they could feel the weather without suffering. It reminded Moffa of a cookout forced inside by rain that poured, then stopped, rained and stopped. He stepped upstairs to the top deck a couple of times to look around in the dark. The bar was open, but the musical combo Formula K, ferried out for their regular Sunday night gig, was breaking down their equipment. At Carlos Arita's suggestion, the group had taken a video camera to film their work, to create a promotional tape. But as they set up amplifiers, squalls blew rain onto them and they feared electrocution. Viewed later, their jerky, grainy video reminded Arita of the scene in the movie *Titanic* where the musicians performed on deck.

As the *Fantome* rocked gently in the bay, Captain March ran up and down the stairs to the bridge. Laura-Jo Bleasdale, the activities mate, remembered a look of disbelief on his face. "He kept coming up to us and saying, 'Make sure you get all their information, flights, destinations, in case they have to get off.'"

At about 8 o'clock, Michael D. Burke called March. He said he had monitored the storm since their 3 P.M. phone call. "It grew tremendously and started changing course. The ship was in a bad situation. I thought it would be safer, it would be a better idea, to cancel the trip entirely and try to get out of the way. I asked him if he had the 1900 (7 P.M.) report. He did."

Between 10 A.M. and 7 P.M., Mitch had grown from 115 to 130 knots. Since 4 P.M. it had turned 20 degrees closer to the ship, to a track of due west. A cruise to the Bay Islands was no longer an option. Burke described their conversation later: "I said, 'I'm not comfortable with the ship stuck in the corner. This thing has grown into a huge beast. The situation is not good. What do we do?' The idea was to try to take evasive action. Unfortunately we are already as far south as we're going to get. There's only one way to go . . . run to the north. Abandon the cruise. The next logical point is, we need to do it now. I suggested we drop the passengers and get the vessel underway. He was uncomfortable with that. Omoa doesn't have the resources. It's 8:30. By the time we hang up it's 9. It would be 11 o'clock by the time they could get to the dock. There's insufficient facilities, no hotel to take them to, no buses, it was raining like hell. He proposed a compromise. He would leave as soon as sixteen more passengers arrived—they were anticipated at 10 P.M.—and run to Belize City. We discussed it in detail. Since we're going to go north, let's go north with our passengers and drop them off in Belize. It won't take us out of our way. It will only take a couple of hours. It's better, more appropriate, he felt, than putting everybody ashore in Omoa in the rain squall which he was experiencing that evening. It was acknowledged that [putting in to Belize City and offloading passengers] was going to cause further delay, but it was not responsible conduct for us to put passengers ashore [in Omoa] that night. Once we got to Belize we would make a further assessment of our options. Having made that decision, time was of the essence."

A run to the north across the path of a Category 4 hurricane 360 miles away was not the only option available to Guyan March Sunday night. Months earlier, in sailor bull sessions, he had predicted that to flee the Gulf of Honduras, he would need two and a half day's notice. Because he was unlikely to get that much time, he had said he would take shelter in the lee of the Bay Islands or in Puerto Barrios, Guatemala. Yet under duress Sunday night, with a storm barreling toward him, nasty weather in an exposed anchorage, ninety-seven wet, scared, and demanding guests and a boss on the phone saying he didn't want to leave the ship stuck in a corner, Guyan March abandoned his earlier reasoning. "Leaving to go up to Belize was his final decision," said March's brother, Paul, later. "If he thought it was the wrong decision, he would have gone somewhere else."

Terry Bewley, the English captain who launched *Fantome* for Mike Burke, said later that he knew what March was dealing with on that Sunday in Omoa. "When you embark all these people you get very wound up in it. It almost rolls you along. Everyone's excitable. Luggage all over the place. The meat hasn't arrived. The cook is in a tantrum. And it's terrible hard to tell them it's all off. If you're his age and background, you would feel insecure, to stand up and stop everything. He was afraid to stop it, and no one in Miami told him to stop it, not forcefully enough, anyway."

Sometime between that phone call and 10 P.M., Captain March went into the saloon and announced to the ninety-seven passengers that the cruise to Belize was abandoned. Because of Mitch, which he showed on a map, the *Fantome* would go east, back to the Bay Islands. Karyn Rutledge later remembered him saying the storm was moving northwest. "It would be better to stay in the Bay Islands," Lori Nicely recalled him saying. "We'll repeat our second week. I'm sorry for those people there for the second time." The crowd groaned, especially the divers and stowaways. "We were disappointed," said Ron Hale, "but there were a lot of things we couldn't do in the Bay Islands the first trip."

That inexplicable announcement was a deliberate deceit, according to purser Laurie Fischer, "simply because there are enough problems with check-in anyway. There's always lost luggage and other issues on boarding night." Captain March, who didn't want to face the unpleasantness of getting passengers back into plastic bags and into lurching launches, also chose not to deliver the bad news that the trip was over.

Months later, the *Fantome*'s shoreside support contractors in Honduras said the decision not to put the passengers ashore in Omoa was shortsighted. Antonio Martínez, the manager of MC Tours, said his buses could have been in Omoa in two and a half hours, and the ninety-seven guests could have found room in two motels of "international quality" in Puerto Cortés, an hour away. They were empty on Sunday. San Pedro Sula, with its Intercontinental Hotel, high-rise Best Western, and a dozen other substantial hotels, was another option an hour past Puerto Cortés up a four-lane road. "To take them to Belize was criminal," Martínez said later. "You have people here who would have taken care of them in Omoa, in Honduras."

As passengers went to bed thinking they would wake up in the Bay Islands, the *Fantome's* crew began calling their relatives and making arrangements for the evacuation. Windjammer chartered a jet from Miami to fly to Belize, arranged a bus from the docks, and reserved rooms at a Miami hotel for Monday night. Melmish Tours in Belize City was asked to meet the ship with their high-speed launches. Belize immigration and customs officials were notified. They would take a Melmish launch to the ship.

Chrispin Saunders called Faith Herrera in Belize and told her to meet him on Monday morning to help him get off the ship. He also called his mother in Grenada.

"Don't go on the ship," Shirlan Saunders said.

"Mom, don't panic. We have to go and take the passengers to Belize."

Onassis Reyes called his girlfriend, Glenn Parkinson, in New York and informed her that the ship was going to Belize to drop passengers before running north to Mexico.

"What?" she yelled. "Have you seen the storm?"

"He was very quiet," Parkinson said later. "He didn't say too much. That was unusual, unless he was tired."

🐚

Though complicated by the incoming passengers, Captain Guyan March's choice had always boiled down to the classic sailor's dilemma in a hurricane: go to sea or stay in port. The answer was not as simple as the question.

Hurricanes pose peculiar threats to harbors not fully enclosed. High winds pushing against a hull can break anchor chains. A hurricane's storm surge of 12 to 20 feet can dislodge anchors and lift a ship onto shore, where waves and winds can dash it to bits. Every year ships are destroyed or sunk in harbors. To make matters worse, winds shift 180 degrees when a cyclone passes. Land that offers shelter as a hurricane approaches becomes a hazardous lee shore when the hurricane passes. Omoa, placid in the easterly trade winds, was entirely open to wind from the north and northwest. Mitch's outer winds and rain bands were already blowing straight in.

Yet it takes a strong stomach to leave a harbor in the path of a hurricane. Before the advent of engines and satellite photos, smart sailors didn't. One month before he arrived in Honduras in 1502, Columbus warned the governor of Santo Domingo (Hispaniola, now comprising Haiti and the Dominican Republic) that a storm was coming in two days. He'd been through two "uricanes"—demon winds—as the Carib Indians called them. According to biographer Samuel Eliot Morison, Columbus remembered the oily swells, cirrus clouds, and low-pressure twinges in his joints. He warned the island governor to delay a gold-laden fleet from leaving harbor for Spain. Columbus was ignored and barred from taking shelter in a river. The gold fleet was destroyed, nineteen ships sank, and many lives and countless millions in gold bullion were lost. Hovering as best they could in the lee of Santo Domingo, three of Columbus' ships broke their cables and were driven out to sea. All survived. "What man ever born, not excepting Job, would not have died of despair when in such weather, seeking safety for son, brother, shipmates and myself, we were forbidden the land and the harbor that I, by God's will and sweating blood, won for Spain," he later fumed.

In the last half of the twentieth century, motor vessels and better hurricane predictions had made going to sea a viable option. Hurricanes are lumbering beasts, not unlike freight trains. With modern craft, it was possible to beat them to the crossing. When a U.S. Navy ship was destroyed by a typhoon after choosing to stay in Hong Kong harbor in 1971, the Navy Research Laboratory wrote a "Hurricane Havens Handbook" and placed a copy on all ships. It walked captains through the leave/stay dilemma. The key, it said, was a clear-eyed assessment of

1. The probability of a hurricane strike, defined as being within 80 miles of a storm's center. That distance would include forecast errors that averaged 100 miles a day.
2. The harbor's potential—did it have terrain with 100 feet of elevation?
3. The ship's speed and condition, the storm's speed, and the time needed to get to "sea room." Sea room, ideally, is hundreds of miles of open water in which a ship can drift if disabled or maneuver around a storm.

In general, the handbook said, a ship should leave port forty-eight hours before the arrival of hurricane-force winds of 64 knots. If a storm took an unexpected turn or change in intensity and a captain was facing a hasty departure in deteriorating weather, "the odds for preventing serious damage . . . swing in favor of using the resources available to secure the ship firmly to her berth." In essence, the navy's answer to the simple question—leave or stay?—was, it depends.

The *Fantome* was not a navy destroyer. She was made of steel and carried lifeboats and many of the same navigating devices, but compared with a modern ship, Mike Burke's flagship was an aging, lumbering Motel 6 with a good restaurant and bar. *Fantome* captains consistently rated her as stout but slow. In flat water, she managed 8 or 9 knots. On sails alone, the best she could do was 4.5 knots. Facing wind and waves, performance dropped to half that. So in forty-eight hours, assuming seas were kicking up, the *Fantome* could have traveled 190 nautical miles. A ship capable of 8 knots in adverse conditions could double that. At 20 knots, a speed common to container ships, mega-yachts, and navy destroyers, a ship could cover 960 nautical miles in forty-eight hours.

Going to sea in the neighborhood of a hurricane virtually guarantees rough sailing. Squalls are constant. Winds reach at least gale force. Waves of 12 feet or more travel away from the storm at 25 knots, for hundreds of miles. Gear breaks. Small problems become major ones. Running from a storm, a ship can get caught in it. Implicit in the navy's matrix is a "well-found" ship. This means well built, well equipped, and well maintained.

Mike Burke and his son, Michael D. Burke, considered the *Fantome* well-found. Her tanklike hull had run aground at least three times with no catastrophic damage. In 1988 she had fallen off blocks in a dry dock in Martinique, breaking off a bilge keel, popping rivets, and opening a leak in a stern tube. She had hung for hours at a precarious angle, her masts askew, before she was refloated. Years later, her keel was repaired. In the late 1990s in Grenada, a confused harbor pilot drove her hard into a dock without any sign of denting. But a ship's integrity only begins with the hull. Pitting a ship against a hurricane requires worst-case thinking. Will her engines keep running? Can she make headway? Can water get in faster than her pumps and freeing ports can get it out? Will she respond to her rudder even in high winds and seas, to maintain course and prevent broaching? If partially flooded, will she float? If knocked over, will she right herself? Are her windows, deck structures, and hatches strong enough to withstand breaking seas or a knockdown? The truth was, neither Burke, his son, nor Guyan March knew.

When the *Fantome* was launched as the *Flying Cloud* in 1927, she was rated by Lloyd's of London as 100A1, meaning she had been built under

Lloyd's watchful eye and was fit for ocean service. Subsequently, she underwent periodic surveys to keep her classification, to certify that she was in good shape and still a good risk for insurance.

When Mike Burke bought *Fantome*, he assumed the risk because he carried no insurance. Although he remodeled the ship dramatically, no insurance company or major classification society, such as Lloyd's or the American Bureau of Shipping (ABS), passed judgment on these changes as required of a ship built to U.S. standards. He avoided oversight because his ships operated among small and poor nations that didn't require otherwise. "I found a way to be legal," Mike Burke said later. "I did what I had to do. I did it because I wanted to stay in business."

To operate legally in international waters, Burke registered, or "flagged," his ships in Third World countries. He also incorporated each ship as a separate, offshore, paper business. Standard among cruise lines, these practices allowed him to avoid corporate income taxes, liability, and high-cost American crews. It also produced a required certificate that the *Fantome* met international cruise ship safety standards, primarily the Safety of Life at Sea (SOLAS) convention of the International Maritime Organization, an agency of the United Nations. Prompted by and written two years after the 1912 *Titanic* disaster, SOLAS requires ships to be stable and buoyant, even when sinking. A whole set of arcane rules tries to assure that in a disaster a ship sinks in a flat, upright position, allowing crews to get to lifeboats. Later, firefighting, safety equipment, and safe-manning regulations were added. SOLAS covers ships carrying more than twelve passengers. Upgraded several times over the years, SOLAS nonetheless gives flag nations wide discretion in approving certificates, and enforcement varies widely among nations.

When Mike Burke first began operating larger ships out of Miami in the 1960s, he bumped up against the U.S. Coast Guard's enforcement of SOLAS, considered the strictest in the world. With old boats, homemade remodeling, and barely enough cash to stay afloat, Burke couldn't meet the regulations. "The law is not fair. The law was written for these big ships. There is no law for smaller vessels that can carry forty or fifty people," Burke argued. "The same set of laws applies to cruise ships with hundreds of people. I can't meet the standard." Burke claimed that a Coast Guard commander, a drinking buddy, advised a loophole—fly passengers to the Bahamas but drop them in Miami—and he sailed through it for a while. Later, the Coast Guard "took the position that he sold a journey that started in the U.S.," said Harvey Schuster, the Miami officer in charge of marine inspections in the late 1950s who once boarded the *Polynesia* on its way back to Miami. "The vessel was old. It couldn't meet rules for carrying more than twelve passengers for hire. We didn't want to put him in jail. We wanted him to stop breaking the law." Eventually, Mike Burke moved his entire passenger operation offshore.

When the *Fantome* sailed away from Miami as a cruise ship in 1971 she was already in violation of SOLAS regulations that prohibited wood cabins and required fire-retarding bulkheads. Windjammer's brochure admitted this. Yet it still could claim compliance with SOLAS because a flag nation or its administrator signed a paper saying she complied. In 1978, *Motor Boating and Sailing* magazine published an investigation of Windjammer's flag status under Panama and Honduras. Editor Jeff Hammond found that under the Panamanian flag, the ships had been registered as "commercial yachts" and did not have SOLAS certificates. Though Burke later received a SOLAS certificate from a Miami agent, Honduran officials said the company's authorization had expired. The vessels were also listed as "merchant" ships, a classification with less stringent standards than passenger vessels. The magazine published a letter from Captain Edward Derr, the U.S. Coast Guard officer in charge of vessel inspections, in which Derr had written to a would-be Windjammer passenger: "These vessels are not in compliance with the Safety of Life at Sea conventions of either 1948 or 1966. . . . In the opinion of the undersigned, none of the Windjammer Cruise vessels are fit or seaworthy vessels. They are catastrophes waiting to happen and it is only a matter of time. You sail these vessels at your own risk, and thank you for your intelligence at making this inquiry prior to jeopardizing yourself and members of your family." At the time of the article, Burke claimed to have carried more than 250,000 passengers in Windjammer's history and was grossing $5 million a year.

When Mike Burke's children took over in 1986, they slowly began to change the reputation and culture of Windjammer. With his sister, Susan, as president of marketing and sales, Michael D. Burke, as head of fleet operations, made no secret that he was trying to outgrow his father's pirate reputation.

"The past is the past. Not to excuse him, my father started with 300 bucks, and through perseverance and dedication to the cause, in his attempt to succeed, he did what he had to do, I guess. Yeah, he's had his battles with the Coast Guard and other regulatory agents. The record will show for the last ten to fifteen years, it has been a focal point of my career to try to upgrade standards, to try to surround myself with individuals with qualifications, with the competence, with capabilities to raise standards. I'm trying to raise the bar. It's also been true of my career that a large percentage of the money this company makes goes back into the ships, because they need it."

But Cap'n Burke's legacy died hard. Jammers fond of the old ships and rowdy, swing-from-the-yardarm days complained about creeping "Foo Foo" ways. The money he used for major upgrades was borrowed from his now-wealthy father, who groused about the new standards. And, like his father, Michael did the work himself, using in-house plans. Harry Reid, the marine consultant who partnered with Mike Burke on his first sailboat, the *Hangover*, said, "Unfortunately for Michael, he was brought up in this environment. You learn this way and don't get exposure to the real world. There is a certain amount of peril to it."

Between 1988 and 1998, young Burke spent $6 million upgrading the *Fantome*. He installed hot water and air conditioning in every cabin. He upgraded electronics. He replaced her engines with two newer 399 Caterpillars. He tore out old tanks and welded "double-bottom" tanks into the hold, replacing metal so thin that a workman's chipping hammer went through the bottom while the ship was in the water, sending a fountain spraying into the hold. The leak was finally stopped after a Keystone Kops routine that included diving below with warmed beeswax, while welding from above. In an attempt to give the ship damage stability under SOLAS, MDB also installed the ship's first watertight, steel bulkheads. For the first time, passengers on Decks B and C had to step over and duck every 20 feet through raised oval steel doors that reminded them of submarine passages.

As part of the 1991 remodeling, MDB moved two stairways between A deck and B deck and positioned them laterally, rather than fore-and-aft. The design was drawn up by a Burke assistant in Miami who was not a marine architect. In order to fit the stairs, two steel I-beams, each 12 to 16 inches wide and running from bow to stern under A deck, had to be cut, and 3-foot sections had to be removed. *Fantome*'s engineer at the time, Roy Alexander, refused to do it. Instead, out of spite, he built the stairways but left the beams intact—to use the stairs, a passenger would have had to crawl under the beams. According to two witnesses, Michael D. Burke showed up at the Trinidad shipyard and ordered Alexander to cut the beams.

"I'm not doing that to my ship," Alexander said.

"It's not your ship. It's my ship," Burke reportedly said.

"You want to cut it? Go get Tony. He's a welder. Tell him you want it cut."

"So Michael got himself a welder and they cut it," said John Taylor, a former *Fantome* captain who was administering the remodeling. One of the beams had already been cut in a different spot for a staircase leading from the saloon to the galley.

When asked later, Michael D. Burke said he didn't remember the conversation. "But was it controversial to cut the beams? Maybe so. There was much in the way of reinforcement done on two decks, on the outside, a piece built around and a piece of webbing built on the hull. So on three decks there was additional structure put in to compensate. The alternative was fore-and-aft stairs, and with the layout we found ourselves in, it just wasn't going to work."

Although completely remodeled with new decks, cabins, stairways, and the removal and replacement of 250,000 pounds of weight, the remodeled *Fantome* was not tested by a Western classification society for intact stability, damage stability, downflooding, or other standards required of ships that carried passengers in U.S. waters. MDB said he hired an engineer to run tests for his own satisfaction. He also called the beam-cutting incident "a learning process." "Without skirting the issue, from the days when my father didn't do things, to the way we do things today, is a process. So the *Fantome* was a stepping stone, to ultimately our building to classification. Each one was done to a higher standard. I don't think the *Fantome* was compromised by less stringent oversight. The issue would be stability and watertightness, structural downflooding, and capsizing—whether they met the requirements. I'm confident she did."

In his efforts to upgrade his father's fleet, Michael D. Burke's proudest achievement was the *Legacy*, a forty-year-old, 294-foot ship remodeled to meet the tough safety certificate of the American Bureau of Shipping and regularly inspected by the U.S. Coast Guard for passenger standards. It sailed into Puerto Rico and the U.S. Virgin Islands beginning in November 1997. "That was totally my impetus, to get a ship in our fleet that's Coast Guard, ABS, and Public Health approved. And that's where we're going from here. Any new tonnage we acquire and feature is going to be built to class. It's taken a long time, but it's just obviously a natural transition for a company to go from its roots to having new ships that are first-class. We are working with good used hulls, but my dream is to have a series of new-builts.

"The cruise industry has grown up, and people's expectations are higher. It used to be, in Windjammer's early days, that it was part of the adventure when there was no dinner and the air conditioning didn't work and the toilet didn't flush. That was part of the fun. Today's customers don't find that too amusing. So we had to continue to upgrade." Also driving the upgrades were new, tougher SOLAS standards for fire-retardant construction that would force the existing fleet off the sea by the year 2010. "In the past it was never important to my dad. As a young adult, I looked forward to having the company provide for me."

In 1996, the younger Burke switched the company's flag of convenience from Honduras to Equatorial Guinea. He did so, he said, after looking at a spreadsheet of advantages, largely dealing with taxes. Equatorial Guinea was a struggling West African nation where, according to the U.S. State Department in 1998, rule of law had broken down and human rights were nonexistent. People were routinely tortured and raped, dissenters were jailed for speaking their minds, and courts were not independent. The United States did not have an embassy in Equatorial Guinea. Aid programs sponsored by the World Bank and the International Monetary Fund "have been cut off since 1993 because of the government's gross corruption and mismanagement." The country had two thousand telephones, a merchant marine of nineteen ships, only one of which carried passengers, and an airport that, according to the country's own Web page, "has a basic degree of development that barely satisfies aviation requirements." Said a State Department official: "There is not much administrative capacity. They don't have people with expertise, qualified to examine issues." Lloyd's List, the marine publication, reported early in 1998 that as many as forty vessels carried Equatorial Guinea certificates that could have been faked.

Equatorial Guinea flagged Windjammer's ships through a Miami agent, Victor Jimeno of Maritime Inspection Corporation. According to MDB, Equatorial Guinea also inspected the Fantome annually and issued a SOLAS certificate, despite the fact that the ship violated 1966 fire reg-

ulations. Jimeno certified SOLAS compliance and, for $200 plus a ré-
sumé and testimonials, issued mail-order licenses to Windjammer's captains, mates, and engineers. Officers did not sit for an exam, though
Burke said that licensing was not a "rubber stamp." Not one of the
Fantome's three chief deck officers was a graduate of a merchant marine
school or possessed a U.S., British, or equivalent license to master a
passenger ship over 1,000 tons. In his native United Kingdom, Captain
March's Yacht Masters license allowed him to run a yacht with up to
twelve passengers. If the *Fantome* were a British-flagged vessel, he would
have needed a Class 1 captain's license, the same as the captain of the
QE2, which required extensive schooling and experience.

In 1998, the U.S. Coast Guard considered any ship flagged by
Equatorial Guinea or certified by Maritime Inspection Corporation to be
suspect. If such ships entered U.S. waters they were automatically boarded
for an inspection. Equatorial Guinea's rate of detention, in which the
Coast Guard actually arrested the ship after a boarding because of serious violations of international standards, was 40 percent above average.
Between 1994 and 1998 the Coast Guard detained four ships flagged in
Equatorial Guinea, including Windjammer's newest ship, the *Legacy*,
which was cited in Puerto Rico for having a starboard lifeboat with "damaged rudder, propeller, and holed bottom from running aground." Any
questions about these matters to the Equatorial Guinea embassy in
Washington were referred to Jimeno, the head of Maritime Inspection
Corporation, who also carried the title of Honorary Consul to the nation.

~

At 10 P.M. Sunday night, the National Hurricane Center recommended
a hurricane warning for Honduras from Limón east to the Nicaraguan
border. Limón is 20 miles east of Trujillo on the mainland, within sight
of the island of Guanaja. A hurricane warning means winds of at least 64
knots will arrive within twenty-four hours. Mitch was 120 miles from
Cabo Gracias a Dios and moving dead west on a bearing of 270 degrees.
In fact, said forecaster Richard Pasch, "the eye has wobbled a bit to the
left over the past several hours, but current movement is estimated to be
westward around 7 knots. Steering currents are not well defined. Track
prediction models are giving a variety of solutions."

The warning, broadcast on the late evening news in Honduras, set off a panic. People piled out of their houses in a mad rush to get to the markets. By 10:30, ice and water were gone. At about 10:45 P.M. Carlos Arita's daughter in Miami faxed him the forecast downloaded from the Internet. Carlos called the *Fantome*'s bridge on his VHF radio. A late launch for arriving passengers brought Onassis Reyes in to shore. Onassis scanned it and, according to Arita, appeared very worried.

"Don't leave. Drop the anchor," Carlos entreated. "Anything we can do for you we'll help." The wind was blowing hard. The waves were crashing.

"I've got to run fast," Onassis told him in Spanish. "I'm scared about this."

"You don't have to leave," Carlos replied. "Jesus Christ, we could take them to city hall, or the fire department."

The last launch, with four passengers, left the dock just before 11 o'clock. Half a dozen crewmen raised the launches into their davits. Like many chores on the old ship, it was not a simple job. Ropes attached fore and aft were snaked through blocks, led amidships, and wrapped around a drum winch. Two deckhands tailed the lines as the drum turned, lifting the 3,000-pound boat free of the waves. Though originally meant to swing inward, so the launches could ride over the deck and be loaded in an emergency, the boats were tied off and left swinging near the blocks, out over the water.

As the *Fantome*'s anchor chains rattled up, Carlos Arita watched the ship rock in the waves. The restaurant's radio crackled. It was Captain Guyan calling from the bridge.

"God Bless you and your family, Carlos. Take them, go to your home in the mountains."

Carlos returned the blessing. Remembering it later, he teared up. "I told him, 'God bless you.' If it was me, I'd get the fuck home. He left because he was a company man."

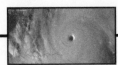

BELIZE AND MIAMI

October 26, 1998

MORNING AND EARLY AFTERNOON

❧

BULLETIN
7 AM EST MON OCT 26 1998
EXTREMELY DANGEROUS HURRICANE MITCH BECOMES
STRONGEST HURRICANE OF THE SEASON

During the night, Hurricane Mitch had moved west 55 miles and be-come a borderline Category 5 storm. A Hurricane Hunter crew, flying through Mitch's clear eye had found the pressure down to 923 millibars, the lowest reading of the 1998 hurricane season. Mitch's surface winds were estimated at 133 knots.

The center of the storm was less than 300 miles east of the *Fantome* when passenger Anthony Moffa climbed the stairs to the bridge at dawn. The sky was overcast and it was raining lightly. The wind was hitting the ship face-on. The sea was gray with 8- to 10-foot waves. A few other people were up, holding on as the ship heaved over each wave. Many passengers were seasick from a rough night. Doors and drawers had banged open. Water had washed onto the well deck and along the side decks past the Admiralty suites. There were no Bay Islands in sight. Moffa looked at the compass in front of the helmsman, who was in bright yellow rain gear. It read 350 degrees, almost due north, which didn't make sense. Down in the breezeway, next to the coffee and sticky buns, a grease-pencil scrawl on the activities board read, "Sailing Lessons" and "Story hour 9:30 A.M."

"I'm sure you realize we're not on our way to Roatán," Captain March began his story hour. "We are directly in the path of Mitch, a Category 5 storm." He went on to say that the hurricane had increased in inten-sity and changed direction. After talking it over with Miami, he said, the

Fantome was going to Belize to drop them. "We need to get you folks off the ship. We are arranging a charter flight home."

The group groaned. March explained that the company would send a letter to allow them to rebook. "You are not going to lose a trip." He paused, and someone in back yelled, "Thanks for keeping us safe." The crowd applauded.

"We were disappointed," said Moffa. "Our vacation changed. But we came to grips that we weren't dealing with a little rain. Looking back, we still really had no idea what we were coming up against."

For once, March did not introduce the ship's personnel but returned topside to a deck crew preparing for battle. Under bosun Cyrus Phillips and bosun's mate Jerry King, deckhands climbed into the rigging to remove the blocks used to raise the fishermen staysails, the upside-down triangles of sail flown (though rarely) in the spaces between the regular staysails. Big and heavy, the blocks could damage the rig or become airborne missiles in a storm. The men also took down the awnings over the bar. Dozens of blue vinyl deck cushions were piled in bench seats and the seat tops screwed down with portable drills. Extra lines were coiled and stowed out of sight. As the crew worked, guests milled about, ordering drinks at the bar. "We took pictures of one another. We watched the crew. There were three or four guys in the rigging," said Moffa. As they packed and set their suitcases outside their cabins, purser Laurie Fischer exchanged e-mails with the Miami office to double-check the manifest. A handful of guests had never shown up. She described Captain March as "very focused. Very, very busy. He was always polite. He took time to answer questions."

By now March had drafted a list of nonessential crewmembers. It included all the women and a handful of male bartenders, cooks, and stewards. Once again, Laura-Jo Bleasdale objected to leaving.

"You know you can't stay," March told her. "You're getting off the ship. I want you to get off. Besides, you have to get off and take care of your sister. Get your stuff."

"You can't make me."

"I can. I'm the captain and you're getting off. Go pack your bag and say good-bye."

"What do I take?"

"You're going for two days. Take what you need."

"Where are you going?

"We're going to go north."

"Is that wise?"

"We've looked at it. That's the best option. Don't worry about it."

Before she left his cabin, March handed her $500 cash. "Use this for your expenses, if you need a taxi. You know the routine. Get a receipt. If you don't have one, write one."

☙

The National Hurricane Center's 10 A.M. advisory, written by Miles Lawrence, described a huge storm drifting slowly westward at 7 knots. Based on an analysis of the satellite photos, he estimated that Mitch's surface winds were 135 knots. Lacking verification, he declined to declare it a Category 5 storm.

Mitch's center, at 16.7° N, 82.9° W, was now 72 miles southeast of Swan Island and 100 miles northeast of the Honduran mainland, where outer rain bands were intensifying. Lawrence warned of 3 to 5 inches of rain that could set off flash floods and mudslides there.

The center's tracking models were a tangle of conflict, U-turns, sharp left and right diversions. But none of the models had the storm going very far very fast. Lawrence interpreted that as "slow, mostly westward drift" for the next 24 hours, followed by a northward turn. "It may soon be time to consider a hurricane watch for Belize and the remainder of the north coast of Honduras."

Lawrence's "northward" turn would begin Tuesday and continue Wednesday and Thursday. He moved Mitch "northward" 40 miles by Wednesday and only another 7 miles by Thursday. His extended outlook—Wednesday and Thursday—contained this standard warning: "Use for guidance only—errors may be large." The hurricane center's average track prediction error on a dozen storms in 1998 had been better than usual, but still sobering to a sailor caught in a hurricane's path. On average, the center's 48-hour forecast was off by 150 miles and the 72-hour forecast error was 200 miles.

From space, Mitch measured in diameter more than the distance from Omoa to the Yucatán. The eye had widened and deepened into an awesome sinkhole in a white swirling platter that was 300 miles across. Rain bands northwest of the eye were already striking Mexico. The *Fantome's* northerly escape route had become a treacherous lee shore.

꿍

If the walls of the Hurricane Research Division of the Atlantic Oceanographic and Meteorological Laboratory weren't so stout, built of concrete to take hurricane winds and storm surge, the voices of Ph.D.s yelling on Monday morning might have carried into the mangroves of Biscayne Bay and scared the pelicans.

"I know what you're going to ask me," Frank Marks began, already irritated at the sight of Pete Black, James Franklin, and Mike Black in his office. They wanted to fly into Hurricane Mitch.

"Why do we need to fly this storm?"

"We don't get to fly a Category 5 storm. We may not get this chance for another ten years."

"How do you know it will be a Cat 5 tomorrow?"

"Even though we missed the rapid intensification, it still is a Cat 5. We should fly."

"You have to convince me."

"We never get to fly a Category 5 storm."

"That's not good enough."

"Well, we need more dropsondes in the eye wall."

"You've already got more data than you can analyze in your lifetime. Why spend the money to go out and collect more?"

The 1998 hurricane season had been a researcher's dream: twenty-nine flights and more than 200 hours of research air time in hurricanes Bonnie, Danielle, and Georges in the government's P-3 turboprop, a plane similar to the C-130s used by the Air Force Reserve's Hurricane Hunters. Some twelve hundred dropsondes had been deployed.

The Hurricane Research Division was filled with brainy, scatter-desk scientists who loved the challenge of gathering data in the middle of a hurricane. Pinned to one of their helter-skelter bulletin boards was a measure of their machismo—the number of "penetrations" into a hurricane eye wall. At the top of the list stood Hugh Willoughby, the director, with 415. Frank Marks had 374. Pete Black was third with 347 and Mike Black followed at 265. Willoughby, a diminutive "Mr. Peepers"–looking mathematician who described hurricanes not with poetry but in physical equations, was the lab's "great penetrator."

"I feel, a lot of times, like a kid in a candy shop in a storm," said Pete Black. "It hits you in all senses, in overdrive. You can feel the bounces, you can hear the rain, sometimes the graupel pellets, the hail, hitting the airplane. You can feel the air motion, up and down. And while that's all hitting you, you are looking at your instruments telling you what is going on outside the airplane: what the winds are, what the temperature is like, the kinds of precipitation particles you are flying through, what the electric charge is on the airplane. You are constantly trying to synthesize the picture as if you are up above this whole thing looking down on it. All of us have this curiosity as to what is responsible for producing such a horrendous system in nature that is capable of such terrific destruction over a large area. By making these measurements you can make a contribution to saving some lives and property."

But while Pete Black argued philosophy, James Franklin was winning the debate.

"We've got no data from a Category 5 storm," he told Marks. "We need more deepening convection events."

"It means going into next year's budget."

"You want something better than this next summer?"

Marks, who later described his job as "baby sitter for ten scientists—we make decisions like the Israeli Army. We're always screaming and yelling, 'No, you're wrong, right.' We operate by consensus"—finally waved them away.

"If you want to do it, go do it."

🌊

By midmorning Monday, tropical-storm-strength winds were lashing the Bay Islands. Ten- to 12-foot rollers had crashed onto the north shore reefs all night. At 6 A.M., Anthony's Key Resort had gotten its guests to the airport and onto a charter flight. Dive master Kevin Brewer estimated winds at dawn of 30 to 40 knots. The staff evacuated their families and moved their ten dive boats, 36 to 51 feet long, into the mangroves of Gibson Bight, a mile and a half away.

The mayor of Roatán, Jerry Hynds, went on local radio and warned: "This animal is coming to Roatán and I don't want to see anybody on the road." In Dixon Cove, east of the cruise liner dock at Coxen Hole, the *Wind Dancer*, a 110-foot diving boat, took refuge.

Forty miles closer to the storm, on Guanaja's West End, David Greatorex, who had been glued to the satellite TV in his tiki beach bar, was spooked by a sudden silence. "I'm used to having birds singing and animal noises. And it just went very, very quiet. No birds. Nothing. I'm looking at the eye on TV. God, the eye is heading in our direction. So I got all the staff together and said, OK, let's get as much from the bar and restaurant as possible and get in the back. We started hauling stuff back, dishes, pans, pots. We put a lot of stuff in one cabin."

On the northeastern corner of Guanaja, Doug Solomon rolled a wheelbarrow and a shovel around a lagoon to a small hill half a mile from the house. There, on the south slope away from the sea, in a natural indentation at the edge of a thorn bush, he dug a one-foot hollow. He made two trips with the wheelbarrow, carrying 10 gallons of water, a jar of *sawusa*—an African meat jerky—plastic sheets, candles, a flashlight, and an ice chest.

Across the island on the south side, veterinarian Alex Patterson watched waves wash under the pilings of his new beach house. Out on the archipelago of private islands, waves were striking the reef and creating spectacular 20- to 25-foot aerial displays of spray. As a precaution he stocked the empty hillside cistern with a cooler containing bananas, cheese crackers, 5 gallons of fresh water, a camera, a VHF handheld radio, and a bottle of Absolut vodka.

Fantome's deckhouse was frenzied late Monday morning, with phone calls and questions about the Belize evacuation, issues over customs, and a growing concern that heading north was a bad idea. Against the wind and 8-foot seas of Mitch's outer rings, the *Fantome's* ETA in Belize had been pushed back two hours, to nearly noon.

At Windjammer's headquarters in Miami Beach, Michael D. Burke had moved upstairs to a "command center," a room on the second floor with a set of charts, a single sideband radio, a red telephone used for emergency calls, and a long folding table surrounded by chairs. Resident computer guru Mike Whiteman provided a steady stream of hurricane information from the National Hurricane Center's Internet site, and Burke was glued the Weather Channel. "We were getting the data, the forecast positions for the next 12, 24, and 36 hours. I was plotting those positions on a chart. Guyan was doing the same thing. We were making the assumption we could be out of Belize by 1300 [1 P.M.]. We figured the distance between the ship and the storm. The more I did that, the more I became uncomfortable. The *Fantome* was heading to trouble. Too strong a headwind. It would not clear land [through the Yucatán Channel] by the time the storm arrived. That wasn't the situation on Sunday evening. On TV, I saw the feeder bands that finally convinced me. The storm was still 300-and-something miles away, but it had grown, in such intensity, that feeder bands were coming into Mexico and that would set the *Fantome* against a lee shore, with no safe harbor. I was never happy or very comfortable with crossing the path of this storm. The *Fantome* had quite a bit of power—2,400 horsepower—but it was a good-sized ship, with a not very fine bow. It had a blunt bow. In heavy seas she would slow down. It was always unsettling in my soul, that we were crossing the front of the storm."

At 11 A.M., Michael D. Burke grabbed a chart, jumped in his car, and drove the few miles to his father's brooding, grandiloquent castle on Miami Beach's bay waterfront. On a king-sized kitchen table, he spread the chart.

"I did it for two reasons: I valued his experience and I wanted him to influence the decision. We sat together at the kitchen table and talked about options. He asked a few questions about the forecast and the speed of the ship, whether there was any safe harbor, north, along the coast. I asked him:

"'What should I do? You've been doing it for fifty years.'"

"Go southeast and get in the lee of the Bay Islands," Captain Burke said.

That was his son's inclination as well. Back at the office, MDB called Captain March. The ship was entering the long, tricky channel off Belize City. When Burke passed along his father's advice, March suggested not making the final decision until he was clear of the reef, on his way out, at about 3:30 P.M.

As the *Fantome* negotiated the channel, Mitch looked from space as if it were draining the northwest Caribbean down into its large, clear eye. The lower portion of its solid central core was chewing the Honduran coast like a sawmill blade. Just ahead lay the Bay Islands. Rain bands circled the storm to the west, interspersed with wide gaps of blue sky and calmer winds. The *Fantome* entered such a gap as March dropped anchor in just 20 feet of water nearly 3 miles off Belize City. He could get no closer in the shoal water. The two Melmish Tours launches pulled up to the gangway platform, and customs officials came aboard. The scene on deck seemed a madhouse to Faith Herrera, Chrispin's lover, who also came out in one of the launches with Teresa Au Gustus, Jerry King's girlfriend.

"Everybody was running up and down. It was crazy," said Herrera. Chrispin led her to his cabin. "He told me to help pack his stuff. He left to work."

Au Gustus said Jerry King had expected to spend a day or two with her and their daughter, Princess, during the normal Belize cruise week. But now, because of the storm, the ship wouldn't be back for several months.

Outside, crewmen began loading passenger baggage into the first launch. It would return shortly for passengers.

"I felt very uneasy," said Karyn Rutledge. "There was never a sense of panic. I would call it quietly worried."

As the second launch slid alongside the gangway, ready for passengers, Guyan March came out of the deckhouse, posed for a few photos at the top of the gangway, and shook every hand, apologizing and making small talk.

By this time, Belizean officials had discovered that two crew passports, those belonging to brothers Alan and Alvin George of Grenada, had expired. They said the brothers could not leave the ship. They also refused to admit the three new dock hires—Jesús Hernández and Pedro Prince from Honduras, and Aníbal Olivas from Nicaragua—because the men had no visas and no way to get back home. All five men would have to stay on the ship. Laurie Fischer handed passports to the departing crew who would find shelter in Belize: steward Enoch Alexander, laundryman Sheldon Alexander, bartenders Castle Hilton and Christian John, and stewardesses Muriel Farquaharson, Beverly McKenzie, and Daphne Smikle.

Chrispin Saunders was in his room packing when First Mate Brasso knocked on the door, according to Herrera. Saunders went out for a minute. "When he returned his demeanor had completely changed. He was, like, sad. After a while he started crying. He said, 'I can't leave. I have orders to stay on the ship. I want to go with you. The captain gave an order. I just want you to take care of yourself.'"

Herrera, pregnant with his child, was trying to stay calm. She'd suffered a miscarriage earlier in the year, and both of them were worried about stressing the unborn child. She pleaded with Chrispin.

"Why can't you come off? Please come off. How will I know you're OK?" Both were crying. "I was holding on to him and he was holding on to me. I took some of his clothes in a bag along with a stereo, a boom box that he bought for me in Omoa. I stayed with him until the last boat, until the captain got on the PA and announced, 'We have to leave. Whoever has to go ashore has to leave now.'"

Teresa Au Gustus, sitting with Jerry King in his cabin, said Captain March came to the door.

"Jerry, we've got to go now. Miami wants us to leave Belize now. We're going back to Honduras," he told them. King stepped outside to talk to March. When he came back to her, Au Gustus asked him if he could stay. King replied, "If we leave the ship we can't come back."

In their last minutes together, King talked "about things he wanted to be taken care of with his baby while he was gone. We were supposed to register the baby under his name. I think he felt like he wasn't coming back to her. He told me, 'When she is six months, quit breast feeding her, and don't spoil her.' A lot of things he told me, like, 'When she is sixteen, she must go up for Miss Universe.' It was like he wasn't going to see her. I felt funny about it. I thought it was a father being worried about his daughter. He loved Princess a lot. Looking at her is like looking at him. She even walks the same."

❦

As the *Fantome* stood off Belize City, another Hurricane Hunter flight approached the eye wall of Mitch. Master Sergeant Mike Scaffidi of the U.S. Air Force Reserve, with twenty years' experience flying into hurricanes, described it as similar to watching a storm arrive in fast forward: first came clear air, then high cirrus clouds, then lower cloud layers, then the ocean kicking up, wind increasing, whitecaps getting bigger, and 100 miles from the center, the rain bands beginning. Then the eye wall, dark gray outside, appeared on the plane's green radar screen as a yellow donut, the yellow representing the echo from a wall of rain. In nine Hurricane Hunter missions, Mitch had stood out for its routineness—a little lightning, a few bumps, nothing outstanding. As flight Teal-23 approached Mitch about noon, Scaffidi was out of his chair, loading a dropsonde into a chamber in the airplane floor.

"It was a beautiful storm. We're getting 150, 160 knots. You could see the eye on radar. OK, it's really small. Great. We really didn't have that much turbulence. I get my other sonde, we're in the eye wall. I plug into the umbilical cord to make sure it's functioning. I'm sitting in my seat at the console and I have the keyboard out, and next thing you know, I'm pinned against the ceiling, looking down at the console. Holy shit. When I came down, I hit my table. I didn't realize I had cut my arm.

"Everything in the back of the airplane went flying. Before we go in we tie everything down. Well, you'd be surprised how much stuff really isn't screwed down. The back of that airplane looked like a warplane. Way in the back, two water jugs flew. I have a backpack where I keep all the plug-in equipment. Everything in its pockets was flying out—pencils, pens, calculators, my lunch. There was lettuce all over the place. All the emergency equipment, oxygen masks that hung on hooks, they were all over the place. My helmet, at the console, went flying. I remember seeing it, as I'm pinned against the ceiling, looking at my helmet. It was an out-of-body experience. Then the jokes started:

"'Hey, Peter Pan.'

"'Oh, look, he can fly.'

"'Drop, you OK?' There was blood all over the printer. My elbow is screwed up. My back hurts. My helmet hit the computer switch. I lost my data."

But not before the barometer in Scaffidi's dropsonde plummeted to 905 millibars.

Pilot Ken Gates, looking at the radar dense with turbulence, radioed: "There is no way to take this bird back into the northwest wall."

As the airplane entered the eye, the bleeding Scaffidi looked out. "It looked gorgeous." Mitch's eye was classically shaped into what is called a "stadium effect." From the opening at the top, the wall sloped inward at 45 degrees like a perfectly round stadium. The sun shone brilliantly down onto the blue Caribbean below.

☙

BULLETIN
1 PM EST MON OCT 26 1998
POWERFUL MITCH STRENGTHENS . . . CATEGORY FIVE ON THE
SAFFIR/SIMPSON HURRICANE SCALE

Scaffidi's dropsonde had found the fourth strongest hurricane in Atlantic history. The reading of 905 millibars matched Hurricane Camille in 1969, and was bested only by Gilbert's 888 millibars in 1988, the Labor Day Storm's 892 millibars of 1935, and Hurricane Allen's 899 millibars in 1980.

On duty at this historic moment, hurricane specialist Miles Lawrence of the National Hurricane Center centered Mitch at 17.0° N, 83.2° W, a little less than 300 miles east of where the *Fantome* was anchored. Mitch's eye would pass over Swan Island that night, he said, but tropical storm winds covered nearly 300 miles. Mitch was moving west-northwest, 290 degrees, at 7 knots. Gusts blew stronger than the sustained winds of 151 knots and "some fluctuations in strength are possible today and Tuesday, but Mitch is expected to remain a very dangerous hurricane capable of causing catastrophic damage."

Any attempt to describe a Category 5 hurricane falls back on the equally incomprehensible model of a nuclear weapon. The Atomic Energy Commission once calculated that an "average" hurricane equaled the energy of 500,000 atomic bombs. The difference is that a hurricane keeps going.

To make a hurricane's power comprehensible to the public—and to get its attention—Robert Simpson, the director of the National Hurricane Center, teamed up in 1973 with construction engineer Herbert Saffir to create a scale of destruction using common objects. Category 1, with sustained winds of 64 knots, what insiders call a "garden variety" hurricane, damages trees and shrubbery but causes no real structural damage. Small craft in exposed anchorages can be torn from moorings. Category 2, beginning at 83 knots, blows down trees, damages mobile homes, and forces shoreline evacuations due to its 6- to 8-

foot storm surge. Category 3, 95 knots, destroys mobile homes, damages roofs, and cuts off low-lying escape routes. Category 4, 114 knots, an "extreme" event, blows away roofs and creates a storm surge of 13 to 18 feet with flooding as far as 6 miles inland. And Category 5, 134 knots and above, a "catastrophic" hurricane, blows away buildings, shatters glass, and creates floods over 18 feet. Anything above Category 2 is considered a "major" hurricane.

The first recorded Category 5 storm to hit the United States struck the Florida Keys in 1935. The barometer on Long Key fell to 892 millibars, and winds were estimated at somewhere between 130 and 175 knots. Called the Labor Day Storm, it killed 409 people. According to David Fisher's account in *The Scariest Place on Earth*, people were sandblasted, and later found with little but leather belts and shoes on. A train was swept off its tracks, killing construction workers. One man, run through with a two-by-four, drank two beers and died.

The only other Category 5 storm to hit the United States, Hurricane Camille, cut through Pass Christian, Mississippi, in 1969, cutting a barrier island in two like a nuclear weapon and killing 259. A three-story wave washed ashore, toppling buildings with partying crowds inside. According to *Newsweek*, four children were sucked from the arms of their father at Trinity Episcopal Church, never to be seen again. A pickup truck flew 50 yards. The storm lasted four hours, and people were found hanging from trees, screaming and crying.

Andrew, which struck Miami in August 1992, killed 26 people, destroyed 60,000 homes, and produced a storm surge of 19 to 23 feet. As the storm came ashore, it blew away radar domes and wind anemometers at the National Hurricane Center. The center afterward moved inland. Andrew caused a record $25 billion in damage, but Andrew was "only" a Category 4 storm.

❦

By 1 P.M., *Fantome* was preparing to weigh anchor with thirty-one men aboard, including almost the entire "hotel" and galley staff. Michael D. Burke said later that he left that decision to the captain. "I can assure you that if he had felt the situation was life-threatening, he would have been sure that people who were not necessary would get off the ship. He didn't arbitrarily pick names. I understand that Guyan asked the heads of departments who was essential. It's unfortunate that more didn't get off the ship. Personally, I don't believe they are needed in heavy weather situations."

Seven of the men approached Laura-Jo and asked her to do favors for them when she got to Miami. She sat on a bulkhead and scribbled little notes. Colin August wanted her to call his wife and send money to her. Brasso wanted her to price a telephone. He also dropped a letter to Louise Reece, his former lover. Onassis asked Laura-Jo to call his girlfriend, Glenn Parkinson, and tell her he loved her. Kevin Logie and Eon Maxwell wanted money sent home. Her own lover, Pope Layne, wanted a linen shirt.

As the last launch filled, Guyan March stood at the top of the gangway. He was dressed in his usual uniform, white shorts and white shirt with "Captain Guyan" embroidered on the chest and four gold bars on his epaulets. But his face had a pinched, pale look. Still, he shook hands with every guest, posed for yet more pictures, and chatted amiably with passenger Anthony Moffa.

"How long have you been with the company?"

"About ten years."

"Will you go north from here?"

"No, we're going to go south, then east, to Roatán. Sorry that we had to cut this short."

"We'll come back and do it again."

"We'll look forward to that."

"When you looked into his eyes, he was doing the job to keep passengers calm," Moffa said later. "Behind his eyes, he was not 100 percent there in front of you. He had probably been up all night."

Laura-Jo Bleasdale descended into the engine room to say good-bye to Pope, and broke down.

"Stop," he said. "I don't like it when you cry."

Near the gangplank, Jerry King was holding Teresa Au Gustus. Chrispin Saunders walked Faith Herrera down the gangplank, knowing she couldn't swim. Then, she remembered, "he got on top of the ship and started waving. I don't think anyone wanted to be on the ship. You could see it in their faces. Before, everytime I go on the ship, they are happy. It was different. It was very tough. Chrispin told me he was going to be OK. I have never been through a hurricane before, so I don't know.

I just believed that he was going to be OK. His last words were, 'Remember, I'll call you.'"

The last to leave were the three women officers: Laurie Fischer, dive master Cathie de Koeyer, and Laura-Jo Bleasdale. "I was hugging all the guys," said Laura-Jo. "They were kidding me, 'Hey, it's party time without Laura.' That's how I remember them."

Laura-Jo hugged her future brother-in-law. "I did a doubletake. He always walked around with a big smile. He looked pale and tired. He looked ten years older. He said to me, 'Take care of yourself and give your sister a big hug for me.' Then he went up and blew the horn."

Guyan March's strained face probably reflected the emotional turmoil around him. But it could just as easily have revealed the unspoken intuition, present in natural sailors, that he was out of good options. He and the *Fantome* and its crew had their backs against a lee shore. The crossroads he had hoped to reach in two hours, at the outer edge of the reef, had become a risky, one-way detour, back the way they had just come. In their ongoing discussions over the last day, March and his bosses in Miami—Michael D. Burke, fleet superintendent Captain Paul Maskell, and owner Mike Burke—had ruled out all options but the one that required the ship to sail 100 miles closer to Mitch.

March himself had eliminated Puerto Cortés, the commercial port near Omoa, MDB said later. "He knew as the storm passed, it would receive wind from the northwest and west. It is open to the west. You get seas rolling around the point and coming into the harbor. It was his opinion that would not be a safe haven."

As for Puerto Barrios, Guatemala, and the newer commercial port of Santo Tomás de Castilla, March, with only two seasons' experience in the western Caribbean, had never been there. "I don't believe he had charts aboard," said MDB. The port had a deep, well-marked commercial channel used by container ships and long banana boats. But MDB said, "It's somewhat of, not having been there, not knowing what you will find, to make that commitment without previous experience, charts, or being there, or an OK from the port authority. Captain Paul (Maskell) had been there. He suggested it was so open to the north that it probably won't be very safe in there."

The option of staying in Belize City had been discussed but dismissed out of hand for the lack of protection. The barrier reef broke seas but did nothing to slow winds that could blow the ship ashore. "Our company strategy is to take evasive action," MDB said later. "We've been successful. I'm not the kind of mariner who blindly believes you're safer at sea than in port. That did not play here. The storm was still 300 miles, two days away. The ship was not in imminent danger. The crew was not in harm's way. It would be totally illogical to anchor the boat and take the crew off with the passengers."

They also eliminated the southern Belizean coast, including a deepwater channel on the Monkey River and the small lagoon behind the Placencia peninsula where the *Fantome* stopped every other week. Maskell ruled them out. The river's anchorage was a small inlet with a dock. "You would want to make sure you had a berth when you got there. There was nobody to call, given the time. With Belize under panic, and we're under pressure, there's not the time to get everything sorted out." Placencia was eliminated because it didn't block the wind. Behind Placencia, banana boats used the 20-foot-deep channel into Big Creek. Captain Paul said later, "If the ship had stayed and anything would have happened, the whole world would have said, 'What fools they were just to sit there and hope for the best.' You go to sea, and you try and put as much distance between yourself and the storm."

That left Captain March with the Bay Islands. Said Michael D. Burke: "We all came to the same conclusion. It was an idea that we had all been considering since 10:30 [A.M.]." By a process of elimination, then, the battle between the *Fantome* and the strongest October hurricane in history was joined. The *Fantome* would go southeast, while its master and owner prayed that the hurricane turned northwest.

The launch circled the *Fantome* once. Laura-Jo was crying hysterically.

Karyn Rutledge was overcome by a sudden sadness. "It was a very different ship than the night before. The romance and the majesty were missing. It was a forlorn-looking ship. The sky was gray and the sails were down and the ship looked sad." She hit Anthony Moffa in the ribs: "Get the camera out. Take some pictures."

The huge boat itself looked gray against the gray eastern sky, as if it were floating in it, ghostlike. "It wasn't like the pictures in the tourist brochure. I look at those now and it gives me the creeps." As the launch sped away, Moffa looked up. Brasso was spinning the big wheel on the bridge.

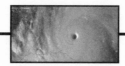

GULF OF HONDURAS
October 26, 1998
AFTERNOON AND EVENING

T HE CHANNEL THROUGH Belize's barrier reef is a twisty mine-
field of coral heads. From the anchorage of Belize City, it runs generally southeast. At every turn on the early afternoon of Monday, October
26, the helmsman on the *Fantome's* bridge would have seen Hurricane
Mitch ahead.

"It was like a wall," said Jack Ramsey, one of the passengers watching from the airport. "Like someone had drawn a black curtain as far as
you could see. It scared the hell out of us."

The *Fantome* was 280 miles from the hurricane's center but only 135
miles from the outer edge of roiling dense rings of heavy rain, squalls,
and lightning. Miles Lawrence had predicted at 1 P.M. that the storm
would continue west-northwest for the next 24 hours but slow down.
"A hurricane warning may be needed for the north coast of Honduras
west of Limón later today." Between the ship and the approaching edge
of the hurricane were rain bands, each large enough to qualify as a tropical wave, separated by gaps of clear, windy weather that were sweet relief.

"All's well," Guyan March e-mailed Miami from the bridge at 3:56 P.M.
The ship had just cleared the barrier reef and was passing the light at the
southern end of the Turneffe Islands. Sheltered by the reef and mainland
and motor-sailing in one of the interludes between squalls, March reported gentle north-northwest winds at 4 P.M., with slight seas and
swells. With the wind on her tail, *Fantome* was making 10.5 knots at 900
rpm. March said he was getting good hurricane information on his single sideband radio.

At some point that afternoon—he remembered 4 o'clock—someone
from Windjammer headquarters in Miami called Samir Galindo, the

manager's son at Anthony's Key Resort on Roatán, and asked about possible shelter. Galindo, frantic with the tasks of battening down a resort and with 15- to 20-foot waves crashing on the outer reef, said he remembered it clearly.

"I was trying to secure boats and [the resort's tame] dolphins on the west end of Roatán. They phoned the resort and the office radioed me. They were saying the boat was in Belize. What did we recommend?"

Samir said he radioed back: "You guys should stay in Belize. Don't come to Roatán, because it's starting to get rough here."

At about the same hour, Paul March called from London to tell Guyan that their maternal grandfather had died the day before. Paul was with their mother at her parents' house, sorrowed not only by their grandfather's death but also because the day was their parents' wedding anniversary. Their father had died in 1991. Paul March said he and his mother knew vaguely that Mitch "was around," but Captain March sounded "matter of fact. He was just coming out of the Belize channel. He was going to run from it. He was going to go down south, to Roatán, and hang out. It wasn't a very long conversation. They had a lot of wind, feeder bands. It was very wet." The conversation, their last, ended with "Carry on. Take it easy. Speak to you in a couple of days." Paul and his mother went back to their Cornwall home.

🐚

Miles Lawrence reported at 4 P.M. that Mitch had strengthened to a "strong" Category 5 storm and that Honduras had issued a hurricane warning for its entire northern coast—the *Fantome*'s destination—meaning that a hurricane was expected in a day. The storm still was moving west-northwest, 290 degrees, at 7 knots. Winds were blowing at 155 knots, with gusts to 180 knots. Lawrence's favorite models persuaded him to bend the forecast track to the northwest over the next three days. But he called it "very slow motion. . . . It is not yet clear which country or countries in the northwest Caribbean are most threatened." In a day, he predicted, the storm would be 25 miles farther north. In 48 hours, it would be 65 miles north. Mitch's "strike" or landfall probabilities, a set of figures used by emergency managers but almost never by sailors, included a 16 percent chance of landfall on Belize in the next 48 hours and a 22 percent chance of a strike on Guanaja in the next 24 hours.

Lawrence assigned a 35 percent chance that Mitch would bend north over the next two days to reach a point 100 miles north of Guanaja.

Mitch was now a "pinup" storm. As word of the 905 millibar reading spread through the warrens at the National Hurricane Center, color printers hummed with downloaded shots from GOES-8, straight down into a whirlpool large enough to circle islands. Around the eye, pure white high-altitude clouds streamed away, hiding the dense weather underneath.

With national borders drawn in on the satellite photo, Honduras looked helpless, Belize doomed, and the Yucatán, sticking up like a thumb, poised for a battering. Looking down, it was inconceivable that a ship would be out there. *Odyssey*, a container ship operated by Hyde Shipping of Miami, had left Belize City at 1:30 P.M., a deadline set by Miami because of the storm. "We left three containers on board in our haste to depart," said Michael Youngman, the company's Miami port captain. The ship was beating north against heavy seas at 14 knots but thought it could outrun Mitch into the Gulf of Mexico. "There was no point in heading east. She would be going into danger." Belize City port director Alfred Coye was clearing his harbor, directing boats to anchorages that would accommodate them. "If they had decided to stay, we would have directed them to Robinson Point, 7 or 8 miles away to the southeast. There is a cement barge. It is very deep. They could have anchored there. It is somewhat protected. But they never asked my opinion," he said. Six container ships that arrived in Puerto Barrios in Guatemala from Friday through Sunday left by 5:30 P.M. "No prudent shipmaster will stick around and wait for a hurricane to come and batter it," said Ian Tull, vice president of ship operations for Dole Fruit. "Mitch was hovering around. Our ships kept out of the area." Nevertheless, three 700-foot banana boats, the *Americas*, the *Frances*, and the *Courtney L*, tied alongside the dock at Puerto Barrios for the storm.

David Jones, the Caribbean weather broadcaster, was aghast to learn that the yacht *Velella* had left Río Dulce, Guatemala, for Roatán. But *Velella* checked in safe from the island that afternoon and agreed to pass Jones' reports on to other cruising yachts on a local Net. Jones' other yacht in the area, *Departure II*, had taken his advice and was running down the coast of Belize toward the Río Dulce, which offered protection to small yachts but not to a ship of *Fantome's* size.

Back in Belize City, a panicked populace was making passenger evacuation a nightmare. The chartered buses had been turned away from the downtown hotel where lunch and a waiting room had been arranged. So they headed for the airport along a road busy with vehicles piled with people and their possessions, fleeing inland. The scene at the airport was simply chaotic. The Weather Channel at the airport bar was projecting landfall in Belize City on Wednesday.

"We were pacing," said Anthony Moffa. "It's getting to be 3 o'clock, then 4. We moved into the main boarding area. It was like being in a high school gymnasium. A poor woman with a dog was in tears. She couldn't get a flight until Wednesday. People were euphoric. People were devastated. One guy at the boarding gate screams, 'Everyone shut up.' I thought somebody had been killed. He was yelling to his girlfriend to come, to get on the flight with them. Meanwhile, they are hammering hurricane shutters on windows. Slowly the airport, internally, is getting dark."

Laura-Jo remembered several cranky passengers complaining about their ruined cruise and demanding, "What are you going to do about it?" A couple from Oregon, for example, was upset to learn that they had to buy seats on the evacuation plane for $250 apiece

Cathie de Koeyer's answer, according to Laura-Jo, was to shout at one point: "You don't realize we've said good-bye to thirty brothers on that ship."

Jack and Deanna Ramsey took pity on a young woman in her late twenties who couldn't get a flight out and was "absolutely panicked, crying. We asked Laurie if all the seats on the charter were taken. She said there were probably twenty-five seats not taken. We said, 'Can't you get them on there?' She said no, because of insurance. We all got sort of ticked."

Laura-Jo called her sister in Wales in tears. "It wasn't until this moment that the severity of it all hit me," Annie Bleasdale wrote later. "They had put crew off. In all my time at Windjammer, I hadn't encountered this."

At about 6 P.M., the Miami charter flight landed in Belize City, and the passengers boarded.

"It had a Hollywood feel to it—getting out of town in the nick of time," said Moffa. "The sky to the east was so dark, you would have thought it was midnight. We all get on the plane and we're getting ready and it is coming closer and the pilot says, 'We would normally take off to the east, but due to the weather we're taking off to the west.' As we turn around, it is starting to rain. Heavily. Great, I thought, we'll be grounded. We start to go. Halfway down the runway the rain stops. We take off, up and out. As we came back around, hard to the right, you could see this enormous storm encroaching. Hollywood couldn't have written a better ending. I was trying to see the boat."

As the plane left Belize, carrying ninety-seven passengers, three crew women, and one crewman, Annie Bleasdale called Guyan March on the *Fantome*.

"He said that everything was OK and that I shouldn't worry. They were sailing southeast to hide behind Roatán. He said that he was very concerned about our friends and agents in Belize, as they were in the direct path of the oncoming storm and the place was about to be devastated. He said that he wished he could have got them on board to run to safety with him. He said he'd call me tomorrow."

Captain March's apparent calm in the face of a Category 5 storm and the biggest, blackest sky of his life, could have been one part relief and one part belief. He had sailed away from the horrible scene in Belize—the hysterical staff, expired passports, last-minute photos, and inane questions from guests—and the *Fantome* was now at sea, rolling in the large, long waves propagating from Mitch's core. A professional calm had come over the ship. It was a feeling familiar to any captain and crew leaving a harbor, particularly in marginal weather. The very act of getting underway, of hoisting and trimming sails, of securing gear and establishing watches, created a purpose that shoved all the "what-ifs" aside. The job was no longer deciding, or dealing with passengers or calls from the office. The job now was sailing, doing battle with the sea and the storm. The crew of the *Fantome* responded as a practiced, familial machine.

March also possessed a sailor's eternal optimism, a belief in his ability to weather a storm and survive. This was boosted by his faith in the National Hurricane Center's 4 P.M. forecast that Mitch would bend northwest late Tuesday and leave him a 100-mile margin.

If Guyan March had been at the helm in the same spot thirty-five years earlier, he might not have been so encouraged. Alone with his ship, his information would have been much more primitive—the waves, the sky, the wind, and the ship's barometer, which by midafternoon on Monday would have fallen 5 millibars below normal. He might have pulled out his copy of the *American Practical Navigator*, known in mariner's circles since 1802 as "Bowditch" after its original author, Nathaniel Bowditch. Its graphs would have told him that a drop of 1 millibar per hour suggests a storm center 225 miles away. If the barometer drops 3 millibars per hour, the storm's eye is 100 miles away. The hurricane's center would have been the darkest spot in the "bar," the outer perimeter of the eye wall, on the horizon.

The captain of the 1960s would have determined the storm's movement by facing the wind. The storm's center would be 90 to 135 degrees to the right, over his right shoulder. Checking this over a period of time, a captain could determine which way the storm was moving. If it was coming toward him, the worst place to be was to the right of its path of advance, or to the north of a storm tracking west, in the "dangerous semicircle" where winds were stronger and were likely to push the boat straight into the storm's path. The safer place—if he had to choose—was to the left of the path of advance, the so-called navigable semicircle where winds blew away from its direction of travel. The idea was to get as far away from the center as possible.

Bowditch advised that once in the navigable semicircle, a captain should put the wind on the starboard quarter—coming across the rear, right-hand corner of the ship—and run like hell. Plotted on the *Fantome*'s charts, this would have meant a course of 195 degrees, almost straight toward Puerto Barrios, Guatemala. Captain March's course was 125 degrees. According to Bowditch, March's course could be considered "safe" only if the storm's track turned northward by 70 degrees. Forecaster Miles Lawrence was predicting Mitch to do that, but not for two or three days. Even then, March would have precious little sea room. Guatemala's shore was only 60 miles away. When he reached Roatán, his sea room would have dwindled to 25 miles.

🐚

At 7 P.M. Monday, the National Hurricane Center reported that Mitch's eye was moving over Swan Island. Belize hoisted a hurricane watch, putting the entire northwestern Caribbean, from Mexico to Honduras, on alert. The storm was moving west-northwest at 7 knots with steady winds of 156 knots and gusts of an astonishing 200 knots. The center now warned of rainfall over Honduras of 10 to 15 inches.

On Swan Island, a small military contingent from Honduras took refuge in ditches. Cows were blown into the sea. Three concrete buildings tore apart as if blasted by an atomic bomb.

On Guanaja, Doug and Mary Solomon gathered their two dogs, Cindy and Penny, their three cats, and their green-naped parrot, Margarita, and left their home for the indentation dug behind the hill. Doug took his barometer, which was dropping steadily. Near the thornbush, they turned the wheelbarrow upside down, spread out the plastic, climbed into their sailor's foul-weather outfits, tried to calm the animals and themselves, and lay down to wait.

On Guanaja's West End, David Greatorex and his staff took refuge in a 12- by 22-foot cabin designed by Greatorex's sister-in-law, an architect in Seattle. Its posts were cement and rebar in 8-inch PVC pipe sunk 3.5 feet into the ground. The building was fastened to the posts by 1¼-inch bolts through four-by-eights. The carpenter who built it told Greatorex, "Good God, you don't need all this." Greatorex told him, "It's not just for sunshine." Greatorex and his four staff put plywood on the windows and went inside. They were in good shape. They had a kerosene stove, 20 gallons of water, and lots of food. They even had lights from batteries.

Planes stopped running to and from Roatán and Guanaja. At the Bayman Bay Club, manager Don Pearly told his guests they were stuck for the duration. He told his staff to go get their families. "We ended up with thirty-three, including a month-and-a-half-old infant."

Across the strait on the Honduran mainland, the wind started howling in the Garifuna village of Santa Rosa de Aguán. Pieces of roofing began blowing off ramshackle houses perched on the sand of the Río Aguán's broad delta. Patrick Cleary, a Peace Corps volunteer who had gone into Tacoa for groceries earlier in the day, reported water running into low-lying homes by the time he returned. His landlord turned on a battery-powered radio Monday night. "He said a big storm was coming but was passing us. It won't hit Honduras. It is going to Belize. We're going to be OK. We were just trying to survive the wind. We couldn't go out. Some roof came off our house. The wind was blowing so hard you couldn't repair anything."

Twenty-five miles to the west, on the hillside city of Trujillo, the wind got so furious that 25-pound tiles began blowing off the house of Jim Davis, an American expatriate. "It sounded like machine guns," he said later. The water, by now, was washing into the dance floor and bar area of his favorite hangout on the beach, the Gringo Bar.

In Miami, Michael D. Burke went home about 8 P.M. Satellite photos on the Weather Channel, shown every hour, made Mitch look horrible, a monster dwarfing Honduras and Belize and everything between. At about 9 P.M. in Miami, Windjammer's marketing chief, Shannon DeZayas-Manno, met the charter flight from Belize, fed the passengers, and found them rooms at a Budgetel. They were told that Windjammer would find new cruises for them and would even fly them to the Caribbean the next day for a berth on another boat. One couple accepted the offer and continued their vacation.

꧁

For crew families aware of the drama, Monday night became an eternity. Glenn Parkinson in New York wanted to call Onassis on the bridge, but she didn't want to bother him. Watching the Weather Channel, she could only imagine what he was going through. At her home in Georgetown, Guyana, Alisa Maxwell went to bed without the promised phone call from her husband, chef Eon Maxwell. He had forgone his summer vacation time to be at home for their son's first birthday in December. Falling asleep, she dreamed that she was on a beach with her husband. "A blue snake was running behind us. He put me on something and he went down to kill it. I don't remember what happened."

In the dark, open Gulf of Honduras, the *Fantome* was making 6 knots. The rising wind was coming from behind, but the waves were growing and the barometer was dropping. Mitch's eye was now 200 miles from the ship, but gale-force winds were only 85 miles away. Periodically, huge bands of dark clouds filled with squalls blew across the ship, with winds gusting to 30 knots. Waves were 12 to 15 feet high, striking the bow on the port side, rolling the ship heavily. Standing at the helm on the exposed, pitching deck in rain gear would have been uncomfortable, but the occasional splash of salt water, blown over the bow, would have been warm, not at all unpleasant. A seasoned deckhand could take a two-hour shift at the helm in stride, supported by an experienced mate standing in the glow of the chartroom ahead of him and an engineer or two below. It may even have been better than going below and trying to sleep jammed into a rolling bunk.

The presence of "old hands" likely eased the tension and discomfort that built through the night. The *Fantome*'s three deck officers had thirty years' combined experience. Guyan March, Brasso Frederick, and Onassis Reyes were strong, fit athletes, good swimmers, and intelligent sailors. The unshakable First Mate Brasso had been knocked about by hurricanes and survived. Second Mate Onassis, who was in charge of ship's safety and the mate normally on duty until midnight, had put the men through weekly drills for fire fighting, abandoning ship, and rescuing a man overboard. Just the summer before, near Belize, the crew had demonstrated its rescue ability when the ship's kitty, Tiki, slipped overboard. "I remember seeing those huge, burly crewmen poised on the lifeboats, ready to drop them and take after the cat," said Carol Frierson-Campbell, a travel writer who posted a story on America On Line. "I remember thinking if it had been a human, how lucky they would have been." It took thirty minutes to drop sails and turn the ship around. Passengers, rum swizzles in hand, ran to the caprail with binoculars and flashlights. It was at the edge of dark. The waters were fortuitously calm. After many long minutes, someone spotted the cat's reflective eyes. The crew dropped a whaleboat. The cat was retrieved. "I was amazed at the time and commitment to saving this cat," said Frierson-Campbell. "Everyone was in tears."

Fantome's deckhands, who averaged four years with Windjammer, were led by twelve-year veteran bosun Cyrus Phillips. He and bosun's mate Jerry King had been graceful and sure as they climbed around the masts and rigging, preparing the ship for the storm. The engineers were headed by nine-year veteran Pope Layne and seasoned seaman Constantin Bucur, although their staff's average sea time was three years and four of the men were first-year rookies. The "hotel staff" under chef Eon Maxwell and chief steward Chrispin Saunders averaged a little less than three years at sea, with very little, if any, hurricane experience. Three of the men were the new dock hires from Honduras, trapped aboard by lack of visas.

The *Fantome*'s seaworthiness, its ability to battle a hurricane and protect them, may never have entered these men's minds. But the *Fantome*, like any ship, was in a constant state of repair. Its age, and the cost-conscious mindset of the Miami office, meant that the list of maintenance needs, compiled on the bridge's computer, never disappeared. "We never seemed to be able to catch up," said Fedor Steer, who left as first mate in April. "Anything serious or safety-related got priority." Engineer Bucur had told his wife that the refit in Trinidad would be lots of work. "He told me that he didn't like how the ship was. . . . It was going OK when he was there, but he put in his mind to change a lot of things around, even about the persons working there."

Most of the wire cable shrouds that held the masts in place, and many turnbuckles used to fasten them to the hull, had been replaced within the previous year. The one remaining to be rerigged was the foremast. During a dry dock in 1997, the hull bottom had been cleaned and painted and the antielectrolysis "zincs" had been replaced. But the ship was short six sails and the old ones were "pretty tattered," said Steer. "The company kept promising that we would get new ones." The *Fantome*'s whaleboat launches, powered by ancient Chinese engines, had been breaking down since Guyan March joined Windjammer. The engineers were constantly fixing them while passengers waited.

In the engine room, thirty-year-old Pope Layne often worked until midnight keeping the *Fantome* running. "Something was always breaking down. There would be a generator out. There'd be an engine out. The pumps wouldn't work. The water would be rusty," said Rhonda Epperson, the mother of Pope's child and the fleet's personnel chief. "Every time I talked to him or anybody in operations there would be problems with the *Fantome*. He begged me to transfer him back to the *Flying Cloud*." Many of *Fantome*'s parts dated from closer to 1900 than 2000. The parts, noted passenger Don Conyngham, "had long disappeared from shelves. All the Windjammer engineers were artists in maintaining equipment that would be in a museum of the modern merchant marines. I remember one split wye for diesel fuel mixing that Pope showed me. He could use it to mix a blend of fuels to keep the specific gravity correct. Modern equipment does that automatically. My company sells replacements. But the older stuff had a mixing wye and a couple of petcocks, and an experienced guy adjusted the mix by hand until the engine revolutions and emissions seemed right. Well, this splitter wye broke. We looked at it. Multiple brazings and chewed-up threads indicated it had lasted far beyond its years already."

"We have to make one," Pope told Conyngham.

"That's a pretty complicated fitting. You're going to need a jig, a caliper, a machine press. You have all that down here?"

"We'll do OK," Pope said.

"And he did," Conyngham remembered later. "Buying loose fittings and cutting them up and brazing them back together with no fancy CAD program or scanning. Not only did it look good, it worked. When I got back Stateside I told this story to a plant engineer. His response was shock. 'We could never do that. Why, the liability. Imagine if it broke, it would all be my fault. Better to replace the machine.' Cultural differences—the American pro with all the toys most concerned with wallpapering his butt, and the West Indies guy who took years to learn the true innards of these old machines, who understands the beauty and inner common sense, who fixed it because it was broke."

At 10 P.M., the eye of Hurricane Mitch was just west of Swan Island and 105 miles from the north coast of Honduras. It was moving west-northwest, 290 degrees, at 7 knots and was expected to continue in that direction, but more slowly. Tropical storm winds extended 175 miles. This monster storm was now producing 12-foot seas for 350 miles in all directions.

"Our track prediction guidance continues to be anything but straight-forward," wrote forecaster Richard Pasch in his discussion. Two computer models aimed it toward Belize or the Yucatán, two others turned it north in a couple of days. The latest GFDL ran the storm southwest for a day, then back, which Pasch interpreted as "a slow meandering motion in 12 to 24 hours and persisting through 72 hours." His forecast slowed the storm, initially, to 2 or 3 knots, with a gradual turn north. But then he expected it to slow even more. The three-day outlook moved Mitch only 120 miles, an average speed of 1.5 knots. "The longer term movement of Mitch remains shrouded in uncertainty," he wrote.

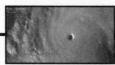

ROATÁN, BAY ISLANDS

October 27, 1998

DAWN—EARLY AFTERNOON

CAPTAIN GUYAN MARCH SPOTTED the long spiny island of Roatán at about 5 A.M. on Tuesday, October 27. A short time later his boss, Michael D. Burke, called from his home in Miami.

"How was it?"

"A little lumpy."

Burke's memory of that conversation, colored by the cool British countenance of Guyan March, filtered out the crescendo of a storm's edge. The waves in the open sea at the time were "probably 20 foot," according to Kevin Brewer, the dive master at Anthony's Key Resort, who was up at dawn checking boats. "One gust blew me across the boat."

"There was a lot of stress," said Burke. "There had not been a lot of concern in the evening. But this is still blowing at 170 miles an hour. It's a huge weather system. He's boxed in a corner. I'm sure he got some sleep, but not a whole lot. Guyan never raised his voice. If anything, there was maybe a bit more hesitation, an edge, not exactly a comfortable tone."

When Annie Bleasdale called March on the bridge, he was more to the point.

"Beam me up, Scottie," March told her.

"He said conditions were pretty bad, Force 10, huge waves. The sails they had left up had been blown out and were now stowed. He still planned to shelter from the huge swell. He told me not to worry, that he loved me and would call in a couple of days."

"Force 10," in sea parlance, is a level on the Beaufort scale used by sailors to estimate wind speeds and sea conditions and their effects on ships. Force 10 conditions mean winds of 48 to 55 knots and waves of 20 to 40 feet, with overhanging crests. The sea takes on a white appearance as foam is blown in dense streaks. Visibility is reduced, though not drastically. On the Beaufort scale Force 10 is just two steps below a hurricane, which starts at 64 knots. At Force 10, ships begin to roll heavily, and control becomes tougher. Overnight, the *Fantome* had gone from the calm behind Belize's reef, 300 miles from the storm's eye, to storm conditions 140 miles from the eye. Based on Bowditch's calculations of an approaching storm, *Fantome*'s barometer would have fallen 25 millibars.

At dawn, Mitch was again moving directly west at 7 knots. A Hurricane Hunter flight during the night had measured the eye pressure at 917 millibars, up considerably from the day before. But wind speeds were still as high as 164 knots. Mexico and Guatemala had raised hurricane warnings. The 4 A.M. forecast bent Mitch's track toward the Bay Islands by just a hair for twelve hours, "with a gradual slowing in forward speed and a bend toward the west-northwest then northwest thereafter." Plotted on a map, the forecast placed Mitch 60 miles due north of Guanaja by 1 P.M. that afternoon, 40 miles closer than predicted on Monday. Three days away it would be approaching Cozumel, Mexico.

Rounding Roatán's West Point, a spot he knew well, Captain March reported that big waves were "boiling" over the sandbar, curling around the island and following the south coast into Coxen Hole, the cruise ship port. His strategy, following standard Windjammer procedure in the eastern Caribbean, would be to stand off the island by one or two miles and steam back and forth, east and west, in the lee of the island. He would not anchor but would stay free to run or even move to the opposite side of the island when the storm passed to the west. Once he reached the south side of the island, behind its 200- to 600-foot-high ridgeline, seas dropped dramatically, to under 12 feet. March estimated the wind at 40 knots from the west-northwest and, according to Burke, put two staysails up again to steady her rolling. At 8:30 A.M. March sent an e-mail to Miami: "Good morning. We will require fuel this weekend because of our side trip we are on. Can we get 10,000 gallons on Friday or Saturday and then we'll top up the following weekend when we get the supplies. Please let the agent know which day so he can get pilots, etc. Capt. Guyan." The ship's tanks held 25,000 gallons of diesel fuel.

❧

At 9 A.M. Hurricane Mitch began pounding the north coast of Guanaja. The sea began to rise, almost as if someone had flushed a plugged toilet. It was that fast: 1, 4, 6, 10 feet. Pushed from the eye wall of the storm like snow in front of a snowplow, the water climbed over Doug Solomon's dock on the northeast end of the island, setting boards adrift. It flooded the sand and flowers, surrounded the concrete block generator room, and began climbing the telephone poles on which his house was perched. A mile to the west, at Mangrove Bight, where scores of homes were built out over the water on pilings, the sea began churning underneath. Boats were tossed about, banging into each other, the docks, and the houses. As the waters reached floor level, people fled out on the rickety wooden walkways suspended between the shore and the maze of homes.

Harriet Ebanks' house was the first to go, at 9:45 A.M. Eyewitnesses said it looked as if a giant sea monster had just lifted it off its stilts. Heavy, wind-blown breakers, nearly 12 feet high, smashed her house as if with a fist, creating a scattered, floating woodpile. "Everything went under—the land stayed underwater," said Kerston Moore, a lobster diver. From the northernmost seawall of Mangrove Bight, townspeople on higher ground watched with horror as the sea popped, floated, and smashed houses one after another. Floating, they banged into each other like loose boats. Then they fell apart. Piles of shattered lumber—former houses—began washing ashore in a great splintered chaos. Panicked people ran pell-mell across the woodpiles, holding their babies, helping their mothers, stepping on nails, cutting their hands. Down the waterfront the surge and smashing came. The waves became waves of lumber, filling the space beneath Moore's house, surrounding the concrete block stilts. Every fifteen minutes or so a larger than usual wave would push the lumber higher. Hundreds of people ran to a church that lay at the center of the village, not 25 feet from the seawall. But lumber and water began wedging around the church, rocking it. "It's time to pray," someone cried. Just then the wind gave a shriek and someone howled, "It's time to run!" The church exploded soon after. People gathered in homes farther up the hill and huddled together in groups of twenty below granite cliffs and in canyons behind the village.

At the Bayman Bay Club, facing north from its cliffside perch, Don Pearly watched his 300-foot dock disappear. The sea rose and the water simply lifted the dock away from its moorings. "It didn't blow up. It just lifted, loosened, and floated off." Pearly and his guests were in a reinforced-concrete basement with a windowed front that looked out to the sea. He had screwed plywood over the windows, so light inside was minimal. They had mattresses and a bathroom. As gusts became stronger, they would speculate on what was going on outside: "There went such-and-such a cabin." The gusts got longer. "It would get scarier and scarier and longer lasting, until finally it was constant. Shortly after that, the noise disappeared from your mind. It was more like a feeling."

Pearly and his assistant manager, Chris Norris, struggled out to check on thirty-three employees and their families in an adjacent basement. It was 53 feet between shelters, but the trip back and forth was torture. "We'd fight to hold on to trees and beams under the cabins. The cabins were creaking and moving." Ten minutes later, coming back, it looked like a different route. New trees had fallen on the path. The noise was constant. The air was filled with salt water—"like a bucket, horizontally. You couldn't stand up. The hillside became a waterfall." Several cabins disappeared. Those that remained were badly damaged, with whole roofs missing.

🐢

At 10 A.M. Miles Lawrence reported that Mitch had moved only 10 miles in the previous six hours, and was 40 miles shy of where the last forecast said it would be. His fix, in fact, showed a 6-mile jog to the southeast from the previous fix. This "jog" involved two successive forecasters' best estimates of the storm's central point, a fix based on a jerky satellite loop with a stated margin of error of 23 miles. A 6-mile shift was "noise" statistically, particularly in a circle of hurricane-force winds 120 miles across. A re-enactment of the storm's track months later showed Mitch did not jog southeast but was making a slow left-hand turn to the south.

Based on his real-time analysis of the models, Lawrence wrote in his discussion: "The GFDL is almost stationary for 72 hours and the NOGAPS shows a slow, mostly northward drift." His official forecast was a "blend" of the models: a bit south of west (260 degrees) for a while, then a slow west to northwestward drift for 72 hours to near the Yucatán Peninsula. Lawrence warned in the discussion, "It would only take a 5-knot error in the forecast speed of motion for the hurricane to make landfall in 24 to 36 hours anywhere in the warning area from Honduras to the Yucatán."

Mitch's winds had declined by 10 knots to 145 knots, still a Category 5 storm. From space, the eye was a perfect hole inside a boiling white vortex. Drawn onto the satellite photo, the Bay Islands appeared as mites, insignificant, the eye itself as wide as Roatán's length.

Plotted on his chart, Mitch's reported 6-mile "jog" to the southeast shocked Michael D. Burke, who was hanging on every word and hoping for the best from the National Hurricane Center. Clutching at straws, the thought occurred to him that if the storm was going southeast, it was "going away. That's good. OK. We'll wait and see."

Aboard the *Fantome*, in the roiled wake of Roatán, March did not have the satellite photo, the weather fax, or the full array of "products" from the National Hurricane Center that were available in Miami. He was, in a very real sense, sailing blind—aided by men far away who could not hear the wind or feel the ship shudder, or sense the mounting fatigue of the helmsman at the wheel on the exposed bridge deck a few stairsteps and a couple of paces away. March himself was tired and stressed. Never very good at mathematics or at estimating time and distance, his keenness wore as he listened to the static-filled single sideband radio or talked on the satellite telephone and plotted Mitch's location on a chart table that heaved and pitched.

"Most of our discussion was about heavy weather preparation," said MDB, who, along with Paul Maskell, called the bridge periodically to check on ship conditions and boost morale. March confirmed that he had taken all possible heavy-weather precautions. Everything on deck had been removed and stored in cabins. The deck boxes had been drilled shut and duct-taped, as had the doors to the Admiralty suites on the main deck. Rope was strung across Decks A and B for safety lines. Watertight doors belowdecks were closed and dogged down, as were the lower bulkhead doors. Two empty fuel tanks had been flooded with seawater to lower the ship's center of gravity. Burke was worried about seawater splashing into the engine air intake, behind louvers near the entrance to the saloon. Water could damage or stop the diesels. March said he had put plywood over them and caulked the cracks with rags and rope. Burke also asked March to secure the heavy saloon doors with plywood. March said that one of the doors had been screwed down, but the other was left open. Burke interpreted that to mean that the crew was in the saloon and needed one door for possible escape. Open to the lobby, which ran with shipped water even in fresh winds, these doors were an obvious point of vulnerability. March reported that the ship was rolling somewhat but handling well, especially on the eastward tack with the wind on its port quarter.

As the morning passed, the ship's barometer dropped intermittently. Squalls washed over the deck. The wind was rising. Daylight was turning dark. It was clear that things were getting worse. When Annie Bleasdale called the bridge again, Guyan March "mentioned that MDB had said they could cut free the launches from the sides if they were rolling too heavily."

Burke, who had worried all morning about the ship being blown into the mainland of Honduras 25 miles away, asked March about other possible strategies, including tying up or anchoring at the cruise ship port at Coxen Hole. March said it was "very rough" at the entrance to the harbor. "Whitecaps were running perpendicular to the harbor. He said he couldn't get in."

"Why not anchor on the south side of Roatán?" Burke asked.

"It is too damn rough."

In his 1991 *Cruising Guide to the Northwest Caribbean*, a book written for small yachts, most of which draw 7 feet or less of water, author Nigel Calder described the southern shore of Roatán as "punctuated by a number of fjord-like inlets cutting back into the encircling hills, each one guarded by a shallow reef with a narrow opening and offering superlative protection." Calder sounded each of the inlets and found water at least 40 feet deep in Dixon Cove Bay, Brick Bay, French Harbor, Caribbean Bight, Bodden Bight, Port Royal, and Old Port Royal. In a second publication, *Honduras and Its Bay Islands—A Mariner's Guide*, another sailor-author, Rick Rhodes, cited Dixon Cove on the west and Port Royal on the east as "viable" options for a ship with the *Fantome's* 19-foot draft.

At the time of the *Fantome's* dawn landfall on Roatán, the west end was already roiling with seas. March did not report conditions for the other inlets to the east. They could have been navigable early in the morning, but he had never been in them, they were not marked with navigation aids, and no one had published GPS bearings to enter in bad weather. As time passed, as the winds picked up and waves refracted around Roatán, these narrow entrances—200 yards in most cases—were most likely covered with breakers, according to Calder. In those conditions there was no way to distinguish the deep water from the reefs.

March could not eyeball the ship in as he did in fair weather. "In heavy, breaking seas they'd all be extremely intimidating," said Calder. "You'd basically be doing it on trust, knowing if you were wrong, you would lose the boat. Even Port Royal, with 80-foot depths, I'm not sure I'd take a 280-foot, 19-foot draft ship and put it in the hands of somebody else's cruising guide." Terry Evans, whose family runs Coco View resort and a boat chartering business on French Harbor, said it would have been "absolutely impossible to find a way in. I put my own sailboat on a reef coming in at night in just 3- or 4-foot seas."

At no point in the morning, according to Michael D. Burke, did he and Captain March discuss a scenario to anchor the ship and get the men off.

As it was, dozens of boats were rocking but otherwise snug in Roatán's harbors Tuesday morning. Numerous shrimp boats were tucked into French Harbor and Oak Ridge. Port Royal harbored several boats. In Jonesville Bight, sixty to seventy shrimp and lobster boats and a dozen yachts cowered. "I had Jack Daniels under my pillow," said one yachtie. Most were tuned to VHF or single sideband radio. "It was kinda fun," said another. "It was like a big party. When you're sitting here, you want to have somebody tell you what is going on—even if it's wrong. You turn to all the channels."

J.C. García, who ran a dry dock used by shrimp boats, was at home in Oak Ridge watching CNN and boarding up his house, which faced Honduras. Sometime late that morning, he noticed a four-masted schooner heading east. "Why," he asked himself, "are they going that way?"

❧

Twenty years before satellite photos were available to mariners, a typhoon overran a U.S. Navy convoy en route to the Philippines to support General MacArthur's invasion. The storm of December 17, 1944, came to be called "Halsey's Typhoon" after Admiral William "Bull" Halsey, the convoy's commander who ignored a precipitously dropping barometer. Three destroyers capsized and sank, several ships were seriously damaged, and 790 men were lost. "It was the greatest loss that we have taken in the Pacific without compensatory return since the First Battle of Savo," Admiral C.W. Nimitz, the navy's Pacific fleet chief, wrote two months later.

Nimitz concluded in a postmortem that there had been too much reliance on weather analysis from Fleet Weather Center in Pearl Harbor and a general failure by the commanders to give up the mission and refocus attention on saving their ships. In a letter that would be codified in navy policy, Nimitz wrote:

"A hundred years ago, a ship's survival depended almost solely on the competence of her master and on his constant alertness to every hint of change in the weather. . . . There was no radio. . . . There was no one to tell him that the time had now come to strike his light sails. His own barometer, the force and direction of the wind and the appearance of sea and sky were all that he had for information. Ceaseless vigilance in watching and interpreting signs, plus a philosophy of taking no risk in which there was little to gain and much to be lost, was what enabled him to survive. . . .

"In bad weather, as in most other situations, safety and fatal hazard are not separated by any sharp boundary line, but shade gradually from one into the other. There is no little red light which is going to flash on and inform commanding officers or higher commanders that from then on there is extreme danger from the weather. . . . Ships that keep on going as long as the severity of wind and sea has not yet come close to capsizing them or breaking them in two, may nevertheless become helpless to avoid these catastrophes later if things get worse. By then they may be unable to steer any heading but in the trough of the sea, or may have their steering control, lighting, communications and main propulsion disabled, or may be helpless to secure things on deck or to jettison topside weights. The time for taking all measures for a ship's safety is while still able to do so. Nothing is more dangerous than for a seaman to be grudging in taking precautions lest they turn out to have been unnecessary. Safety at sea for a thousand years has depended on exactly the opposite philosophy."

❧

By noon on Tuesday, half the homes in Mangrove Bight on Guanaja had been reduced to woodpiles, awash in the surf. A mile to the northeast, lying in his slough with his wife and pets, Doug Solomon watched as leaves on trees and brush blew away. If he lifted his head above the ground, he estimated the wind at 35 knots. Sitting up, he encountered a rush of 80 knots. Twenty-five miles across the strait, on mainland Honduras, the power went out in La Ceiba, the banana port.

Aboard the *Fantome*, conditions had deteriorated to such an extent that a helmsman could no longer stand outside. He was sent below, and March and his mates in the deckhouse took over steering using a joystick, a round, 3-inch black ball that moved the rudders with hydraulic power. Engines were varied by hand in the engine room, with orders radioed down from the bridge. March reported that the staysails had blown out again.

"How is the rig standing up?" Paul Maskell asked March from Miami. "Fine. It looks fine."

March sounded normal to Maskell, but the satellite phone shielded the rising noise of the storm, the groans of steel, unfamiliar vibrations, and unsettling lurches. Winds of 50 to 75 knots—roughly Category 1 force—were now sweeping over Roatán and through the *Fantome's* thicket of wires, wearing on the ears and nerves of those on board. The tops of waves 10 to 15 feet high were beginning to blow off and streak the sea white. The sky was turning a battleship gray. It was still possible to walk around the *Fantome*, but except for the mates in the deckhouse and the engineers below, most crewmen were believed to be jammed into the booths of the dining saloon. It was the most comfortable place on the ship—their bunks forward had become like bucking mechanical bulls, uninhabitable. In the saloon they could group together for moral support and they could get a sense of conditions outside through the quarterdeck windows. It was also the closest enclosed mustering spot to the lifeboats.

🐚

As he puzzled over the war room's computer models shortly after noon, Miles Lawrence was having twinges of doubt. For a full day Hurricane Mitch had defied the computers and official forecasts. It had not turned northwest. It was drifting southwest. Virtually all the models showed the hurricane curving slightly northwest and blasting across northern Belize and the southern Yucatán. Only the GFDL meandered, showing a little loop. But Mitch was moving so slowly that it occurred to Lawrence to fall back on an old-fashioned practice—if the storm's movements were slow and erratic, call it "stationary" until it showed its true track, or, if moving, extrapolate the current movement forward. With this on his mind, and Mitch clearly having a mind of its own, Lawrence sat down to write the 1 P.M. advisory.

"Mitch is moving slowly toward the west-southwest near 5 knots, and a slow west-southwest to westward motion is expected to continue for the next 24 hours." The winds had dropped to 134 knots, a Category 4 storm. Using shots from several satellites—GOES-8 had gone down at 2 A.M.—he centered the storm at 16.9° N, 85.4° W. The center of Mitch was 30 miles from Guanaja and 60 miles from the *Fantome*.

"The goddamned storm is coming right at you!" Michael D. Burke blurted when he plotted it and called Captain March. Later he recalled, "Our hearts sank. It's hard to describe the feeling inside, a feeling of trepidation and fear, of the worst happening in front of your eyes." March, until now the picture of calm, uttered one line Burke remembered.

"It doesn't look good."

"What do we do, Guyan? We can't stay in its path and hope for the best."

"It wasn't an easy conversation," Burke said later. "Obviously we were in trouble now. We had this huge, powerful storm bearing down, with few options."

The storm's edge, on the horizon the day before, was now on deck. Satellite photos clearly showed the terrible rush of air that was striking the hull, heeling it. March estimated the wind at 60 to 80 knots. Burke thought he was exaggerating. "He didn't have instruments. Past 60 it was a best guess."

"What are we going to do, Guyan? We can't stay in its path and hope for the best."

They talked over options that were rapidly falling away. They couldn't go south. It was 22 miles to the marshy mainland. With winds roaring from the west-northwest and waves of 20 to 40 feet in the open sea, they could not head west toward Guatemala and the port of Puerto Barrios. Northwest, back toward Belize, was out of the question. It was also too late to try a risky plunge through a boiling reef into one of Roatán's harbors. Nightfall was six hours away. In the storm, darkness would come sooner.

At 1:15 P.M., Captain March told Burke that on his last tack to the west, he had had difficulty getting the bow through the wind. The twin Caterpillar engines barely pushed the nose around. The high bow and tall masts were like sails. He could no longer point the bow north, to turn or stay near Roatán. Even if he had jibed the ship, worn the bow around in the other direction, away from the wind, he could not have swung the ship up into the wind, and would have wound up pointing southwest, away from Roatán and back toward the Honduran shore. The farther away from the island he got, the stronger the wind and the less control he would have. "So," said Burke, "he was committed to run to the east." Captain March and the *Fantome* had run out of options.

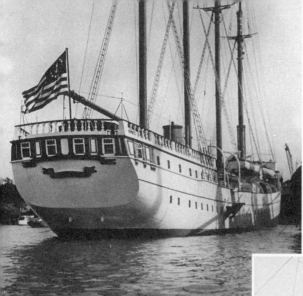

The Flying Cloud, *the most luxurious private yacht in the world, was launched in Italy in 1927. Here it flies the American flag under the ownership of Nelson Warden of Philadelphia while anchored near Monaco, circa 1932. Warden bought the Flying Cloud (later the Fantome) from the Duke of Westminster. The big windows aft would later illuminate Fantome's dining saloon.*

The entrance to the quarterdeck private suites, a carved, concave shell, was designed to resemble the front door of a typical Cotswold cottage. The Duchess of Westminster described the suites as "almost too odd to be believed." The shell and the ornate stairways to the poop deck were retained by Windjammer when the well deck (foreground) was bridged over to become the "lobby" on A deck. A portion of one of these banisters was found on Guanaja after the Fantome disappeared.

The stairway leading to the six original guest suites on B deck, with one of the ship's masts in the foreground. This stairway was retained by Windjammer for access from the dining saloon down to the galley.

PHOTOS BY MARTIN BUSLER VIA BILL WILLISON (3)

The original deck, showing the swinging lifeboat davits. Mike Burke replaced these with davits on the party deck from which the whaleboats (launches) were carried, suspended over the water. The original skylights (right) on the well deck admitted light to the suites on B deck below. Burke bridged over the well deck between the forecastle and quarterdeck to form the top (party) deck. MARTIN BUSLER VIA BILL WILLISON

A.E. Guinness purchased the yacht and renamed her Fantome, and in 1939 it was sailed to Seattle, where it sat out World War II. After Guinness died in 1945, the "million dollar yacht" was sold for $50,000. SEATTLE MUSEUM OF INDUSTRY AND HISTORY

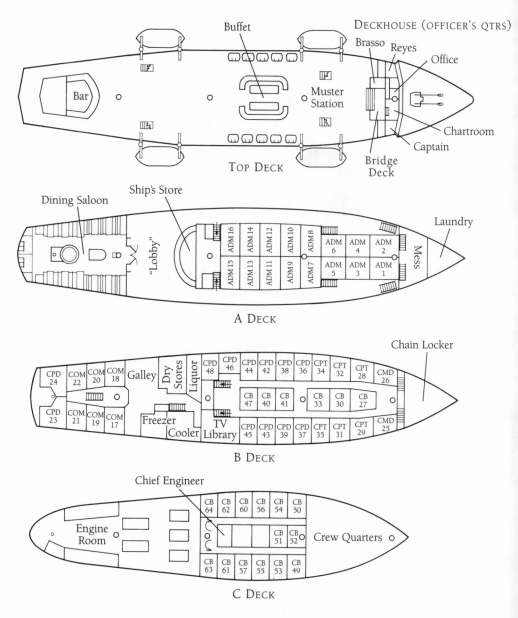

TOP DECK

Buffet

DECKHOUSE (OFFICER'S QTRS)

Brasso Reyes

Office

Bar

Muster Station

Chartroom

Captain

Bridge Deck

A DECK

Dining Saloon

Ship's Store

Laundry

"Lobby"

ADM 16	ADM 14	ADM 12	ADM 10	ADM 8
ADM 15	ADM 13	ADM 11	ADM 9	ADM 7

ADM 6	ADM 4	ADM 2
ADM 5	ADM 3	ADM 1

Mess

B DECK

Chain Locker

Galley

Dry Stores

Liquor

Freezer

Cooler

TV Library

CPD 24	COM 22	COM 20	COM 18			CPD 48	CPD 46	CPD 44	CPD 42	CPD 38	CPD 36	CPT 34	CPT 32	CPT 28	CMD 26

CB 47	CB 40	CB 41		CB 33	CB 30	CB 27

CPD 23	COM 21	COM 19	COM 17			CPD 45	CPD 43	CPD 39	CPD 37	CPT 35	CPT 31	CPT 29	CMD 25

C DECK

Chief Engineer

Engine Room

Crew Quarters

CB 64	CB 62	CB 60	CB 56	CB 54	CB 50

CB 51	CB 52

CB 63	CB 61	CB 57	CB 55	CB 53	CB 49

ADM Admiralty Suite   COM Commodore Suite   CPD Captain's Double
CMD Commodore Suite   CPT Captain's Cabin   CB   Standard Cabin
     Deluxe

Lines plans of the Fantome.
BASED ON DRAWINGS SUPPLIED BY WINDJAMMER BAREFOOT CRUISES, DETAIL COURTESY
STUART LARCOMBE OF WINDJAMMER. REDRAWN BY JIM SOLLERS.

[TOP] *Under Windjammer ownership, the Fantome flew jibs forward and staysails behind all four masts. Topsails could be flown above the "upside down" triangular fishermen staysails, but they were only rigged for the rare "photo op." The ship "sailed like a pig," her captains said, and for the most part motored around the Caribbean. Note the elevated bridge forward, the small windows in the ship's side that let light into the B deck cabins, the saloon windows aft, and the loading stairs amidships.*

[MIDDLE] *The carved "dragon" bar, in the shape of a boat, on the stern quarterdeck. Bartenders beneath a blue tarp sold drinks for "doubloons."*

[BOTTOM] *Crewmen in striped shirts, with help from guests, haul staysails and jibs into place by hand as "Amazing Grace" plays from a bagpipe recording. Winches (left) were used to raise launches. The horseshoe buffet in the middle of the party deck can be seen at right.* PHOTOS BY ED BUSCH (3)

Fantome *crew, January 1998, on a St. Lucia–Grenada trip. Captain Guyan March is kneeling in the center, with Annie Bleasdale (wearing a cap) to his left. Chief Steward Chrispin Saunders, in bow tie, towers at left. The crew rotated weekly depending on leave and other assignments.* KATHY PTASNIK

[INSET] *This orange life ring, mounted in the ratlines, was found on Guanaja and recycled as a wall decoration in a bar. Malabo is the principal port of Equatorial Guinea, Africa, the flag nation of the* Fantome. ED BUSCH

[ABOVE] *Underway, looking forward on the party deck. Guests relax as the helmsman on the raised bridge steers* Fantome. *The canister life raft (lower right) was one of eleven aboard. Only two were found.* TOM GUY

[LEFT] *Looking aft from the bridge deck. Underway, a buffet of "snacks and swizzles" was served at 5 P.M. daily on the party deck. The stairway in the foreground leads down to A deck.* ED BUSCH

[LEFT] *The view aft from the bridge shows the teaklike angelique wood of the party deck, the horseshoe buffet area, the white fiberglass "ski slope" cover of the ornate stairway leading to A deck, and, at rear, the bar, minus the blue shade tarp. Bits of angelique and cabinetry covered Guanaja after the hurricane.* KATHY PTASNIK

Former mate Wade Church and Captain Guyan March in the deckhouse. The small window behind them looks forward and was March's only view out during the storm. KATHY PTASNIK

The electronic equipment in the deckhouse included radar, GPS, single sideband radio, and satellite telephone. CRAIG STUCKER

Guyan March, 21, fresh from his Yacht Masters test and a year of ship-handling experience in England, looked like a teenager when he joined Windjammer in 1987.
PADDY SHRIMPTON

Captain Guyan, 32, after 10 years at Windjammer, had risen to captain's rank and was considered the "golden boy" of the fleet.
ROCKY RAISEN

Thursday nights were party nights, and the deck officers dressed in drag. Left to right: Second Mate Onassis Reyes, Captain Guyan March, and First Mate Brasso Frederick. DAWN SHELBURNE

Chrispin Saunders, 26, chief steward, from Grenada. A favorite of guests, he elevated his salad making and flambé desserts to a performance art. Behind him is the stained glass window in the "lobby." ROCKY RAISEN

Colin August, 36, deckhand and launch driver, from Guyana. Known as "Dovey" at home because of his gentle disposition and "Coffee" aboard Fantome, he was married to Marcel. His brother, Brian, was on leave during Hurricane Mitch. ROCKY RAISEN

Cyrus Philips, 40, bosun, from St. Vincent. He had been with Windjammer for 12 years and hoped to buy a freighter and start his own business of sailing between Caribbean islands. ROCKY RAISEN

CLOCKWISE FROM TOP LEFT: *Deonath Ramsudh, 42, refrigerator specialist, from Guyana: he kept the air-conditioning and freezers working aboard Fantome. In January, nine months before Mitch, he won $69,000 in a casino and set up an education trust fund for his three daughters. Jerry King, 38, bosun's mate, from Guyana: part of the "oiled machine" that kept Fantome running, King had girlfriends in several nations and children in two. Vernon Brusch, 27, electrician, from Guyana, left home in 1997 telling his mother, "Mommy, if I get work I won't be back." Canute "Pope" Layne, 30, second and sometimes acting chief engineer from St. Vincent: Pope kept Fantome running by making parts for the old equipment. He and Laura-Jo Bleasdale, activities mate, were lovers. He was the father of a child with Rhonda Epperson, Windjammer's human resources chief. Alvin "Spice" George, 28, cook, from Grenada: his brother, Alan, was also part of the crew.* PHOTOS BY ROCKY RAISEN (5)

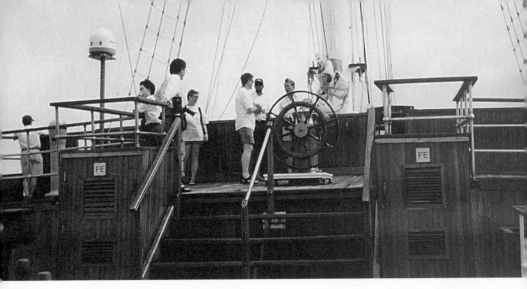

En route to Belize on Monday, October 26. Guyan March talks to guests on Fantome's bridge, which was made of angelique wood on an angle-iron frame. Note the antenna for the satellite phone to the left. The entrance to the deckhouse is ahead and to the right of the wheel.

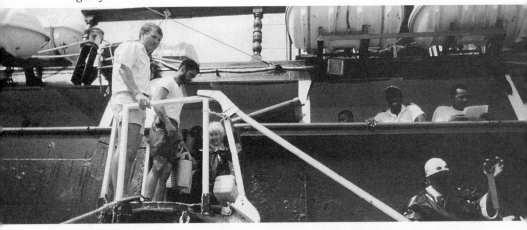

ABOVE: Guyan March and Onassis Reyes see off the last guest launch at Belize on Monday, October 26. Brasso Frederick is at the rail. Next to him, Jerry King is reading a letter. BELOW: Brasso Frederick took this photo of the departing launch with guest Lori Nicely's (center, waving) camera. PHOTOS BY LORI NICELY (3)

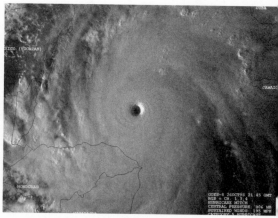

Hurricane Mitch, 4:15 P.M. EST, Sunday, October 25. Mitch is a strong Category 4 storm and still intensifying. Sustained winds are 130 knots and pressure is 924 millibars. Mitch is moving 290 degrees, west-northwest, at 7 knots. Tropical storm force winds cover 300 miles of the Caribbean from Honduras to Cuba. One hour and forty-five minutes later, 97 guests will begin boarding the Fantome in Omoa, Honduras.

8 A.M. EST, Tuesday, October 27. Pressure has risen to 917 millibars, but winds are still as high as 164 knots, so Mitch remains a strong Category 5. The storm is beginning a slow left turn into the Bay Islands, while Fantome tacks in the lee of Roatán.

4:45 P.M. EST, Monday, October 26. Mitch has been a Category 5 storm for several hours, and has now reached its most severe point. The pressure of 905 millibars makes it the fourth strongest Atlantic storm on record. Sustained winds are estimated at 155 knots, with gusts up to 200 knots. The Caribbean Sea is visible through the eye, which is 12 to 15 miles in diameter.

3:20 P.M. EST, Tuesday, October 27. Pressure has risen to 930 millibars, and the eye is filling in. With winds of 115 to 180 knots in the eye wall—perhaps 140 knots at sea level—Mitch is still a borderline Category 4–5 storm. Eighty minutes later, Windjammer loses phone contact with the Fantome, and a NOAA research plane enters the eye.
PHOTOS BY NOAA (4)

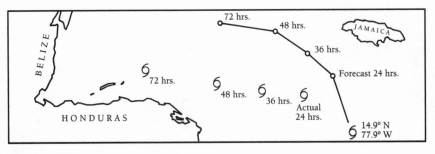

Saturday, 10/24, 11 A.M.

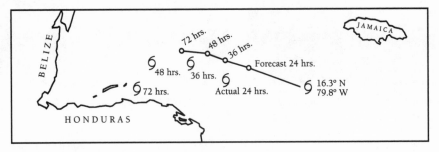

Sunday, 10/25, 10 A.M.

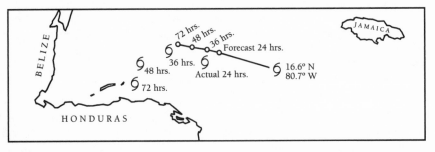

Sunday, 10/25, 4 P.M.

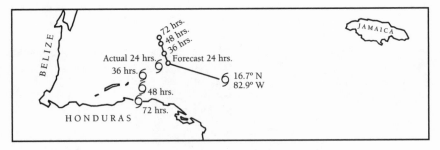

Monday, 10/26 10 A.M.

Forecast versus actual tracks of Mitch from four points on the timeline.
TRACKING MAPS DRAWN BY JIM SOLLERS.

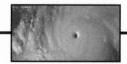

BAY ISLANDS
October 27, 1998

AFTERNOON

❧

A LESSER SAILOR might have panicked by now. A Category 4 hurricane was bearing down on him. The ship he'd been able to handle so well would no longer track and go west. The waves and wind around him were the worst he'd seen. But Guyan March was not given to panic. On the bridge of a ship he wore a look, born of ability, seasoned with success, of calm and assurance. "Never in his life did he lose control of a situation, certainly not at sea," said his brother Paul. "Calm and controlled was the way he managed and thought things through. He was very methodical and calculating."

So successful had March been as a young sailor that problems almost surprised him. Those who knew him saw this aspect occasionally—a passing, stunned look. "He would never actually express it verbally, mainly because there were people around who would pick up on it," said Jeremy Linn, his old sailing instructor. In 1986, while still in sailing school, March was motoring the 72-foot *Hoshi* into a lock in Scotland when the engine failed. He was doing 4 knots. If he had kept going and popped the gate, the ship would have dropped 30 feet. "A look of total horror appeared—only momentarily," said Linn. "He was very quick thinking. We both dove into the engine room and turned the key. The old diesel had been running too slow and stopped. I saw the same thing in handling sails when things weren't quite right. There would be a look of just complete horror. He would take a moment to think about it, and come up with the right solution ninety-nine times out of one hundred. He was calm and collected. He wouldn't shout or scream."

March also impressed his shipmates from the start of his Windjammer career. As a mate on the *Fantome* in the late 1980s, he took control of the bridge when the ship went aground in Antigua. When the captain seemed powerless, Guyan "was all business," said Sharon Patterson, the purser. He was "so self-assured and confident about all things pertaining to sailing that no one ever doubted his suggestions. He could weigh the large and the small, the crew, passengers, weather, ship, responsibility, business, fun, girlfriend, life, love, and laughter and keep them all orbiting in pretty much a well-balanced scheme. Like juggling a dozen balls at once. There were times when you could see rings under Guyan's eyes and knew he needed rest badly, but he never complained about it. I don't understand how he did it, but the man never showed a grouchy side."

Ed Snowdon, who served as mate under March aboard the *Yankee Clipper*, recalled, "I have never met a man, and I've been around a lot of circles, who had more of a sixth sense and innate ability to make the right decision and know the right thing to do. It was uncanny. He didn't have to stop and scratch his head. He was not at all daredevil. He was always making the most prudent decision. When I was sailing down a coastline, he might say, 'Ed, you're 2 miles off a lee shore. What happens if you lose an engine and a squall comes up? You're going to be set down. If you're another mile off, you're in better standing.' He taught me that kind of thing. He would always err on the safe side."

March had tasted rough weather. He'd crossed the English Channel in small boats with winds of 40 to 50 knots. "At home, in the dinghies, we would be the first ones out and the last ones in," said brother Paul. "In marginal, rough seas, everyone waited. If we started in, they knew it was time to head in. Everyone gauged it on us. It went to ability. If we thought it was marginal, it really was time to go in." At Windjammer, Guyan had seen waves sweep the top of the *Fantome* and felt its heeling in big waves. He'd known the edges of several hurricanes. March, like most sailors, had a fascination with sea storms and disasters and an encyclopedic knowledge of them, according to Patterson. "He told me about rogue waves: massive waves that appeared unexpectedly and took ships and crew by surprise. We talked at length about disasters at sea, ships that encountered storms and lost crew."

March must also have known that a career at sea sometimes requires periods outside the comfort zone. That's how sailors grow, through longer crossings and bigger waves. If they survive, the bold ones revel in newfound confidence. "Every time you go out there is a risk," Windjammer owner Mike Burke believed. "That's part of the beauty of it. When you've got a bone in your teeth? And you wonder. That element of danger. It's a good feeling—if it holds together." But the wise ones recognize that their survival sometimes has as much to do with good luck, or a guardian angel, as with their own ability. On Tuesday afternoon, October 27, Guyan March, full of pride and trim, was in the hands of the gods.

"I started to feel fear from him," said Michael D. Burke. "He wasn't too forthcoming with his acceptance that we needed to run to the east. I think he was afraid. Look at his circumstances. He is leaving a lee. He is heading out. It's going to get dark in a few hours, if it's not dark already. He's in hell. He's already facing pretty horrendous conditions. His circumstances will get worse, right at dark. There wasn't a whole lot to say."

Almost immediately, Roatán's protection disappeared. From the high point of a 700-foot peak, the one used to find Port Royal, the land sloped off rapidly into the sea to the northeast. Two low islands, Morat and Barbareta, stood offshore with no lee. Then came a 14-mile stretch of deep water before the ochre bluff of Guanaja, invisible beyond the dark squalls and veils of spume, rose abruptly from the depths. Running under bare poles, the *Fantome* was making 7 knots on a compass bearing of 90 degrees. As Roatán passed by the port beam, the wind on deck increased gradually, from a "garden variety" hurricane to something above 80 knots. Sea conditions worsened dramatically and rapidly. Within an hour, waves jumped from the 10- to 15-foot range to 20 to 40 feet. The waves generated by Mitch's outer winds were still piling in from the west-northwest around Roatán's south side, more or less behind the ship. But in the open channel these waves encountered others refracting around both islands, as well as monster seas surging directly south through the channel from Mitch's eye wall, which was now just 30 miles to the north. The highest sustained winds in the eye wall were 133 knots. Gusts could have reached 198 knots. Mitch was right on the border between a Category 4 and Category 5 hurricane. The 282-foot steel *Fantome* plunged on, unprotected from the most powerful force on earth.

"Confused seas," the term used by March to describe the colliding wave trains, could not come close to describing the steep, irregular boiling that now surrounded the ship and its crew. The water leaped and sank, built mounds and cut cliffs. There was no rhyme or logic. According to wave theory, when 20-foot seas from one direction meet 15-foot seas from another, the coincident crests rear up an average of 25 feet, with periodic peaks of 37 feet and an occasional 50-foot giant.

Around the *Fantome*, steep waves appeared from nowhere, then broke into cascading faces that crashed like breakers and hissed over a sea surface already white with wind-blown spume.

The rolling of the boat increased violently—30 to 45 degrees to port and then to starboard—March reported to Michael D. Burke. Waves struck the hull and poured water into the A-deck "lobby," forward of the dining saloon, and over the sidedecks between the bulwarks and the Admiralty suites. The top party deck was 20 feet above the water. B deck was a mere 12 feet. "He had gotten hit by a bow wave, a big wave, with lots of water on deck," said Burke. MDB was worried about broaching, a loss of control in which a ship heels wildly to windward, exposing its broad side to wind and sea. He questioned March about ways to prevent broaching, using a launch as a drogue trailed astern, or sails—jibs or staysails—tied to a mooring line as a sea anchor deployed over the bow. But the ship was rolling so much it would not have been safe for crewmen to be out rigging lines or wrestling a 3,000-pound boat over the ship's stern. Plus, March said he didn't think it was necessary. "The bow of the ship is broad and deep, so it is not squirrelly. So when it surfed, the ship would ride straight. It didn't turn off," said Burke.

At some point, Guyan March apparently left the deckhouse—when Burke telephoned, Brasso answered and said the skipper wasn't there—which would have required him to open the sliding hatch and struggle out onto the bridge. Grasping ropes and railing, or clipping a harness into one of the jacklines the crew had rigged, he would have pushed or perhaps crawled through wind and spray capable of etching a bloody tattoo on his face. The 20 feet across the exposed party deck to the closest stairway at the muster station would have seemed like traversing an earthquake. "He must have been blind as a bat," said Neil Carmichael, captain of the Windjammer ship *Polynesia*. "I don't think people appreciate what it's like when you start getting 50, 60, 70 knots and rains as torrential as that. I've been in 50 to 60 with a snorkel mask on. You can't see 10 feet." Having descended the forward stairs, March could have staggered aft along the port or starboard sidedeck between the Admiralty suites and bulwarks, crossed the "lobby," and pulled open the unsecured wooden door to the dining saloon in an interval between periodic deluges of solid seawater. Or, making his way forward 20 feet, he could have opened a watertight hatch and descended a ladder to

Deck B, and from there reached both the engine room and the saloon. He might even have braved the length of the top deck and descended the duke's original stairway into the lobby.

Guyan March and Michael D. Burke never talked about where the men were, but Burke assumed that engineers Constantin Bucur and Pope Layne were in the engine room, perhaps with other engineers, sealed off by waterproof hatches. They would have kept busy, monitoring engines and hydraulic pressure, watching the water level in the bilge beneath them, thinking about sediment in the fuel. Routine work would have been impossible as they grasped pipes and worried. Pope Layne had been through Hurricane Marilyn in 1995 aboard Windjammer's *Flying Cloud*, the company's smallest ship, which was too slow to outrun hurricanes and was tied to a mooring ball off Peter Island in the British Virgin Islands when storms threatened. Pope and other crew stayed aboard to run the engines against the force of the wind. "He was scared to death. He said he had to crawl, literally crawl, on deck," recalled Rhonda Epperson. "You couldn't hear anything. The wind and rain were just so intense. The wooden covers to the benches were flying off. He couldn't communicate over the radio because of the noise. So people were sending messages back and forth by crawling on the deck."

By Tuesday afternoon, the rest of the *Fantome*'s men were presumed to be in the saloon. "That's where I'd be," Burke said later. That would have put twenty to twenty-six men in a room that had once been filled with rum and laughter and the twinkling brass lights of a cruise. Now grunting, nauseous men, trussed into bulky life jackets, strained to stay in their seats and hang on to the macramé-covered posts. The burnished brass lamps, if not dismounted and stowed, would have described crazy arcs, as would the gold chains on the crew's necks. The men would have been suffering great fatigue. Their muscles had been tense for twenty-four hours as they moved or hung on in the rolling ship, fighting to stay in a bunk or not be tossed about. Their last good sleep had been Saturday night, three days before. Ever since, they had been in a flight-or-fight mode. They were scared. Several of the men couldn't swim.

Deckhands and the more experienced crew, including bosun Cyrus Phillips and bosun's mate Jerry King, probably would have walked through escape routes in their minds. From where they were, they would have to climb an exposed stairway and make a suicidal dash to the top-deck muster station and life rafts. The hotel department heads, chief steward Chrispin Saunders and chef Eon Maxwell, and their staffs most likely were petrified. Without normal duties to occupy them, their minds were free to roam, to their wives and kids, to plans for the future, to beautiful women, to random promises, prayers, and regrets. The scene outside the saloon's windows encouraged their worst fears.

Phillips, at forty the "old man" of the *Fantome*, Bequia-born and with twelve years with Windjammer, was the closest any of the West Indian crew came to being a sailor from birth. He "wanted to get money together and have his own boat for freighting through the islands," said his brother, Julian Peterson, who crewed on Windjammer's *Yankee Clipper*. "It was supposed to come time in 2005."

Jerry King, in his last call home, had told his sister how homesick he was. He hadn't been home since January. When the ship next docked in Trinidad, he told her, "I'm going to roll in all that mud."

Friday, three days away, was electrician Vernon Brusch's twenty-seventh birthday, and he had promised his mother he would be home to celebrate. In his last phone call from Omoa, Brusch had laughed and said that he would be the one bearing gifts. "Oh God, Mommy, my cabin is full." Piled on his bunk before the storm were a VCR, more CDs, and a plastic tricycle for Otaphia, his pretty child who liked to wear red and white beads in her hair. "He had no room on the bed to lie down," said Athelene Brusch, who set her mind to a birthday cake, a homecoming meal, "and those kinds of things."

Kevin Logie of Trinidad, who had followed his brother to Windjammer, was due to leave the *Fantome* in a week to become lead chef on another Windjammer ship. He still dreamed of saving money to open his own tailor shop. On his last trip through Miami, Logie had twenty minutes to spend with brother Neville. "He had footage on his camcorder of my three-month-old baby. I told him I would look at it another time. He was coming back to Miami with the camcorder, CDs, a TV, VCRs—everything was in that little cabin."

Jesús Hernández, deckhand, the Honduran dock hire without a visa, was 25 miles from his estranged wife and two children, who were soon to be in the hurricane themselves. When he was ten months old in 1974, Hurricane Fifi barreled through the strait between the Honduran mainland and the Bay Islands and devastated the country. A small stream running through the village of San Marcos became a roaring torrent through

Jesús' mother's house. "I couldn't hold all the children," she said later. "The river was taking Jesús away. But a neighbor came and grabbed him by the hand."

Alvin and Alan George, the Spice Brothers from Grenada, men taught to cook by their grandmother, were chefs at heart. Alvin, the neat one, had two kids at home. Alan, the good-looking brother, the life of the party, was saving his money to open a restaurant in Grenada. "I'll see you in November," he had said in his last phone call to their mother, Margaite. When she protested again about his life at sea, he had said offhandedly, "If I have to die at sea, I'll die there, instead of on land."

Francis Morain, deckhand and father of six in private school in Grenada, had turned thirty-seven on October 10. After enduring a $350-a-month job, he had the letter he'd worked for, the letter from Windjammer recommending a visa to the United States. He had told his wife, Elizabeth, to join him in Trinidad for Christmas shopping.

Carl "cool and deadly" James, engineer, was looking forward to Christmas, when he could take his sister's children downtown in New Amsterdam for ice cream.

Deonauth "Django" Ramsudh, refrigerator mechanic, had been an acolyte in the Lutheran church as a child. If he was to meet his Maker, at least he'd taken care of his three children with the $69,000 won at the casino.

Colin August, the launch driver, no doubt wished he'd taken some leave, like brother Chuckie, who was safe ashore.

Rhon Austin, deckhand, was experiencing his first tour at sea.

Maxwell Bhikham—Blinky, they called him—was a Muslim deckhand who never missed prayer time with Mohamed Farouk Roberts, another Muslim and first-year engineer. They were from Guyana, too.

Steadbert Burke and Vanil Fender were Jamaicans, a first-year carpenter and a cook. They had wives at home.

O'Ryan Hardware, the ladies' man, had followed his brother to Windjammer and become an engineer. Brother Orville had reached his dream—enough money to marry and get off the boat.

Deodatt Jallim, another first-year carpenter, had followed his brother Harry to sea. He had called his wife from Belize and told her to expect him in two weeks.

Carlisle Mason, deckhand from St. Vincent, and Wilbert Morris, the quiet, muscled welder from Guyana who helped keep the ship together, huddled with the others. Aníbal Olivas, the Nicaraguan dock hire, two weeks on the ship as steward, was there. Pedro Prince, the Honduran galley aide stuck without a visa, was thrown together by circumstance with Rohan Williams—Dr. Stone, they called him—another deckhand. Bobby Pierre from St. Lucia—so helpful and joyous as Chrispin's assistant steward and such a good dancer—was there too. He looked remarkably like a smaller version of Horace Grant, the basketball star, and lately had been dating Chrispin's sister, Beverly McKenzie, who had gotten off the ship in Belize. Whatever these men were thinking was shoved aside with each bang and howl that brought the storm back like a question from Saint Peter. At some point, they became too seasick to care.

When a storm is violent enough, even experienced mariners will eventually begin to suffer from a type of motion sickness, not the nausea most think of, but an enveloping fatigue—the "feeling that we want to close our eyes whenever we get the chance," according to Carlos Comperatore of the Coast Guard's research branch. By itself, that might not be a problem. But when it combines with sleep loss, stress, and desynchronosis—the maladjustment of the body clock—endurance drops significantly. Even the most durable mariners begin to retreat into a personal shell, walled in and enervated by the motion of the ship, lack of sleep, the physical exertion of staying upright or in a bunk, and worry. It is the first sign of deteriorated performance that sooner or later overcomes any sailor. First, the man gets quiet. As conditions worsen, he becomes forgetful. It becomes tougher to do mental arithmetic. He is apathetic and slow to respond. He might forget to check critical information, or he might act when what is called for is no action.

When he reached his men, Guyan March would likely have told them the truth about their plight, about the loss of Roatán's lee and his hope for the run east. He would likely have reviewed safety matters, especially the use of life jackets and life rafts. His presence may have had a calming effect on the crew, who would have been praying and pushing back moments of panic. These would have been held back only by the rational thought that of all the Windjammer officers they knew, Guyan March, Brasso Frederick, and Onassis Reyes were the best. "He would have gone through every single scenario in his head," said crewman Julian Peterson, brother of bosun Cyrus Phillips. "If there was one person I would want to be with, it would have been March because of his control over himself and his ability to handle the vessel."

At some point, March rejoined Brasso and Onassis in the deckhouse. Knowing what they knew, the minds of these three men likely would have raced with all the things that could go wrong. How far would she roll before the ship no longer cared whether she came upright or kept going? At what angle of roll would water downflood, and from where? Would watertight doors hold? Would the square portlights on B deck shatter and flood? If the *Fantome* was laid over, would the large, rectangular saloon windows surrounding the crew stand up to wave crests? Could the ship's most vulnerable spot—their deckhouse—stay together? The highest, forwardmost, and flimsiest shelter on the ship— 25 feet above the water on calm days—must have been hell, the rolling and pitching exaggerated, the noise debilitating. In one grunted exchange with Miami, March described a chair flying.

Their conversation limited to brief shouts, the officers, too, likely withdrew inside, to that private space forced open by the knowledge that they could die. When the weather was rough, Brasso liked to sleep below the saloon, in a C-deck cabin near the center of the keel, where motion was dampened. Now, in the worst possible place on the ship, he could well have imagined time at home in his big new house on Antigua. Built from scratch on his Windjammer earnings, it was probably worth $400,000. So big in body and spirit, a rock in the midst of crisis, even Brasso could have legitimately concluded that if the ship came to grief, it would be impossible to get anyone into a life raft.

Onassis, full of vigor and promise, could have flashed on the crewmen he knew who couldn't swim, his girlfriend Glenn and their Christmas plans, or the feeling of being trapped underwater that he had experienced when a launch had flipped and he'd been snared in the canvas top. It had scared the hell out of him, Parkinson said later. "It was a realization of the reality, a random fluke. He knew how dangerous it was." He must have considered the irony that failed love had put him there to replace a heart-sick mate. Or maybe he recalled his last e-mail to his mother, sent Friday night for her birthday. "Remember that you finish a new year every time you begin a new day. So it's never too late to start something new. Like doing more exercises or writing a new diary, etc. . . . My time in these waters will end soon because I finish on December 26. . . . I'm very healthy. Running 30 miles a week (in the mud) and lifting weights. I have to buy some vitamins. Take care of yourself, Mama, and you will be hearing from me soon. Your son loves you. Onassis."

At 2:30 P.M., on Guanaja's southeast shore, veterinarian Alex Patterson watched his beach house slide into the ocean. He was 100 yards away in his sister's hillside house. "There was so much salt spray, I could only see the top of it." Shortly after, the house he was in began coming apart. "The roof started leaving. The walls started leaving. There were seven of us inside. Two of them were seventy-five years old." He helped them into the crawl space beneath the house. He and his wife, Monique, then fought their way 50 yards behind the house to the 2,000-gallon concrete cistern. The others stayed behind because they didn't think they could make it there. The cistern, 8 by 8 feet, had a square hole on top covered by a heavy concrete lid, 2 feet square. The shed over it, used to collect rainwater, had blown away. "The wind was blowing like crazy. The sand was coming out of the ground. It felt like it was sandblasting us, hitting us from the back. It would blow like crazy for twenty, thirty seconds, and you'd have a three- to five-second lull. You've got pieces of trees falling around you. I got there ahead of my wife. I waited behind the cistern to get out of the sandblast. I waited for the lull and then, here she came. She probably got blown down three times in 100 feet." They climbed into the cistern.

North, across the island, Black Rock, the size of a barn, and a cute cottage tucked in its lee were underwater. The storm surge, at least 20 feet high, poured into the raised home of Doug and Mary Solomon. By 3 P.M., all but 8 of the 150 homes in Mangrove Bight were gone. In his elevated home on land, Kerston Moore could feel the waves slapping against the plywood over his windows that faced the bay. Looking out through a crack, "it was like an airplane in fog. Like a white wall. It was too much for a person to witness."

At 3 P.M., the *Fantome* was midway between Roatán and Guanaja. The storm's center was 40 miles to the northeast, but the eye wall was less than 20 miles away. Winds and waves from the outer edge of the eye wall surged straight south at the ship through the channel. The wind speed rose to Category 2 level, 95 knots. Since the wind's force increases with the square of velocity, the effect on both the sea and the ship was torturous. March reported waves so high that 3 feet of solid "green water" poured repeatedly onto the ship's main deck. On the top, party deck, barrels of water arced over the bow and sides and surged around like surf on a rocky shore. "As the water sloshed, it would break up a lot of benches and tables," said Michael D. Burke. "It was not unexpected. They were made of one-by-threes. There was a lot of water on deck." The deckhouse, the nerve center of the ship containing all the electronics, was built of the same wood, bolted to an angle iron frame. The roof over the officers' heads was plywood reinforced with fiberglass mat.

March also reported water cascading into the whaleboats that hung 25 feet off the water on the top deck,

"Cut 'em off. Don't worry about it," Burke said.

It was a moot point. The deck of the *Fantome* had become a no-man's-land. Walking anywhere was impossible with the deck at a 45-degree tilt, steeper than a home stairway. As the ship's well deck rolled toward the water, Guyan, Brasso, and Onassis, trapped in their deckhouse, braced and fought to remain upright. In Miami, Michael D. Burke paced by the phone, biting his lip. "Shit," he kept saying. "Oh shit."

At 3:40 P.M., the *Fantome* cleared the channel between Roatán and Guanaja and was 7 miles south of the tip of Guanaja's West End. Burke asked March if he could get into the lee of the island, which lies northeast to southwest. The wind was blasting the ship on its port rear quarter.

"There's no way," March replied.

"What about turning, putting the wind on the beam and running northeast?"

"No way." Even if Captain March could have done that, exposing the full length of the ship's topsides, superstructure, and rig to the force of the hurricane was what he had been struggling to prevent.

Fantome plunged east.

꽃

Flying toward Mitch in NOAA's P-3 turboprop, researchers James Franklin and Michael Black were afraid that they had missed their hurricane party. As their boss had warned, Mitch appeared to be weakening. When they had taken off from Tampa just after noon, Mitch's eye was clouding over, and Miles Lawrence was reporting winds down to 135 knots, a borderline Category 4/5 storm. In keeping with their habit, Franklin and Black had stocked up on junk food. Black, who never got sick, usually carried a greasy burrito. Franklin, who always got sick, still tried to eat a lot to keep his stomach "busy." He'd gone to Subway for a sandwich and "really good chocolate chip cookies—good and buttery. I like Hershey's chocolate with almonds. Barbecue potato chips. Generally, nothing healthy. I've never thrown up. I get nausea and incredible headaches from the noise and vibration. The whole airplane is in a low-grade vibration from the turboprops."

The scientists still hoped to observe other details within the eye using Doppler radar and GPS dropsondes. Armed with a belly radar, spearlike wind probes, and the "score" of two hundred hurricane penetrations painted on its fuselage, the P-3 was a veteran. "It's a four-engine turboprop. It can take a beating. We frequently overstress the airplane past its design specifications," said pilot Phil Kenul. "You don't do it intentionally. Sometimes the storm flies you."

Black-bearded and with the roundish, gentle look of a manatee, Michael Black was typical of hurricane researchers. One side of his brain loved the mystery of storms, while the other mourned their havoc. He loved flying into hurricanes.

"I've been flying into storms for fourteen seasons. I always look forward to it. Sometimes it is extremely rough, though usually not. You never know what you're going to get. The strength of the storm is not equal to the roughness of the flight. We flew into Gilbert, the lowest pressure on record—888 millibars—in 1988. The stronger ones are like being on a roller coaster; the upward motion is so broad that the plane will rise up and descend very smoothly, down into the downdraft. At times you actually float. Briefcases have flown and hit me. We've had computer paper fly around the cabin. We have a coffee urn, a commercial cylinder with a bungee cord around the top, and at times that has come off and coffee grounds go all over the back. We have obvious scientific objectives. Hurricanes, still, in a lot of ways, are mysterious. There is a lot we don't understand. It is such a potentially beautiful sight when you go into a strong storm, with a clear eye and mountains of clouds. It is truly an awesome sight."

At 3:30 P.M., an hour from penetration, the storm showed up on the nose radar.

"You can see the outer and inner rain bands and the eye wall—a circle. It is phenomenal," said Kenul. On the plane's belly radar, the colors were measured in "decibels," a measure of return echo from the rain. "Black is innocuous. Green not much. Yellow, caution. Red basically means stop, you're going to get the shit kicked out of you. Magenta is for extremely high decibels, plus turbulence. That we avoid like the plague. Red and magenta are basically the 'holy shit' colors." As they nosed toward Mitch, red and magenta stood out in its circle of doom.

Coming up to his 4 P.M. deadline for another forecast from the National Hurricane Center, Miles Lawrence surveyed the computer models with dispassionate dismay. The storm had been moving southwest for twelve hours, but none of the models showed the slightest interest in going along. Lawrence began to sketch out a track with a bit of southern motion, and then a landfall in Belize in 36 to 48 hours. He fixed the center of Hurricane Mitch at latitude 16.8° N, longitude 85.8° W and described its motion as west-southwest at 4 knots.

Mitch's center was now directly north of the ship, 32 miles away. With an eye radius of 10 miles, Mitch's eye wall was now over northern Guanaja. Winds were still near 134 knots with gusts 50 percent higher.

Doug Solomon, lying soaking wet beside his wife and cowering dogs and cats on Guanaja's northeast coast, tasted the eye wall's arrival. The rain mixed with salt water blown out of the ocean. "The worst thing was the sound. You have no comprehension. It was like having an express train blowing steam right next to you. What we could see were huge, high, wide mangrove trees self-destructing. They were 40 or 50 feet high. Gradually they wore down to stumps. Breaking off to nothing." As the sky darkened prematurely, Solomon watched his barometer drop to 960. "I knew we were in real trouble then. The wind speeds picked up. It felt like it was right above us."

In his little West End cabin with five employees, David Greatorex described the hurricane noise by inhaling and making the sound "Wvzzzsssss. And every ten or fifteen minutes, it would go Who Who WhoWhooooo. And the cabin would go Ssh Shhh Shsssh, shaking, then all of a sudden, Whoo whho whooowhoo and quit."

Greatorex tuned a portable radio to a station from La Ceiba, on the mainland. Someone was interviewing a weather station in Florida, with translation to Spanish.

"What about the Bay Islands?" the Honduran interviewer asked.

"The Bay Islands. Just a moment. Oh, you mean Isla de Bahía?"

"What should they be doing there?"

"Oh dear, everyone on those islands should evacuate immediately."

In Omoa, *Fantome*'s home port, the storm was now upon the little fishing village, with wild surf and winds of 50 to 60 knots. Waves were striking the wooden window pulled down over Carlos Arita's tiki bar.

🐚

At 4 P.M. the *Fantome* was approaching Mitch's longitude. Michael D. Burke thought that was good news.

"Soon," Burke assured Guyan. Soon, the ship would be east of the center. It would be in the "navigable quarter." Wind would be blowing the ship away.

Shortly after, Captain March reported that, in fact, the wind was clocking more westerly. It was coming over the stern. Burke was elated. Things were working out. Things couldn't get worse. "I asked Guyan to bear a bit south of east, to get as far away as possible." March toggled the ship's big rudder to 93 degrees.

But aboard the *Fantome*, the suffering only increased. The ship was surrounded by chaos. The sky overhead was turning a charcoal gray-black. The rain beating on the deckhouse was horizontal and as heavy as a fire hose. If he could have opened his copy of Bowditch, Captain Guyan would have seen the book's classic description of the view now outside his ship:

"As the center of the storm comes closer, the ever-stronger wind shrieks through the rigging and about the superstructure of the vessel. As the center approaches, rain falls in torrents. The wind fury increases. The seas become mountainous. The tops of huge waves are blown off to mingle with the rain and fill the air with water. Objects at a short distance are not visible."

In good times the *Fantome* creaked comfortably. Now she would have brayed. The hull, rising and falling, would have shuddered, slammed, and struck water as if it were stone. Rolling through a 90-degree arc, the beefy masts waved like willows. Even well-stored items would have come loose. Cans on shelves, glass in the refrigerator, spilled milk, rum bottles, books, CDs, toys for kids, and VCRs for their mothers would have mixed in a great, cacophonous salad. Standing water sloshed around. Doors, windows, and seams would have leaked water.

If they could see anything, March, Brasso, and Reyes in the deck-house and the men in the saloon would have watched the slate-gray, white, and turquoise mountains rise above them. Then, as if riding an elevator, they would have risen to look out on a frightful battlefield where wind and spume raged. Down again they would go, into a trough, the seas hissing around them before cascading seawater covered everything. "The radar, if working, would be giving a dubious picture," said Neil Carmichael, captain of the Windjammer ship *Polynesia.* "They're inside the bridge, with limited visibility, three or four small windows. The bridge wasn't set up to be used on the inside." Maneuvering to avoid the worst breaking seas would have been impossible, even if visibility had permitted it.

Michael D. Burke remembered the captain's description: "It was terrible, squalling, dark and dirty, yet it was not like he was about to die," said Burke later. "He was not out of control. We didn't have far to go. It was a race. If we could get to the east, with the winds southwest, we'd have the Honduran mainland to protect us from heavy seas. It was a matter of time before we and the storm got further apart. We never discussed getting into rafts or the lifeboats. We weren't of the opinion that all was lost."

🦈

In *Typhoon: The Other Enemy*, retired navy captain C. Raymond Calhoun sketched the domino effect of a hurricane (called a *typhoon* in the Pacific) on his destroyer, *Dewey.* Halsey's Typhoon, which struck the Third Fleet in the Pacific on December 18, 1944, was similar in strength to Hurricane Mitch. When the typhoon's center was 50 miles away, the aircraft carrier *Monterey* reported rolls so heavy that airplanes on its deck broke loose, caught fire, and rolled into the sea. Steering systems on light carriers failed. Two men went overboard on the *Independence.* The carrier *Cowpens* had a fire on deck. The *Langley* began rolling 35 degrees to both sides.

"At 0911 our voice radio went out. . . . electrical failures now became a recurring problem. Everything was being short-circuited by the driving rain and spray. Our helmsman was having to use from 20 to 25 degrees of right rudder to maintain a heading. At 0928 with the ship rolling 40 degrees to starboard the *Dewey* lost suction on the port main lubricating oil pump. We had to stop the port engine in order to prevent wiping the main bearings. . . . the *Dewey* was corkscrewing and writhing like a wounded animal. The inclinometer registered 55-56-57, then 60 degrees. I tried to recall the stability curves . . . my recollection was they had shown that the *Dewey* could recover from a roll of 70 degrees."

The wind "drove spray and spume with the force of a sand blaster. Capillary bleeding was etched on any face exposed directly to it." The doctor reported several men injured by falling, some with fractured ribs.

The navy ship was "tossed, shoved, beaten." Metal covers ripped away, despite heavy screw-down hasps. In two hours, despite "watertight" hatches, a foot of water filled every living space. "The pounding and rolling grew worse. We were now going over consistently to 68 and 70 degrees. Each roll I would dispatch a silent prayer, 'Dear God, please make her come back.' Engineers reported that on each starboard roll, the blower intakes, on main deck, were submerged and 500 to 1,000 gallons of water gushed into the fire rooms. Water tenders grabbed fittings and hung like monkeys. Sometimes they fell into the starboard bulkhead, shoulder deep into sloshing water, striking machinery and pumps. During one roll, a starboard hatch sprang open. Seawater poured on switchboards. There were flashes, short circuits, fires. The power went out. Steering went out. The wheel required 6 to 8 men.

"Many times I found myself hanging by my hands, with feet completely clear of the deck, in such a position that if I released my hold, I would drop straight down, through the starboard pilot house window into the sea. Several times I looked down past my dangling feet and saw the angry sea through the open window, directly below them," Calhoun wrote. The men prayed aloud: "Don't let us down, now, dear Lord, bring it back, oh God, bring it back." Each time it did, they shouted, "Thanks, dear Lord."

Outside, guy wires on exhaust stacks slackened and snapped taut with each gust. One broke with a noise like a cannon. The stack collapsed. The steam line broke. A whistle and siren and roar went off. When a fireman burned his pants, he told Calhoun: "It didn't really matter, Cap'n, I'd probably have had to burn 'em anyway."

At 4:20 P.M., Glenn Parkinson called Windjammer's headquarters and learned that Onassis Reyes had relayed a message to her. "He loves you," said a voice in Miami.

"Tell him I love him, too," she answered. Later she said, "I don't know if he ever got the message. I went home and watched the storm on TV."

For moral support as much as anything, Michael D. Burke asked Captain March to stay on the phone, to keep the satellite line open. "Me and Captain Paul [Maskell], we were not doing a lot of talking. He's in a battle for his life."

Captain March reported waves of 30 to 35 feet, "right on the stern—except for confusion. He was saying the sea was terrible. Rough. He indicated it was getting worse. He was starting to lose the lee, which was all the more scary to me. I fully realized what he was going into over the next few hours."

"Don't worry about the lifeboats," Burke repeated to March. "Even if you lose a mast, don't worry. The debris on deck—it's not an issue. Get through it. We'll fix the ship later." He asked March if the water pouring on deck was falling off.

"It's discharging," March said.

The seas were terrible. "Confused," March yelled. The ship was making 7 knots. March reported a GPS fix of 16°15′ N, 85°51′ W, about 10 miles south-southeast of Guanaja.

"You could feel the grimace," Burke later recalled. "The ship was rolling heavily. And that's pretty scary in itself. He would have to hold on. You'd hear sounds of exertion. I heard him groan. I heard him say, 'That was a big one.'"

"Is it falling off? Is it shedding?"

"Yes, that's not a prob . . ."

At 4:30 P.M., the satellite telephone went dead.

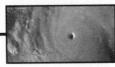

MIAMI AND BAY ISLANDS

October 27, 1998

O H S H I T . "
Michael D. Burke redialed the *Fantome*'s phone. An intercept recording came on: "Out of service."

"Shit."

He punched it again. Nothing. He dashed to the tiny radio room and tried raising the ship on the single sideband radio.

"*Fantome, Fantome.*"

There was nothing but static in response.

Seconds later, at 4:30:45 P.M., NOAA's P-3 turboprop with Michael Black and James Franklin aboard entered the eye wall. Their approach, from the northwest at 10,000 feet, was "fairly bumpy," said Black, the chief scientist on the flight and a veteran of 275 hurricane penetrations. Just before the eye wall, the plane had flown for thirty minutes through rain bands, an experience that pilot Phil Kenul likened to "getting hit by a fire hose. The turbulence can go from mild to severe. It can knock your hands off the yoke. Mitch was approaching that."

The eye wall itself was "like being in a bad elevator ride, out of control, going up and down," said Kenul. "You get restrained against shoulder harnesses. We had a couple of microbursts that took us down 2,000–2,500 feet. You could see it on the vertical speed indicator, down, up, 2,000 feet per minute. The change in G load—in Mitch we were pushing 3 positive and negative 1.4. We got to the bottom and got pushed upwards, back to altitude. That's pretty common." Outside, the view was "like flying in a lightbulb. Everything is a suffused white. You're in instrument conditions, but your eyes are bouncing so much you can't focus on the gauges. All you're trying to do is keep the airplane at a constant airspeed, the turbulent penetration speed of 210 knots. We don't try to maintain altitude. As long as we have plenty of airspace, we let it drop. The eye wall lasted only eight seconds, the same eight seconds that you'd be on a bucking bronco or bull ride. It can go on forever."

The change from wall to eye was dramatic. "All of a sudden you break out into the eye. It is extremely bright and calm," said Black. Pilot Kenul described the feeling as being "spit out" by the storm.

Mitch's eye was classically shaped, though ragged. From the top, the dark gray eye wall sloped inward like a velodrome. The eye was filled with clouds, a sign of weakening, so neither the sky nor the sea was visible. The pressure had risen to 931 millibars, up 25 from its low point the day before.

On their radar screens, Franklin, Black, and Kenul could see that the eye was 12 to 15 miles across, elongated north to south, and surrounded by an 8-mile-thick eye wall of horrendous winds, tornadoes, updrafts, downdrafts, and thunderstorms. Large cells—huge thunderstorms red with rain and magenta with turbulence, the "holy shit" colors—rotated counterclockwise from the southeast quadrant around to the northwest, then dissipated. The updrafts were strong on the east wall. Strong downdrafts filled the west wall. During their minutes of calm inside the eye, the team used the radar, its screen filled with circles and splotches of green, yellow, blue, and red, to pick a path through the other side. "The wind direction starts to turn, you hit the eye wall and immediately you're back on that elevator ride," said Kenul. "It's nonstop turbulence, and then the outer rain bands." Kenul, with 120 penetrations in twenty storms, called the Mitch flight the "most notorious, roughest ride all year, including Georges. It was moderate to severe. We got knocked around pretty good."

Though the barometer had risen considerably, James Franklin, busy shoving the dropsondes into Mitch and watching the data flow onto his computer screen, found that the storm had not weakened at all. "I was amazed at what I was seeing," he said later.

At 10,000 feet, the airplane measured 125 knots of wind. Using the standard 15 percent reduction to calculate sea-level speeds, Franklin expected speeds below to be in the 100- to 110-knot range, a Category 3 hurricane. But Franklin's dropsondes showed the wind speeds increasing the closer it got to the ocean. "They just kept going up and up and up." Actual speeds of 115 knots were found at or near the water, but readings of 150, 165, and 180 knots also were found in places in the eye wall. Several dropsondes stopped working in the turbulence.

If they had kept working, speeds of 140 to 150 knots might have been found at sea level. One sonde, dropped into the clear air of the eye inside the northwest wall, recorded winds of 150 knots some 300 feet above the sea.

"Wow," Black radioed to his colleague Franklin, "This looks like it is still a Category 5." Black, recalling his reaction later, said, "Here is a storm weakening, yet surface winds are as strong as or stronger than the day before. This was new. We hadn't seen these observations before. There was scientific excitement about that. Also, gee, I was glad we decided to go." The flight crew settled in for a four-hour visit with Mitch, back and forth, with six full penetrations and forty-six dropsondes.

✑

That a lost ship and a research plane should be in the same hurricane at the same moment, separated by only 2 miles of vertical distance, was a small irony in the midst of a cataclysm. Windjammer's headquarters on Miami Beach was less than 10 miles from NOAA's Hurricane Research Division on Key Biscayne, yet neither knew of the other's presence in the storm. The airplane was monitoring standard emergency frequencies but heard no distress calls, nor did it pick up any transmission from an emergency locator beacon like those carried on the *Fantome*. As the scientists above went about their rambunctious study, the *Fantome* just disappeared.

One man would later claim to have heard a Mayday. Winfil Alegría Palma, a trucker and fish buyer who survived Mitch at his beachside home in Puerto Castilla, near Trujillo, was monitoring VHF 16 on Tuesday afternoon. At 3:30 P.M. local time (4:30 P.M. Eastern Standard Time), he said, "They called and called. I heard him say *Fantome*. 'We are the *Fantome*.' They said they were coming from Roatán and that they were going to pass between Guanaja and Castilla. He was asking for someone to give him a position. He said that a wave had entered and the sea was getting even stronger. He asked for help. It was in Spanish. The sea was *caudaloso*—great volumes of water. Three calls came, one right after another. I called him, because I heard him say he was the *Fantome*, a tourist sailboat. He was asking for some kind of rescue. You could hear he was nervous. It was a voice of fear. Like when somebody's about to fail at something. They didn't report anything about machines. Just that the sea was very high and that a wave had bathed them and that's why they were asking for help. I didn't hear 'Mayday.' A wave had entered and they were about to sink. The boat had started filling up with water." No one else reported the Mayday.

At Windjammer, it was too early to assume the worst. Michael D. Burke called in electronics chief Dennis Newsome, who said the phone antenna was rated for 100 knots.

"Dennis, what happened? Did they capsize?"

Newsome didn't think so. His assumption was water damage from wind-blown water. Newsome called the antenna's manufacturer. The company said the satellite transceiver should stay focused on the satellite until the ship heeled 45 degrees.

Burke paced his office. The winds had clocked to the west, the ship was surfing its way to safety. "I didn't feel the worst," he said. He kept waiting for the phone to ring from the bridge of the *Fantome*.

At 7 P.M. EST, Windjammer Barefoot Cruises learned that Hurricane Mitch had drifted directly south toward the *Fantome*. The National Hurricane Center estimated the storm's fix at 16.6° N, 85.6° W—25 miles from the *Fantome*'s last position. The storm's center was 12 miles from Guanaja. By the looks of the satellite picture, Honduras and the Bay Islands were being battered.

"Mitch has meandered slowly over the last few hours, and may meander further tonight," the center's discussion reported. "A slow southwestward to westward motion is expected in 12 to 24 hours. However, the center of the hurricane is coming very close to the coast, and hurricane conditions are spreading onshore over Honduras and the adjacent Bay Islands. Ham radio reports indicate significant damage on the island of Roatán."

Mitch's sustained winds, as reported by Franklin in the NOAA research plane, were 130 knots, and the radius of hurricane-force winds was 60 miles.

"Are you sure?" Michael D. Burke said when told of the hurricane fix. The taste of desperation rose in his throat. He called the National Hurricane Center and asked someone where the strongest winds were. He was told 10 to 12 miles from the center.

"What about 22 miles out?" Burke asked.

"It's a damn strong wind."

Based on the fixes, Burke thought Mitch had taken another bizarre

jog to the southeast. Based on later analysis, the storm had arced toward Guanaja and the *Fantome* at a steady pace. The worsening conditions reported by Captain March as he left Roatán were the result of a
hurricane getting closer.

"It is very difficult to describe, the palpable fear," Burke said. "I was
desperate to reach the ship. We tried constantly, on sideband, the telephone. It's like losing your kid. Deep down in your soul, something
terrible is happening, or has happened." In his helplessness, Michael
D. Burke's mind wandered from the ship, to memories, to guilt, to his
decisions over the last two days.

"The feeling in your belly. You try to reestablish contact with the ship.
You are visualizing what the captain was going through. It's a terrible
feeling. Especially with the size of our company. They're family. I crewed
on the *Fantome*. Many men have been with us for years. I grew up with
these guys. At 1 P.M. we realized we were in trouble. Prior to that our
strategy was successful. Only at 1:15 did we realize we were in trouble." At some point, he blamed the National Hurricane Center. Its forecasts seemed terribly wrong.

Lying in the dark on the ground, water running down inside their plastic sheets and inside their storm suits, Doug and Mary Solomon started
seeing lightning. "It must have been the wall of the storm. I knew it was
real close then. I figured it was about 200 miles an hour plus in the
gusts. There was a dramatic wind shift. It started blowing from the east,
so I knew the storm was coming south. And that's where we stuck."

In Mangrove Bight, the tidal surge dissipated, wind and rain picked
up, and darkness became a menace. Corrugated tin roofs, called "zincs"
on the island for their galvanized steel coating, began flying around
like medieval instruments of decapitation. Townspeople, huddled below
the marble cliffs, saw them sail through the air. In Kerston Moore's
house, 250 people had crowded in with standing room only. "You couldn't
lie down. You could feel it shudder. I moved the men to one end to hold
the thing down." As the roofing blew off, seawater poured in through
the boards. "It was raining salt," said Moore. "People were packed so
tightly they stayed warm. It was everlasting."

Many ran around the bend of Mangrove Bight to the home of Greg

Park, a Canadian whose sturdy house on the hillside, above the sea, held together. Essentially a large, open house with louvers for cool air, it became home for 150 people, many of whom braved the dark, flying zincs, and falling debris to go back and get their relatives. Orven Johnson went back for his mother and found that the wind made him almost weightless. As he ran, each step would span 6 to 8 feet, as if he were running on the moon. "They say you can't see wind. But the salt water had become a vapor, and you could see that. I cried because I couldn't get back to my mom."

As darkness enveloped the Bay Islands, the P-3 research plane flew a wide pattern, swooping down to Santa Rosa de Aguán and along the Honduran coast, across Roatán twice, and across the northern shoreline of Guanaja, where Michael Black caught a glimpse of the shattered isle.

"My God, this storm is not moving anywhere. They are going to be in devastating conditions for twenty-four hours," he said to himself at the time. "I experienced Andrew in Miami, but that was two hours of extreme winds. I couldn't imagine a day or longer in these kinds of conditions. The terror and uncertainty. It was obvious, when we got out of there, and by the time we compared our fix on the storm with the Air Force's, that the storm was hardly moving. It was drifting to the south. We were concerned about Honduras."

The island of Roatán was outside the wall, which "makes all the difference in terms of damage," Black said. "When you get over 100 miles an hour, every additional 5 to 10 miles an hour makes a tremendous difference. It is not 1 to 1. The force goes as the square of the wind speed. That's why the difference between Categories 3 and 4 is huge. Going from Roatán's Category 3 to what we found over Guanaja, Category 5, makes a tremendous difference in destructive potential."

After dark, pilot Phil Kenul reported Saint Elmo's fire, static electricity that shimmered like balls of green electric fuzz on the windscreen and the forward gust probe. By now, James Franklin was feeling "really lousy."

"I'd put my head on the desk. I remember feeling really sick," said Franklin. "I like going through the center, but when the flight is done, I'm devastatingly tired."

Still, Franklin realized that Mitch had again demonstrated how little scientists understood about hurricanes. The historic relationship between atmospheric pressure and wind was wrong in Mitch. The winds were inexplicably higher at lower altitudes. Mitch raised a lot of questions about past storms and the way they had been estimated.

The flight team dropped their last sonde at 7:31 P.M. Pilot Kenul circled inside Mitch's dark eye until all the data were transmitted to Miami, then flew home. The plane landed in Tampa a little after 10 P.M., after nine and a half hours in the air. As they landed, yet another Hurricane Hunter plane droned south from the base in Mississippi for a 1 A.M. fix.

After five hours of futile calling, waiting, and hoping that *Fantome* would call in, Michael D. Burke called the U.S. Coast Guard to ask whether they had received an emergency signal from the *Fantome*. The ship carried three emergency position-indicating radiobeacons (EPIRBs) that, once activated, would emit an emergency signal to guide rescuers. Two were 406 megahertz beacons designed to beam an SOS and the ship's identity and location to a satellite. The *Fantome* would have been identified if one of them had been transmitting. These beacons could be turned on manually, but one was attached to the outside wall of the deckhouse in a housing designed to release automatically when submerged under 10 feet of water. It was then supposed to float to the surface. The second 406 EPIRB, with an out-of-date battery, was kept inside the deckhouse, along with an older EPIRB known as an emergency locator transmitter (ELT). If turned on manually, this ELT emitted a homing beacon to airplanes at 121.5 MHz, but without vessel identification.

Sometime after 10 o'clock a crying woman claiming to represent Windjammer called MC Tours manager Antonio Martínez in Honduras, asking, "Have you had any contact with the ship?" She asked him to put an announcement on an FM radio station that covered most of Honduras and had become the storm source for the country. She said the ship had been pumping water when contact was lost.

An operator at the Web site Honduras.com apparently heard this broadcast and typed: "Reportedly all contact has been lost with a cruise ship. . . . We wonder what it was doing around here anyways!"

At 10 P.M., the National Hurricane Center reported that Mitch had stopped moving 12 miles east of Guanaja. The storm was "weakening," with winds of 122 knots. The eye pressure had risen to 933 millibars. With hurricane-force winds out 60 miles, Mitch was battering a 100-mile stretch of the Honduran coast centered at Trujillo. Despite the friction of land, if the center of the storm remained over the warm Caribbean water, sucking up energy, Mitch would "likely remain a formidable hurricane for at least another couple of days," according to Richard Pasch's discussion. Puzzling over "inconsistent" models, Pasch wrote, "It suffices to say that the steering flow remains ill-defined." Still, guided by several models, he drew an official track forecast moving the storm westward, with its first landfall at Ambergris Caye in northern Belize Thursday evening. Prophetically, Pasch said that while storm surge and winds were very dangerous, "rainfall from this slow-moving system is particularly life-threatening. Fifi, a Category 2 hurricane in 1974 which moved along the north coast of Honduras, claimed over 3,000 lives from flooding and mudslides."

Beyond Honduras, Mitch's effects spread north and west, its outriding seas prompting a high-surf advisory in New Orleans. Along the unprotected Yucatán coast, sailor Bob Gates of Niantic, Connecticut, was swept off the 34-foot catamaran *Ocean Gypsy* as it tried to navigate a reef in near darkness and high seas. The *New London Day* reported that the boat was washed ashore and six men survived. They were en route to Placencia, Belize, to start a charter business.

🐚

As their long, howling night of misery continued, people on Guanaja lost their sense of time. "I didn't know if was Tuesday night or Wednesday night," said David Greatorex on the West End. "We were getting used to the howling, howling wind. Two girls had their Spanish Bibles out. I was trying to keep them from going crazy. It was extremely scary. When the cabin would shake, every ten or fifteen minutes, I would say, 'Ah, that's nothing.'"

In their damp cistern on the east end of the island, Alex and Monique Patterson tried to lie down on their little benches with their feet on the walls and heads hanging off. They got soaked from water splashing inside. "It was like lying under a running freight train, a shaking noise.

Almost like sonic booms occasionally when the wind buffeted across the hole. It was constant noise going all the time. It was pitch-black darkness. You got chilled to the bone. I had been in several storms. They never lasted this long."

As the center of Mitch edged directly east of Guanaja, the people on the south shore began to feel its brunt. Many gathered at the Pelican Reef home of Dr. Keith Taylor, the only cement building in a neighborhood of wooden shacks. Sima Setti, a teacher living at the doctor's house, said a group of 40 grew to 120 by Tuesday night. "There would be quiet times, a couple of hours, then all you would hear was a nearby roof, caught at one end, flapping like a banging hammer. Things flying around. I just wanted the roof to just go," said Setti. Most of the people crammed in with her spoke Spanish and were Seventh-Day Adventists. Most of the time they stood, praying and singing. The many children stood or lay where they could, silent.

❧

As the night dragged on, the women of the *Fantome*—wives, lovers, mothers, grandmothers—stirred in troubled sleep across the Old World and the New. A perturbation disturbed their dreams. Had it visited only one woman, it might have gone unnoticed. But every woman who loved a man aboard *Fantome* felt something awful.

Chrispin Saunders, the steward, came in a dream to his grandmother, Veronica Welsh. He was laughing and kissing and hugging her, but he wasn't happy. "Don't cry," the old woman told him.

In his mother's dream, Chrispin was crying. "I held him and he held me and we are rocking," said Shirlan Saunders. "Mom, don't give up on me," he said. "I won't give up on you," she said and woke up.

In Guyana, Vernon Brusch appeared to his mother, Athelene. "I see him coming in. I said, 'Junior, where have you been?' He just bowed his head. I looked and there were tears. They were coming out of his eyes. He was crying. I don't dream often."

Norma Jean King smelled death in her dream that night. She saw her son, Jerry, but there was a foul smell, a stink about him, like mud, feces, or a body decomposing. "I go to a river. I see this place dug, near the water. The mud is creamish. I see this big hole. I smell human, like a dead body. It worried me."

Jerry's father, estranged from the family for twenty-five years and visiting in England, dreamed that Jerry was calling him. He was in the woods, beckoning and saying, "Come. Come." His father, Glen, replied, "I'm coming," but though he hurried he couldn't catch him in the trees.

In Belize, in a school being used as a hurricane shelter, Jerry King's baby, Princess, woke up and cried all night. She and her mother, Teresa Au Gustus, were lying on a classroom floor. As she was crying, the windows and doors burst open—the only portals to be disturbed in the entire school.

In New Amsterdam, Guyana, Ruby Ramsudh, the seventy-four-year-old mother of refrigerator specialist Deonauth, saw a person on a bed in her house. He was crumbling, like a sculpture of sand. "I couldn't make him out. I was trying to shout," she said. She slept later than normal, woke up, and knew that her son had died.

One of Colin August's sisters dreamed of a hole, a grave, in which a man wearing black pants lay in a white sheet. Colin's father, a pensioner traveling in England, got sick that night and was taken to a hospital for tests that proved inconclusive. "Maybe," he said to a relative, "something is wrong with one of my children at home."

In Miami, the *Fantome*'s three female officers, Laura-Jo Bleasdale, Cathie de Koeyer, and Laurie Fischer, went to bed after learning that the ship was missing.

"I woke up in a cold sweat. I was crying and crying," said Laura-Jo. Cathie sat up and Laurie woke up, too. She whispered to Cathie, "They're gone."

In England, Annie Bleasdale "woke up and saw this haze over my bed. I sat up and reached for it. I remember being upset and angry. I could have been dreaming, but even now it's still so real—it was like an energy field just hanging there. I turned back to my pillow in tears. The next morning, I knew I had to get out of bed. I was awake, but I rolled over and shut my eyes and drifted back off. I dreamed that Guyan was there in bed with me. He had his white epaulet shirt and stripes on. He was holding me so tight. We kissed. We hugged. It was so real. I knew that as soon as I opened my eyes, it would be over and he'd be gone. I know he had come to say good-bye. He was very sad and didn't say anything. He just looked so sorry. I cried!"

BAY ISLANDS, MAINLAND HONDURAS, AND MIAMI

October 28, 1998

🐚

IN THE EARLY MORNING hours Wednesday, Hurricane Mitch came to rest 17 miles southeast of Guanaja. The eye wall was mauling the southern side of the island. Forecaster John Guiney described it as "meandering" between Guanaja and the mainland. Mitch's eye was filling in. Its pressure had risen to 941 millibars. A Hurricane Hunter plane estimated sustained winds of 115 knots at sea level, still a Category 4 storm.

But the models insisted that Mitch would move west, toward Belize. Guiney described the ensemble as "displaying considerable scatter. The solutions vary from a west motion to a northwest to north motion." He forecast a westerly track in 12 hours and a "gradual bend toward the northwest by 36 hours," with landfall on the Belizean-Mexican coastline.

At Windjammer headquarters, the sound of shortwave static filled the situation room. Michael D. Burke sat staring at a Bay Island chart covered with tracks and circles. His sister Polly brought him a sandwich. His sister Susan gathered staff, divided them into shifts, and buoyed them. Though exhausted, Burke wouldn't leave. He paced the length of the cafeteria table, waiting for the red phone to ring from the *Fantome*, while dreading that it would be the Coast Guard.

"That was the worst time of this whole event, those early morning hours. I kept visualizing what they were going through," he said later.

For more than eight hours Burke had drawn and redrawn the *Fantome*'s last GPS fix and watched with helpless agony the southern drift of Mitch. At 4 P.M. Tuesday the storm's eye had been at 16.8° N. At 7 P.M. it was at 16.6° N, 12 miles closer to the ship. Three hours later it was at 16.5° N. By 1 A.M. Wednesday, Mitch had drifted to 16.3° N—only 3 miles from the *Fantome*'s last latitude.

"Then the worst thing happened," he said. "Mitch stalled for thirty hours.

"I did a little work. I plotted the *Fantome* at the closest point. They would have been 22 miles apart. This wind was 140–150 miles per hour. There were two scenarios: [one was] that the *Fantome* continued eastbound for hours and the storm, given its course, would have blown them away from land. I was hoping for that. They suffered only damage: antennas, communications gear, maybe dismasted."

The other scenario that seemed feasible to Burke was that the *Fantome* was driven into the Mosquito Coast. "There's as much as a mile of mangrove out from shore. If that's the case, he would have been blown into the mangrove. Even though the storm was shit-kicking them, I had confidence the vessel was not going to sink because of the watertight bulkheads we had installed." The steel bulkhead walls with watertight submarine-style doors had been installed on Decks B and C in 1991. "Even though she was seventy, I knew her. I had been involved in the refurbishing. I'd been her manager for eighteen years. I didn't think it was going to break up. Even if it rolled and would not come back up, it would not sink."

As he watched Mitch come to rest atop the *Fantome*'s last known position, waves of despair rose and subsided. One minute he thought about Captain March. "Guyan's a smart guy. I surmised he was alive and didn't transmit on 406 (EPIRB) because he was in 100 knots of wind and knew that nobody was going to come and get him. He had the mental acumen to wait until the weather calmed down." The fact that the EPIRB outside the deckhouse had not been automatically activated by immersion gave Burke and Windjammer a shred of hope. No beacon seemed good news.

The next minute, Burke dwelt on the fury of the storm and allowed himself to think that the boat was in trouble. "Given the washing machine with 100 knots plus, it's inevitable that water was going to find its way in and wear men down to where they can't survive. I came to my personal conclusion it was not likely that they were just going to come out on the other side intact. I thought she might founder."

At 4 A.M., Windjammer's red phone rang. Burke leaped. It was the Coast Guard, asking him to repeat the *Fantome*'s EPIRB number. Burke shook as he looked it up. The guardsman asked him to repeat it again.

"Do you have an EPIRB?" Burke asked.

"Yes, we do."

"Is it the *Fantome*?"

"No."

"Jesus Christ!" Burke began laughing, his mood and hopes soaring. He called the Coast Guard back four times to confirm that it wasn't the right number. He began to assume the best. The ship was adrift but OK.

On Guanaja, lying on the ground in the eye wall, Mary Solomon thought she heard an engine. She couldn't believe it and yelled to her husband, who was wrapped around her with the dogs and cats. She had to yell, to be heard above what she would later describe as a "shrieking, this incredible noise."

"My God," said Doug Solomon. "There's a ship out there. The seas must be at least 50 feet." Most likely, they heard the Hurricane Hunter plane that was flying through Mitch in the early morning hours of Wednesday.

At dawn, on the north side of Guanaja, guests and employees of the Bayman Bay Club awoke in their basement shelters to silence. "We opened the door that had taken three men to hold. There was no rain. No wind. We thought we were home free," said manager Don Pearly. "The kids got out. We were congratulating ourselves. I looked out and saw a solid wall—a charcoal-gray wall with a smooth surface, as if it were stuccoed."

Pearly thought it was the inside of the eye wall. As he watched, he was startled to see a government airplane skimming the surface of the water. A Hurricane Hunter plane was taking a fix at 7 A.M.

"It went quiet," remembered David Greatorex, who emerged with his staff on the West End to find every tree down, his guest cabins flat, his bar gone. Two islanders from the south side of the island came crawling through to check on him. He warned them that it was only the hurricane's eye, and to get back. When high winds returned, they retreated to the cabin. A piece of plywood started ripping away. "The guide with me, Carlos, he grabs a hammer and nail, opens the door, and steps on the front porch. The next thing, he is 20 yards away. It blew him into a mangle of trees. He had to crawl back, bleeding."

Five miles to the northeast, Doug and Mary Solomon felt no lull. "A twelve-hour storm turned out to be a nightmare. It went on and on and on. The wind speed must have been 150 to 200 miles an hour for sixteen hours, and then, when it started to die off, the sustained winds were a bit less. But we'd get spin-offs hitting the islands and mountains, like williwaws."

On the south side of the island, at Posada del Sol, manager Buddy Thompson watched as the waves toppled a rock and concrete retaining wall and began throwing salt water sideways. Windows and doors blew out. Fourteen feet of roof peeled off the bar end. When all the furniture went flying, he told his men, "find someplace safe. We can't hold this." The penetrating seawater wrecked everything electrical: light fixtures, fans, water heaters.

Just to the east, in Savannah Bight, a group of shrimpers tried desperately to keep their boats afloat. Tied to mangrove trees in the shallows, they were running their engines full tilt, trying to lodge their bows in the mud. As the storm surge rose they took up slack in the lines to keep the boats grounded. In the struggle, the *Jamila Sue* broke loose. A mooring line may have gotten caught in her propeller. The boat began drifting, rocking, heading toward the archipelago just offshore. One man jumped off and swam to shore. Three others, including Captain Randy Tatum, remained with the boat. It bobbed and listed and finally turned upside down as it approached privately owned Clark Cay, which was covered in spectacular eruptions of waves. There the fishing bridge of the capsized boat scoured a hole in the reef before halting 400 yards east of the island's shore.

By midmorning Wednesday, an impression of Mitch as a whirling dervish with a crazed, maniacal mind of its own had settled over the National Hurricane Center in Miami. Forecasters simply could not explain or predict what it was doing. While most of the models forecast a westward motion with landfall on the Yucatán Peninsula, Mitch had gone nowhere. It was battering Honduras as a Category 3 storm, dumping huge quantities of rainwater on the mainland while whipping the sea and islands with hurricane-force winds that now extended out 105 miles in a strange, northeasterly elbow. The forecaster on duty at 10 A.M., Dr. Ed Rappaport, laid out his dilemma: "There are currently two camps of future tracks." One was north, the other northwest. Neither would turn out to be right. Because his forecast moved the storm somewhat north, he warned the Gulf Coast of the United States to beware.

Shortly after 11 A.M., the U.S. Coast Guard broadcast to Caribbean mariners that the *Fantome* was missing. It also contacted Honduras' search-and-rescue organization, which, though overwhelmed by the rising floodwaters and mudslides of a national disaster, tried to contact the ship by radio. Hurricane Hunters also called out the *Fantome*'s name as they flew into Mitch. There was no response.

The alerts were relayed by ham radio networks. In the distorted, sometimes garbled language of the single sideband frequencies, some heard the words "*Fantome*" and "missing" as cries for help from the ship. Captain Neil Carmichael of Windjammer's *Polynesia*, for example, asked David Jones, the weather forecaster, if he had anything from the *Fantome*. Jones, in turn, called out for the *Fantome* several times. Hearing these calls, the Windjammer office in Miami went crazy with hope. Two Florida ham radio operators told the Coast Guard they had heard what might have been SOS calls in a West Indian accent. The Cuban freedom-fighting "Brothers to the Rescue" group relayed one ham report from a clandestine base in Cuba. Windjammer's marketing chief, Shannon DeZayas-Manno, Cuban herself and bilingual, retrieved the tape but could make little sense of it.

Each of these reports was like an electroshock to the chest of Michael D. Burke and his colleagues at Windjammer. Their hopes peaked—it must be Brasso calling—only to drain away as the reports led nowhere. Burke focused on his mangrove theory—the boat had drifted south into the Mosquito Coast. He faxed a photo of the *Fantome* to the military in Honduras and Nicaragua. He also chartered a private plane from Grand Cayman to search the coastline, but it couldn't fly because of Mitch. Neither could the Coast Guard.

That afternoon, as the Caribbean's "coconut telegraph" spread the word that the *Fantome* was missing, Windjammer began to get calls from relatives of the crewmen. Shannon DeZayas-Manno divided the personnel files among her staff and asked them to compile a phone list with next-of-kin information. Some minutes later she found her assistant, Roy Bower, sobbing at his desk. "When you opened a crew file and saw their photograph, that was the first time you saw them. You realized who was on that ship. You'd heard their names time and time again. Brasso. Chrispin. Onassis. Certain people who stand out. So I took the files. I told Roy, 'I'll take care of it.' The first one I opened, I started crying. We started going down the list and calling everybody to let them know that the ship was missing. The first phone call I made was to Maxwell Bhikham's mother in Guyana. She started screaming on the phone. I don't know what I expected, but I didn't expect that. It was really emotional. I ran over to MDB's office and I plopped the files on their desks. He gave me a blank look. He had enough to deal with."

By midafternoon Wednesday, some people in Mangrove Bight had stood shoulder to shoulder, packed in houses with salt water pouring on them, for thirty hours. The children among them were amazingly quiet. They crawled into cupboards and lay down where they could.

Soaked through, Doug and Mary Solomon suddenly remembered that they had shut their parrot in the cooler. Opening it, they found it full of water and Margarita clinging to a floating orange. "Hello," she said.

Ignoring his wife's pleading, Alex Patterson stuck his head out of their cistern to look around. He watched in astonishment as people ran from collapsed houses to other houses in Savannah Bight. "The Parchmans lost their house. They left and walked to the village in water that was up to their armpits. The man next door, Wilson, and his family came running up when their house disappeared. My next-door neighbor and his wife tried to stay in their house. It started blowing away. I think they were in three or four houses during the storm. They'd run to one and it would disappear. It ended up with forty or fifty people in one house." His sister's house, just below, had lost its roofing, and the old people inside were huddled under the crawl space, watching through the eye wall as Savannah Bight collapsed, one house at a time. "I'd been in typhoons before. I'd gone through Andrew. That was four hours. This went on and on."

At Dr. Keith Taylor's block house in Pelican Reef, 120 people filled the dripping interior with religious fervor that helped drown a noise that Taylor described as like "a 737 or an F15. It's as if they are getting ready to take off, but they never take off. It was like an airplane for thirty hours." Inside, Catholics, Adventists, Jehovah's Witnesses, even the unfaithful, made promises, sang, and played hymns on his wife's piano.

"Everybody was praying to somebody," said Taylor. For some reason, his phone still worked, and it rang with a call from Kodel Kelly, one of his nurses from the island of Bonacca.

"Is my house still standing?" she asked. Taylor put down the phone to look out his window. "I could see the entire house moving. It was in the water, floating." He picked up the phone. "Kodel, you will be relocating to Sandy Bay."

At Guanaja's Bayman Bay Club, the noise and isolation were taking their toll. Humans, trapped in basements like rats, began acting like them. When a manager checked on the thirty-three employees huddled in a separate 20- by 15-foot basement, they accosted him.

"We know what you're doing."

He stared, dumbfounded. "What?"

"You're going to get a helicopter to take the gringos out!"

He fought his way back to Don Pearly's basement and told him to deal with it. Pearly knew logic was not at play. "I'll be the last to leave," he promised. He also made a mental note of where his guns were.

Pearly returned to the other basement to find his guests in near revolt.

"We used the phone, Don."

His satellite phone had less than an hour's remaining battery life. But they'd called a governor, an ex-ambassador to Belize, and a general, all of whom told them there was nothing they could do. Spooked by someone's wild fear that a mudslide would tumble their shelter into the ocean, they had also tied themselves together with a long rope, with loops for their wrists. Pearly said later, "It was radical."

A few miles west, the island of Roatán was counting itself lucky. Mitch's outer winds and waves raked the northern shore, destroying most homes in Punta Gorda, but residents there had scrambled to higher ground and, miraculously, no one had died. Ben's Resort disappeared in the surf. Anthony's Key Resort would later report on the Internet that it lost "a few rooms, but by no means all and will be opening again as soon as possible."

On his weather net, David Jones had been trying repeatedly to raise the yacht *Velella*. No one answered. "I could only believe the worst had happened and that *Velella* had failed to survive the storm." In fact, the southern side of Roatán had escaped beautifully. In Coxen Hole "winds are calm and have been most of the day. Telephones are working for the most part," a professor reported to Honduras.com. In the fjord of Oak

Ridge, there was no wind in the harbor. As proof, a bar owner later pointed to his rickety establishment, built on stilts near shore. "Anything would have blown this down."

🦅

Slowed by the friction of Honduras, Mitch weakened to 100 knots— Category 3—late Wednesday afternoon and edged westward. There was no visible eye, and from the satellite the storm looked like a white swirl, dredging moisture from the entire Honduran coast and dumping it in great swaths on the countryside. By now, 2 feet of rain had fallen in La Ceiba, the coastal city used by tourists to catch a commuter plane to the Bay Islands. Water from overflowed rivers had reached the take-out window of the Burger King. Witnesses watched cows, horses, and houses tumble into the Río Cangrejal. En route to rescue children in a flooded orphanage, La Ceiba's police commandant, a captain, and three officers disappeared when a bridge collapsed under them. They were never heard from again. The Wednesday afternoon tides were 12 feet above normal. The city was an island, and people were catching fish in the streets in front of their homes.

To the northwest, debris began building up behind two low bridges where CA-13, the main highway across Honduras, crossed the Río Aguán. Two lakes began to fill the wide fertile valley. The chocolate tide spilled through irrigation ditches into banana fields, soaking the roots, then climbing the fragile trunks.

On Wednesday evening, shortly after he went to bed in Trujillo, the port city 25 miles south of Guanaja, Daniel Díaz was awakened by a Mayday call on his VHF radio. He recognized the voice as that of a fellow fisherman who lived in the village of Santa Rosa de Aguán.

"Please," the voice cried. "The river has cut the city in three pieces. The power is gone." He was using his car battery to broadcast.

Díaz was the forty-three-year-old president of the Federation of Fishmen, known as Moderpesca, a group that used GPS, VHF radios, and other modern equipment to fish in Japanese-supplied 25-foot fiberglass dories with 25-horsepower engines. He alerted several colleagues, hooked his boat to his truck, and drove toward the Río Aguán, 20 miles away. Topping a rise, he was shocked to find the river only 5 miles away and the whole valley filled with water. With six men in three boats, he set out to launch a rescue to Santa Rosa, some 20 miles away. But they didn't get far in the dark before they encountered people in trees and on roofs of flooded villages who cried out to the boatmen. The fishermen filled each craft with fourteen people and returned to the shore. Díaz then called for more boats.

"This," he radioed, "is a big emergency."

On his radio, he could still hear his friend pleading, but the disaster at hand kept him busy. He and his partner, Nandito Fernando, headed out again. Díaz saw a foot in the midst of a tangle of tree branches. Maneuvering his boat close, he shouted, "It's a man." They pulled him in. He was dead. In his cradled arms was a one-year-old boy, also dead. With his own children, a boy, eleven, and girl, seven, at home braving the storm by themselves, Díaz broke down. A few minutes later, they found five people dead in one place. Díaz and Fernando hauled them into the boat, took them to a sandbar island, and buried them in a hole. As they maneuvered through the night, they passed cows swimming and people crying out in the dark.

"I feel real close to God," he said later. "They were crying, 'Please! Please.'"

They pulled a fourteen-year-old boy from the current. "My mom and dad are on the roof of the house," he said.

"Trees were sticking in the boat, and making the motor come out of the water. It was running fast, rrrr, rrrrrr. Whining." Díaz maneuvered where the boy pointed, and a mother, father, and six boys were straddling the ridge of a house, all in a row. Their feet on each side were in the water. Díaz pulled them off and found an island on which to deposit them. When he went back, their house had broken and washed away.

Moments later, he turned his head and saw a man clinging to a tree caught in a cascading current. Their only hope was to run up the current, tie a rope to a tree, and ease back to where the man was. He asked his partner, "Nandito, can you hold the boat?"

"No problem."

"OK. Let's go."

Getting to the man was like climbing a half-mile of white water in a cataract. They roped a tree and backed off and rescued him. All this while Díaz could hear his friend calling from Santa Rosa on the radio.

"Please, please. There are ten persons on a house in a current. Daniel, the river has washed away a house with seven people. I think they are dead. There are three hundred to four hundred people in real danger."

Díaz, muddy, exhausted, soaked by the rain, couldn't get there.

At 11:30 P.M., in the eastern section of Santa Rosa de Aguán, Peace Corps volunteer Patrick Cleary was awakened by a neighbor's cry. He'd gone to bed exhausted at 7 P.M., after two nonstop days of dealing with wind damage in the village. Through his grogginess, the voice chilled him:

"The river is here."

That was followed swiftly by a yell from his landlord, village elder Sebastian Solano, who never raised his voice. "We've got to get out of here!"

"I feel I'm dead," said Cleary. "I get out of bed and step into a foot of water. It's pitch-black. I go out the back door and the whole backyard is a lake. It's filling up, not running like a river. I run into my room. What do I need, what can I save? It's too late. I grab my passport and work card and my headlamp."

As Solano's family waded out, stepping across a lumpy sand landscape, two of his grandchildren, twelve- and fourteen-year-old girls, screamed. The water was 4 feet deep in places. "Hardly anyone there can swim," said Cleary. "They don't go into the ocean. They're afraid of the ocean. They go to the river. Now the river's on us. I hear people yelling. Glimpses of flashlights. People in the dark. There's still wind. It's still raining. And it's midnight."

☙

During their flights Wednesday, Hurricane Hunters had detected an emergency signal north of Guanaja. It was one of the older-style homing radiobeacons that broadcast to planes on 121.5 megahertz but do not identify themselves. The *Fantome* carried one inside the deckhouse. When told about it that evening, Michael D. Burke assumed it was not the *Fantome*'s. It would not have made sense for Guyan March to activate that beacon but not one of the 406 EPIRBs that would identify the vessel and its location to satellites. The 406s remained silent. "I think she's out there," Burke said, plotting the ship's course if driven south. Burke had one of his men call Alden, the 406 EPIRB manufacturer. Made nearly bulletproof, to high technical standards and with a battery life of a decade, the Alden beacon was now keeping Windjammer's spirits afloat. "They roll up on the beach," a company spokesman told Windjammer. "It's durable."

At sixteen minutes past midnight, a late-night correspondent on Windjammer's Web bulletin board typed a single, frenzied line:

"The news stations here in South Florida say that the *Fantome* is MISSING!!!! Does anyone have any info????"

Minutes later, Windjammer shut down the site.

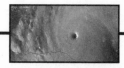

BAY ISLANDS, MAINLAND HONDURAS, AND MIAMI

October 29, 1998

🐚

A S THURSDAY BEGAN, Hurricane Mitch was officially "stagnant," its center 14 miles from where the villagers of Santa Rosa de Aguán, in pitch-black panic, were fleeing their homes. Sebastian Solano led his family to a neighbor's house, where hysterical women speaking Garifuno huddled around a single candle. Rain poured in. "I heard a creaking noise," recalled Patrick Cleary, the Peace Corps volunteer. "The kitchen crumbles. Everybody's screaming. We all run out the back door and dive out into complete black in 4 or 5 feet of water. Solano goes off in the dark. We are in a chain, five of us. The dogs are paddling behind us. We cross barbed wire. I lose the soles of my hiking boots. My headlamp goes dead. Now I can see part of the river running through pretty fast. We go through, fording with a pole to keep our footing. We go up to a friend of Solano's, a Garifuna who lived in New York and is now retired. He has an oasis. The water is not there. His wife makes us coffee. It's 4 in the morning. I'm just praying for light.

"Solano is outside with a radio. We tune in to Miami. All they're talking about is Mitch. It's wiping out all of Honduras. I'm interpreting. There are thirty people in the house. Babies, kids, crying. Dogs. Total chaos. That's the first we knew of Mitch. At 5:30 we go outside. It looks like a bomb hit the place. I ford a couple of rivers and see that the river has now completely busted through. It's roaring through our house, my room. The door's open. My stuff's gone."

The bridges that had formed huge lakes in the Río Aguán valley had given way during the night. Concrete abutments were dislodged and tossed downstream. Muddy torrents ran to the sea, creating new rivers through the village. The river rose through the entire town, washing sand away from foundations, cracking homes, flushing pigs and chickens into the sea. Cleary noticed people running toward a cliff from where they could see the other side of town, across the river. The river was three times its normal width, and running with 8- to 10-foot waves. One end of the village was gone. Six people were on the roof of the school, and two school buses had toppled into the swirling river. A Japanese fish-processing plant was in ruins. Thirty percent of the homes were destroyed.

One of the missing homes on the sandy delta belonged to school-teacher Isabella Arriola, a heavyset, thirty-six-year-old Garifuna with an expansive grin. She lived there with her husband, Ricardo Guity, and their three children. Seven neighbors had taken refuge in the house. According to witnesses, the river engulfed the house gradually and forcefully, a roiling bulldozer that climbed 6 feet in two hours. When the waters gushed through, she grabbed her youngest child, six-year-old Anderson, in her arms and followed her husband and two other children, Elizabeth, eight, and Ricardo, ten, through the rushing water toward higher ground. They were overcome by the current and swept into the sea. At the time, Hurricane Mitch's eye was 3 miles from the village, and anyone in the water was washed under the eastern eye wall and swept northward off the coast into 4,000-foot-deep water. Arriola, her entire family, and seven neighbors were counted among Santa Rosa's forty dead.

At dawn a Hurricane Hunter plane fixed the center of Mitch on the Cape of Honduras, the peninsula that protrudes from Trujillo directly south of Guanaja. Slowed by the friction of land, the eye's pressure was up 41 millibars to 979, and the wind had dropped to 75 knots, a Category 1 storm. Though half of Mitch was over land, forecasters followed their computer models, which persisted in sensing a west-northwestward drift with an eventual landfall on the Yucatán Peninsula.

On Guanaja, Kerston Moore, the lobsterman who had been standing in his house with more than one hundred neighbors since Tuesday, noticed that the water dripping through his roof tasted fresh. It was rain, not salt water. "Hurricane Francera lasted four hours. Greta and Fifi seven hours. But Mitch, the son of a bitch, he lasted thirty-seven hours," said Moore, who emerged to find Mangrove Bight gone. People who hid in the canyons above the village descended to find lobsters and crabs scattered in the woods.

When Mary and Doug Solomon awoke, they did not recognize their tropical paradise. "We were lying in what looked like Verdun. Not a blade of grass or shrub." They were soaked inside their foul weather gear, salty, dirty, bug-eaten. Mary was the first to walk to the brow of the hill and look over toward the house. Myopic, she yelled to Doug that she saw the house. He went to look.

"It's gone, Mary. It's all gone." In the warm remnant rain of Mitch, four more streams of salt water wet their cheeks. Three houses on the beach and one on the island were gone. Walking back around what remained of the mangrove swamp, they found the shore scattered for 2 miles with debris, as if a huge plane had crashed at 200 knots. Water and wind had taken their boats, water heaters, diaries, a red carpet, diving bottles, batteries, solar panels, ham radio, and bathtub and deposited them 1,000 yards inland.

On the site of their dream home, only the concrete generator room and an in-ground circular pool remained. The Solomons' generator room was an oily, salty mess. Mary and Doug gathered palm fronds and spread them on the floor. At the height of the storm, one of their cats had panicked and run off, severely scratching Mary's arm when she tried to restrain it. Now her arm was badly infected, and Doug lanced it. With two bottles of single-malt scotch that they found, they lay down in the rain and slept like the dead. When they awoke the island had turned black. The salt spray had poisoned and killed much of the vegetation. Even the rocks looked black. For as far as they could see, everything was black.

After thirty-six hours in his cistern in East End Village, Alex Patterson pulled himself and his wife out. Winds still blew at near hurricane force, but by comparison, they seemed like a breeze. Only four of the village's thirty-nine houses had enough structure left to live in. None of the native houses had survived. The neighboring village of Savannah Bight, where most homes had balanced on stilts, was a pile of splinters. "There wasn't enough lumber left to build caskets," said Patterson later. "I'm still amazed. The wind blew so hard, with so much particulate matter, that the galvanizing was stripped off wire fences." Patterson's handyman, Carswell Bennett, emerged from his home to find little but assorted debris: "mattresses, tanks, clothes . . . shit."

Sima Setti, the Guanaja teacher, who had gone three days without sleep at Dr. Keith Taylor's house, came out to find only one house standing in the neighborhood—the one she was in. The ground was littered with dead pigs and chickens.

Across the island, nine hundred homes—95 percent of the dwellings—were destroyed. Yet gallows humor began to percolate among the survivors. Dr. Taylor heard this exchange on VHF radio between shrimpers who had been running their boat engines now for nearly forty-eight hours in the desperate bid to stay sheltered in the mangroves:

"We can't take another six hours of this."

"We don't know what's going on."

"Is it still over us?"

A voice he recognized as Rolphe Merrin's broke in.

"Let me tell you, it's over."

His transmission was followed by an almost tearful, "How do you know?"

"I can feel the sand fleas eating my ass."

The first reports from Roatán indicated that one hundred houses had been destroyed in Punta Gorda on the north shore. In Coxen Hole, one of the hurricane shelters on the south side, people reported minor damage and no deaths. In the West End, aside from roads awash and seawalls damaged, even Foster's, a Windjammer haunt on stilts over the sea, had escaped serious damage. Port Royal, the old English hideaway, had barely a riffle of wind.

By 4 P.M., the National Hurricane Center downgraded Mitch to a tropical storm and reported an official landfall in Honduras, nearly over the village of Santa Rosa de Aguán. The city of Trujillo was recording 50-knot winds, and tropical-storm winds extended out to sea, over Guanaja, nearly 175 miles. The GFDL model predicted a southward motion through Thursday evening, and then a turn to the northwest—something the models had been predicting for a week—"with a landfall on the Yucatán in 72 hours."

Though the storm was diminishing, the wounds it was inflicting on Honduras and Nicaragua were not. Gathering in the mountain streams, several feet of water headed downhill. In some places, 2 feet of rain fell in six hours. Rivers were rampaging, carrying cars, trees, and cattle to the sea. Three teenagers, watching from a levee, joined the flotsam when the earth beneath their feet collapsed. In La Lima, headquarters of

Chiquita Brands International, an Associated Press reporter found water waist-deep in the streets. Bananas, grain, and citrus growing in the 250,000-acre Sula Valley were awash. The death toll by Thursday afternoon was estimated at thirty-six, fourteen of them on the Bay Islands. Some fifteen thousand homes had been destroyed. Honduran TV showed flooded plantations and reported that in the Miskito province, entire villages had dissolved into the sea.

"God save Honduras," said President Carlos Flores Facusse after a flying survey of his country's destruction. Yet in the capital of Tegucigalpa, there was little sign of pending doom. A note posted on the Caribbean Hurricane Page, www.gobeach.com, reported "only some small rivers flooding lower parts of the city . . . it is not raining . . . the day is much brighter than yesterday." The correspondent did not know that much worse was in store.

The search for the *Fantome* began at 8 A.M. Thursday when the U.S. Coast Guard dispatched its first search-and-rescue flight, a C-130 turboprop, from Clearwater, Florida. NOAA pilot Phil Kenul, who had flown through Mitch on Tuesday, accompanied the flight as an advisor.

The Coast Guard had several search-and-rescue missions on that flight, including an ELT (Emergency Location Transmitter) signal in the Bay Islands that could be coming from the *Fantome*'s 121.5 megahertz radiobeacon. En route to Guanaja, however, they were also to search for six individuals thought to be Americans on Swan Island. Descending through clouds for a low-altitude run over the island, the plane's traffic collision avoidance alarm went off in the cockpit. Five miles away a "contact" was coming toward them at their intended altitude.

"We're thinking, 'What the hell?'" said Kenul. "We held up our descent and called on the radio. What kind of moron is out in a storm at 500 feet? We're the only idiots."

It was a Hurricane Hunter plane, returning from Mitch, answering the same search-and-rescue call. "As luck would have it, we're in the same place. We never even saw them. Without collision avoidance it would have been a very unpleasant experience."

Swan Island is a skinny, rocky Honduran territory once valuable to the United States as a military air base. Patrolled by a half-dozen Honduran soldiers—not Americans, it turned out—it now looked like Mount St. Helens, according to Kenul. "We didn't see a single blade of grass, not a leaf on any tree, and every tree was snapped off halfway down. Everything was laid down. The island was totally denuded from the wind." The men later were found alive, having hidden in culverts and ditches.

As the C-130 flew on toward the Bay Islands, the news of the missing *Fantome* spread into homes throughout the eastern Caribbean. Twelve hours after hearing about the ship on the news, Chrispin's mother, Mrs. Saunders, in Grenada, got a call from Windjammer. Across town, Alice George, Alvin and Alan's sister, got her own call from Windjammer and went to see her mother.

"I want to tell you something. Sit," she said, in tears. "Alan and Alvin—they haven't seen the boat. In Mitch. I can't believe it."

In Guyana, Vernon Brusch's sister got the news by grapevine and went with a friend to tell Athelene Brusch. They asked her to sit down. She searched their faces.

"Mommie, you know what I heard? The ship disappeared."

"I didn't take it for nothing," Athelene said later. "I felt the hurricane had shifted the ship and took it to another island."

In Belmopan, the capital of Belize, Faith Herrera's sister approached her.

"Faith, did you know the ship is missing?"

"How in God's name can't they find a ship?" Herrera remembers saying. "I didn't believe."

She called the company with an emergency number Chrispin had provided. A voice replied that yes, the ship was missing, "but we'll find it. Everything is OK."

Windjammer's headquarters was in chaos. People were sobbing at their desks. The phones went crazy with stricken relatives and the first nosy reporters making inquiries. Michael D. Burke and his team were marshaling airplanes, ham radio operators, and island agents to search for any sign of ship, crew, or debris. Susan Burke set up a task force of ten people on phones, from all departments, to handle incoming queries. Friends came in to help. Many passengers called, as did crewmen's friends, relatives, second cousins, and especially mothers. All were seeking news, reassurance, any scrap of hope. "It was constant and insatiable," she said later.

At 6:45 P.M., with dusk approaching, the first Coast Guard search-and-rescue flight finally reached Honduran waters to look for *Fantome*. Phil Kenul described the conditions as a "Sunday picnic" compared with his Tuesday flight: widespread thunderstorms and rain, winds from the east at 40 to 60 knots, seas 10 to 30 feet high with visibility 1 to 3 miles—"beautiful. The ride was pretty nice. A lot better than flying in a light bulb. We could see the sea and islands." The crew circled Guanaja's eastern reef and the harbor at Savannah Bight, homing in on the EPIRB signal thought to be from the ship. It was beeping just off-shore in what appeared to be a sandbar near Bonacca, the main port of Guanaja on the south side. There was no sign of the *Fantome* or her crew. The airplane circled and circled, looking. Several shrimp boats were seen intact. Two vessels were beached on a barrier island with no one around. Offshore, the plane flew a rectangular search pattern, call-ing out "*Fantome*" on the radio. They dropped a transmitter-type data marking buoy into the water to mark current drift for the next search plane to follow.

As the C-130 headed back home at 8:30 P.M., the first stories of the search moved on news wires. Agence France Presse quoted Jeff Hall of the Miami Coast Guard as saying the ship was "still missing." There were several errors in the first report—passengers got off in Omoa and the ship went missing on Monday. Windjammer spokesman James Canty was quoted as saying that the ship was experiencing 10-foot seas and winds of 65 knots. At the time of the news report, the death toll in Central America was reported to be thirty-two, only one more than the *Fantome*'s crew. Canty told the *Fort Lauderdale Sun-Sentinel* that in the absence of an emergency signal, the company felt the boat was safe.

As the official news spread, Windjammer encouraged families to check in, and the company was inundated with calls from relatives. Families were divided up among the staff, who were directed to focus on immediate families. They soon learned that "family," to island residents, meant children, a wife or two, cousins, and half-sisters. They tried to funnel news through one member of the "family," a tac-tic that satisfied no one. Windjammer's reservations clerks became grief counselors, armed with an American Airlines crisis manual bor-rowed from a friend of the senior Mike Burke. "We are sales and mar-keting people," said marketing chief Shannon DeZayas-Manno. "We're selling fun fantasy cruises. We had never had to deal with a crisis like this."

By Thursday's end, some at Windjammer began to give up hope. Polly Burke, who designed the company's artwork, heard her brother Michael say, "I think they're gone." Her stomach fell. She ran out of the building and broke down.

The Internet began humming with news about Mitch: its damage, lost loved ones, and the fate of the *Fantome*. Earlier in the day, Lori Brandt of San Diego, a member of a Windjammer chat forum, had e-mailed two public bulletin boards, Honduras.com and gobeach.com, asking for news. Gert van Dijken, who ran the Caribbean Hurricane Page for gobeach.com, posted her note at 12:56 P.M. "We are worried that the worst has happened, and if anyone has seen the ship at Roatan or could confirm that they are OK we would be very appreciative."

At 8:47 P.M., Honduras.com, a Web tourist service, replied to Brandt's e-mail plea with this exciting news: "Correspondents report the ship was tied up and fine, but got loose and now they are uncertain of its whereabouts."

Asked to confirm that, a message at 9:02 P.M. read: "It has been confirmed by our San Pedro Sula correspondents that the ship is fine :)"

At Windjammer, the news was like a whiff of oxygen in a tomb. Could it be? DeZayas-Manno and others at Windjammer made frantic calls to anyone they could. One woman dialed Carlos Arita in Omoa. When he called back, he blurted out how happy he was that the ship had gone to Belize.

"No, we sent them to the Bay Islands," she said.

"You killed them," Arita said.

The company caller hung up. For the next three days Carlos Arita called out for the *Fantome* on his VHF radio.

By the end of Thursday, Web sites like the Caribbean Hurricane Page were getting agonized personal queries:

"I would like to know if I can get any news from my friends from Roatan. Their names are McNab, Mr. Bob, Evan and their family."

Late Thursday, an official plea from Windjammer staff member Miguel Moreno appeared on the Caribbean Web site.

"Sailing Vessel *Fantome*. 31 persons on board. Please, anyone who has seen her or knows of somebody that has seen or heard from them after Tuesday afternoon, pls write back."

The next message was another plea for a victim of the storm.

"I am trying to locate the family of Douglas and Jane Kothenbeutel. If anyone knows of their whereabouts, please let me know."

🎏

At 10 P.M. Thursday, tropical storm Mitch was still near the Honduran coast. Its pressure had risen to 995 millibars and winds were 45 knots. Richard Pasch, the forecaster on duty in Miami, tried to convince the models that the storm was moving inland and not north, as they had consistently forecast. He injected into the modeling calculations of southeasterly motion. "In spite of this, almost all of the models predict a west-northwest to northwestward motion developing almost immediately. . . . With this guidance, the current official forecast is very similar to the previous one.

"Rainfall continues to be a problem with this system. More flooding and mudslides appear likely for another day or so. Satellite images show an area of persistent convection over western Nicaragua, so the flood threat in that area appears to be particularly serious."

Late that night in El Progreso, an industrial city east of San Pedro Sula, thousands climbed on the roofs of their homes after the Río Ulúa burst its banks. The fire department, short on boats, called the situation "desperate." By now, the capital city of Tegucigalpa had received 60 inches of rain in five days.

"GOD HELP US!" someone typed at Honduras.com.

🎏

At around 11:21 P.M., a small group of Windjammer fans signed on to a live Internet chat room and began to discuss the missing ship. The Windjammer bulletin board was down, and they didn't expect it to come back up until *Fantome* was found. Shannon DeZayas-Manno had shut it down "to keep the info on the *Fantome* correct," said Lori Brandt, "to avoid rumors and fear spreading." The Jammers shared theories, hopes, stray bits of intelligence—straws in a virtual wind. There had been a message on Yahoo chat about "problems."

"I still think they're in that bay," said one.

"He could also have taken the western side of the storm, and be anywhere from Costa Rica to Colombia," typed another.

"Many reports that the south side of Roatan was fine. That's where we think *Fantome* is," said the first.

"Webmaster at Honduras site says *Fantome* is fine," said another.

"Wonder how San Pedro Sula knows and Windjammer doesn't?"

"Am surprised to hear they might even still be in the area. They told Windjammer on Tuesday that they were going around the South End to try to miss the storm."

To the rest of the world, the *Fantome* story unfolded this way: in bits and pieces, rumors and questions, almost in slow motion, obscured and confused not by a lack of words, but by too many.

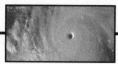

BAY ISLANDS, MAINLAND HONDURAS, AND MIAMI

October 30–November 1, 1998

🐚

FRIDAY, OCTOBER 3 0, brought the full blooming of disaster in Central America. In the immensity of the saga, the story of the *Fantome* was a paragraph.

"ANYONE—IN ANY COUNTRY . . ." began a bold-faced scream from the tourist Web site Honduras.com. "The Fire Departments of Honduras are in desperate need of small motorboats, swamp boats, hydrocrafts. . . . ANYTHING that can transport people through water."

Rain was falling at the rate of two feet per day. Four feet had fallen, and another foot or two was possible. Tegucigalpa, the capital, was declared a disaster area.

"We are drowning here! Lots of houses have been flooded," came a Web note from the capital. "Please pray for our nation, because we are confronting the worst disaster of our history."

By Friday night the Río Choluteca had washed away factories, hospitals, and several neighborhoods. There was no way of knowing the number of missing in what a U.S. State Department report later called "blood waters . . . mud and debris that emit a nauseating smell from decomposing animal and human remains." The "true horrors," as the *New York Times* would later describe them, began Friday night when mudslides buried people as they slept. At Casita Volcano, in Nicaragua near the Honduran border, the old crater filled with water, a wall gave way, and fourteen villages with 1,500 people were buried in mud.

Because 80 percent of Honduras' telephone service was gone, the accounting Friday morning was incomplete. Nonetheless, authorities estimated 1 million homeless, 70,000 homes destroyed, 5,000 people in treetops, and more than 100 dead. In scattered Web postings, these stories emerged on Friday: The seaside village of Miami, with 40 thatched-roof homes, had dissolved and disappeared into the sea. Bodies were floating in the Río Ceiba. People had tied their children in trees to keep them from being drowned in mud. In San Pedro Sula, water was up to the second floor of the new airport terminal. There were 30,000 people in shelters in San Pedro Sula alone. They slept on cardboard while chickens and dogs wandered about. Hundreds of bridges were washed away. A family of six in Choluteca was buried in mud. Fifty people were missing in Comayagua after the Río Salistroso swept away 150 houses.

After forty-eight hours of rescue work in the delta of the Río Aguán, Daniel Díaz's absence left his family thinking he was gone, too. But he was still in his boat, following the road to Santa Rosa by the utility poles sticking up in the water. On one of his last trips, his partner saw a plastic bag in the water and shouted.

"I think it's people."

"It's a man in here."

They tried to get him off the crotch of a tree, but he wouldn't let go. He was crazy with fear. As they pulled, they realized that he had wrapped his left hand to the tree with barbed wire. "The hand was this big. I didn't have any pliers. No hammer. We broke the wire by bending it back and forth, for fifteen minutes." As they laid him in the bottom of the boat, his arms remained frozen in the clenched position.

"My bag!" he cried.

They grabbed the plastic bag. It was empty.

Bay Island survivors emerged from their makeshift shelters to a bewildering, random world. The archipelago of private islands off Posada del Sol on the south coast of Guanaja had been whipped and beaten into a few scraggly palms—the resort of Half Moon Cay was gone. Yet nearby, a concrete dome on stilts known as the "igloo" stood untouched. In Sandy Bay, a floating hotel was stripped of its rooms, and boats were blown right out of the water, tossed into the mangroves. Nearby, though, on a spit of land, an outhouse with a palm roof appeared not to have noticed the storm.

The atmosphere was still miserable: salty and sandy with nonstop rain. People described the air as "white" with clouds. Robert Abella felt famished and began scavenging food from shops that had been blown apart. Dr. Keith Taylor found himself walking in circles. "There was too much debris, and the wind was still 70 miles an hour. You couldn't go anywhere. You didn't have a boat."

Although most of the structures were destroyed, the death toll on Guanaja was remarkably small. Two people died under collapsed homes as they tried to flee in Savannah Bight. A ninety-six-year-old woman in Bonacca Town died when a refrigerator fell on her. The bodies of the three fishermen lost off the shrimp boat *Jamila Sue* Wednesday morning were found, and a woman emerging from shelter after the brunt of the storm passed fell dead from a heart attack.

Walking around his blighted estate, Doug Solomon found metal parts from a boat, a huge swivel socket off a gantry or small mast, and some three-quarter-inch electrical cable. He kicked over a CD boom box and books. He didn't know about the missing *Fantome*.

Across the island, at Posada del Sol, vacationing diver Hector Castro set to work with a buddy to restore the resort's water system. Back home, they were utility engineers for the city of Fort Lauderdale. While returning from the generator shack, they found what looked like a stairway floating in the water. It was ornately carved, with portions of steps and the banister. Lying on the beach nearby, where they'd been stranded by the receding storm surge, were two orange life jackets stenciled with *"Fantome."* With no knowledge of the ship, communications cut off, and unending repair work ahead of them, the men went back to their tasks. Their discovery remained unknown to Windjammer.

Officially, Windjammer Barefoot Cruises was still full of hope. Unofficially, people at the company were looking for reasons to be optimistic. Annie Bleasdale called often from England, desperate for news. Despite her bad dreams, she kept up a façade of bubbly good cheer: "They're fine. They're having a beer." Michael D. Burke was finally able to charter two private planes to search the Honduran coast, including the Mosquito Coast around Cabo Gracias a Dios. Assuming the worst, he asked skin divers to follow the ocean currents toward Belize in their search for debris or bodies. At the same time, hoping against all odds to find the men huddled in mud huts somewhere along the Honduran coast, he hired Jeeps to penetrate remote areas of the devastated coastline. The company also relied on the handful of Internet-savvy Jammers who spread word of the search to ham nets and bulletin boards, relayed tips to the Miami office, and propped the staff psychologically. Sara Sommers, for example, a medical equipment technician in Jackson, Wyoming, chased the tantalizing tip from Honduras.com that "the ship is fine."

"Can you please confirm and give location of *Fantome* and source of information?" she inquired.

"Correspondents report the ship was tied up and fine, but got loose and now they are uncertain of its whereabouts. As soon as we hear anything more, we will let you know."

"Did your correspondents mention in what location the S/V *Fantome* was tied up? We are wondering if she returned to Roatan after losing radio contact and perhaps holed up in Coxen Hole or other protected areas on south shore."

"We are trying to get further info. We have lost contact with our office in San Pedro Sula and are in the process of trying to reach them. This request is at the top of the list."

"Please, please tell us WHERE the S/V *Fantome* was tied up, and WHICH DAY she was seen???" Sommers' increasingly agitated queries, over twenty-four hours, produced nothing concrete.

As such tips flooded and ebbed through the phone lines and computer workstations at Windjammer, all sailor bravado subsided, giving way to classic symptoms of mourning: shouts of anger, jags of tears, and an occasional, hysterical, "They're gone! They're gone!" In their crisis—the first of its magnitude in Windjammer history—the company reacted in ways that, in retrospect, seemed ungraceful. Michael D. Burke, for example, dispatched two people to the West Indies with cash enough to pay families of missing crewmembers two months' salary. He considered it a humanitarian gesture and a "starting point," but payments of less than $1,000 per man made him look cheap.

Also on Friday, Susan Burke's office mailed letters to the ninety-seven passengers who had been evacuated from Belize. Backdated Monday, October 26, the day of the evacuation, the letter declared the aborted trip a "travel delay." As a result, the evacuation flight cost of $251.60 per person was deducted from their travel insurance payout of $500. The letter, which arrived amidst news reports about the missing ship, then invited them to rebook their "missed cruise" in the coming year. The company listed four available weeks in January aboard the *Fantome*.

🐚

A second Coast Guard C-130 flew over Utila, Roatán, Guanaja, and the surrounding sea on Friday, calling the *Fantome*'s name on VHF Channel 16 to no avail. Windjammer had provided details of the ship's three 38-foot whaleboats equipped with VHF radios, orange smoke, signal lights, red handheld flares and parachute flares, plus the eleven 25-person life rafts "colored orange." The Coast Guard's briefing papers also instructed air crews to look for "PIW W/PFD"—persons in water with personal flotation devices, or life jackets.

Over the Bay Islands, the pilot reported 35-knot winds, occasional waterspouts and isolated tornadoes, and confused seas of 10 to 14 feet. The ceiling was 1,200 feet. He also tracked a 121.5-megahertz emergency radiobeacon signal near Guanaja's airport, and said it appeared "to be coming from a boat that had washed ashore near the runway." As the C-130 flew over, veterinarian Alex Patterson used his handheld VHF radio to report damage on the island. The pilot asked Patterson to go to the airport and turn off the emergency signal, which might have been the same one Thursday's C-130 flight had homed on.

That evening, Coast Guard spokesman Jeff Hall told the Associated Press that another flight was under consideration but hadn't left yet. "There's still not a lot we can do with the way the weather is down there."

James Canty of Windjammer told the press, "We believe the vessel is out there and it's just a matter of damage to the communication system that's preventing communication with the crew."

🐚

As Saturday, October 31, arrived in Honduras, Tropical Storm Mitch continued to defy all attempts by the National Hurricane Center to get its arms around a system that now looked like an angry child's scrawl over Central America. The beautiful hurricane eye was long gone. Forecasters stared at the jerky satellite loop, unable to say with certainty where the center was. Winds were down to 35 knots near Tegucigalpa, then up to 50 knots on Roatán, with tropical-storm-force winds spread over an area 400 miles wide, from the Pacific Ocean, across Honduras to the Bay Islands. The worst convection, in fact, was on the southern edge of the system, near the Gulf of Fonseca on the Pacific coast, and not in the center, where the pressure had risen to 1000 millibars. Mitch now appeared to be dredging up Pacific moisture to dump torrential rains on Nicaragua, Honduras, El Salvador, and Guatemala. Mitch also continued to make liars of the center's computer models, which never had done well with predictions over land. The storm was drifting southwest to latitude 14.0° N.

On Saturday morning forecaster Miles Lawrence, back on duty after two days off, reversed the long-held prediction that the storm would move back out into the Caribbean. Honduran waters were now barely riled enough for small-craft warnings. But Lawrence did follow model guidance that the storm would eventually turn north over land toward Mexico, perhaps reaching the Bay of Campeche in the western Gulf of Mexico. Not until 9 A.M. Saturday did Mitch turn westward. By then, the 8,000- to 13,000-foot mountains between Guatemala and Honduras had sapped so much energy from it that Mitch was downgraded to a tropical depression.

Any excitement that Mitch had generated among the weather professionals in Miami by now had drained away. The news that a ship was missing—perhaps because of their forecast failures—now combined with the dreadful realization that their forecasts didn't contain adequate language to warn of the disaster happening underneath Mitch's miserable cloud cover.

"My people like these storms," said Jerry Jarrell, the director of the National Hurricane Center, in an interview months afterward. "These are exciting storms, and this was one of the most severe storms of the century, probably the strongest any of them have ever worked on. There is a bit of excitement. You hear about a person dying, or suffering, and it reminds you that these are not fun and exciting things. These are killers. Us giving names to them gives them a bit of humanity that they don't deserve. They are wicked, cruel things. Whereas when you look at these pictures, they are beautiful. We're torn between these two emotions—one that we really like them, and one when we are jerked down to earth."

Jarrell said the tone in the center's war room changed with the news that the *Fantome* was missing. "That was the first confirmation, or first suggestion, that really, people are suffering."

Then came the rain, which had loomed in the backs of their minds because of Fifi. "Even if Mitch didn't go over Honduras, if it went west or northwest, they were going to have a disaster." But the center's predictions fell short of actual rainfall amounts, and the Saffir-Simpson hurricane scale of 1 to 5 missed the mark in Honduras, Jarrell said.

"The problem is that we and the media try to use the scale to do something it was never meant to do. It was meant for you and me, who have never seen 100-mile-an-hour winds, to show what it would do, in words—trees down, roofs off. It has done a wonderful job at that. But when you have a Category 5 hurricane, all kinds of things happen, and the Saffir-Simpson scale just talks about wind speeds, and by inference, storm surge and wave heights. Most rain events have been weaker storms. Storms over land get weaker, and who cares if it rains over water? The problem was, when Mitch went up and up, everyone was watching it—a disaster blooming—then it peaked and went down in intensity and everybody lost interest in it just as the disaster was going off the scale. So the Saffir-Simpson is going one way and the potential for disaster is going the other. Wind speed doesn't determine rainfall at all. Is it possible to develop a scale or a model that does? Yeah, it's going to be possible. I don't know when. At this point it is an idea."

❧

On Saturday morning, at the family's weekend house in Panama, the mother of Onassis Reyes began screaming. Her husband, Gilberto, who'd been napping, came running, thinking someone had broken in. She frantically showed him a newspaper she'd been reading. A small headline read: "Sailing Vessel from U.S. Company Disappears in Hurricane Mitch." It named the *Fantome*.

"I think Onassis mentioned he was on the *Fantome*."

"Are you sure, the *Fantome*?"

"I think so. I think so."

Reyes called friends in the government, who, within an hour, found a Windjammer hotline number in Miami. Rhonda Epperson, who took the call, said Windjammer had been trying to reach him.

"That's a lie," he barked. "Was Onassis on board?"

"Yes."

"There are no words," Reyes said later. "That's how the company managed this tragedy."

Most of the *Fantome* families knew of the ship's disappearance by the weekend, directly from Windjammer or by word of mouth, and had called the company for updates. Athelene Brusch, mother of Vernon, said Windjammer called her at home in Guyana on Saturday and told her the ship had disappeared. "They kept calling and giving me news. They kept telling me they saw no trace." They gave her a calling card number to call Miami without cost.

Jerry King's mother, cutting logs in a remote area of Guyana, was stricken with a cramp on Sunday. When she lay down, Jerry appeared to her "almost in a daydream." "What are you doing? Go home," he said. When she went to town, she found a message that had been left with the police department on Friday. "I knew it was him who talked to me. We were very close."

In Grenada on Sunday, a crewmember of the *Yankee Clipper* who knew Francis Morain called his wife, Elizabeth, and informed her that the *Fantome* had been missing since Tuesday. No one had called her from the company. When she telephoned the Windjammer offices, someone told her they had lost her number. "Don't be alarmed. Everything will be OK." Her questions flooded out. "Why not drop the crew, too? There are other people's lives at stake, too," she said. At home with her six children, Elizabeth Morain began to imagine a life without Francis and his income. "He could do cabinetry. He was good with his hands." Close friends gathered around her. She waited by the phone for some good news. "Every time the phone would ring, the children ran, waiting for their daddy."

❧

The first reports of bodies reached Windjammer on Saturday when Jerry Hynds, the mayor of Coxen Hole, Roatán, called. A Belizean Web site also carried a report of two bodies found north of Ambergris Caye, and the correspondent reported speculation that the bodies were from the *Fantome*. The news plunged Windjammer headquarters into despair. Rhonda Epperson, the outgoing human resources director for the fleet, said she volunteered for the gruesome job of flying to Roatán to determine the identities of the bodies there. But Michael D. Burke dispatched two other employees. The company issued its first formal press release, describing the ship's last known location and its efforts to search the coast with private aircraft. It made no mention of bodies.

The Coast Guard flew two C-130 sorties on Saturday afternoon. The weather had improved to showers and thunderstorms, southeast winds of 20 knots, and confused seas of 4 to 8 feet. One plane flew the Honduran coastline, buzzing the water at 1,000 feet and reef areas at 500 feet. It found 55-gallon drums and a large white picnic cooler north of Roatán. A second plane flew the entire Yucatán and Belizean coastlines. The floating locator radiobeacon dropped on Thursday by an earlier Coast Guard flight had drifted north around Roatán, indicating a current setting 360 degrees at 1.42 knots that might have carried the ship's debris in that direction.

On the Web, news stories about the *Fantome* were gathered by Dean Dey, a university computer systems operator who had built a small, private Web site devoted to the joys of vacations on Windjammer ships. "No New News," he reported late Saturday. Scores of Windjammer fans posted prayers, poems, and photos of the *Fantome* and its crew. Their chat rooms exchanged memories, condolences, half-informed views of "standard Navy procedures," and newfound knowledge about EPIRBs. Saturday evening, Windjammer reopened its official bulletin board. Dean Dey typed a note that over one hundred Jammers had e-mailed him for information. "The concern of my fellow shipmates has been touching. I know of few other events that have evoked a response like this . . . it is a family response. A member of our family may be in trouble, and we care."

The British helicopter that suddenly appeared over Guanaja Sunday morning seemed like an angel to islanders in their sixth day of stunned isolation. The chopper had launched from the HMS *Sheffield*, a British warship assigned to the international drug interdiction effort in the Caribbean. Anchored off Bonacca harbor, the *Sheffield* was sending teams ashore with medicine, food, and water.

"When we landed it was bizarre," said Dr. Sue Davies, the ship's medical officer. "Not a single bush had any leaves on it. Not a single green thing. In Mangrove Bight, a cemetery had been built next to the sea. It eroded away and the graveyard was no longer. What would have been graves were open. The wood planks destroyed. I remember the smell —the total destruction of absolutely everything."

Davies treated seventy people for injuries, mostly "trivial" cuts and infections. She evacuated three people: one crushed by a refrigerator, a diabetic without insulin, and an elderly man with gangrenous feet. Davies reminded people to boil water—they seemed childlike in their shock—and left behind chlorinating tablets.

On the other side of the island, *Sheffield* crew repaired the Bonacca water line, restored power to the hospital, began controlling air traffic to the airport, and allowed people to make calls from the ship's phones. Mary Solomon paddled a kayak to the ship and called her children. David Greatorex, who had kept his British upper lip stiff and his staff calm through the storm, fell apart when a crewman from the *Sheffield* greeted him with, "How you doing, mate?"

"Then I cried," Greatorex said later. "Six people and we all survived. The rest is immaterial."

As the *Sheffield* crew dispensed aid, many in the outside world frantically sought news of loved ones. By Sunday, the Caribbean Hurricane Page, www.gobeach.com, had swollen with missing persons reports:

"We are desperately trying to find out anything about our father JC Morgan who was in (Guanaja). He had a small house there but we feel sure it is washed away probably along with his boat. PLEASE . . . He was well acquainted with 'Arlo.' I think he knew Jim Miler. His neighbors are Gilbert and Petey (sorry these are the only names I know) . . ."

"I am looking for information on Jack Meyers, an evangelist from Oklahoma, who is down there on a mission trip. Our church is in prayer for him . . ."

"Everyone in my family is going completely insane. I am trying to locate my aunt, Esley Chavez. She has not been seen or heard from since Friday night and her house is almost 6 feet under water."

Or this one, described as if searching a morgue: "Caroline has a dark complexion with scar on her forehead and throat from a tracheotomy. Terry has scarring on face from dog attack when he was small."

Each posting was a drop in a tidal wave of grief, and many readers responded. Loretta Miles, whose husband survived on Roatán, set up a bank account to help people in Punta Gorda. The Florida headquarters of the Bayman Bay Club organized Guanaja Relief. Jean Greatorex, wife of David, alerted people to relief planes and ships leaving the Caymans for Guanaja. Churches, unions, shipping companies, and Continental Airlines gathered food, medical supplies, tarps, tents, generators, and plywood to send in aid.

On Guanaja, the *Sheffield* and its helicopter, aware of the search for the *Fantome*, began taking a closer look at the reefs and shorelines.

On the Honduran mainland, so many bridges had collapsed "that watching them has become a macabre spectator sport," the *Miami Herald* reported. "When the rain slacks off for an hour or two, [residents] forage for food through streets swamped in backed-up sewage and garbage that rain swept in from the local dump." When asked by a reporter what a shelter needed, Desi Elvira shouted: "Milk! Milk! Milk! Milk for the babies. And diapers. Look around you. There are 10 babies in the room and every one of them is wet."

"Poor Tegucigalpa," someone reported on Honduras.com. "All seven bridges down, houses from entire neighborhoods buried with people inside. Radio reports over 1,000 dead. Mitch apparently saved the worst for mainland Honduras."

The view from El Progreso was "just one big ocean that covers miles and miles," reported Ernesto and Sherree Banegas, pastors of the Lord's Gathering Church, on the Caribbean Hurricane Page. "When the river broke it came with such force, hundreds drowned. We took babies and children out of trees. It is so desperate that one cannot even imagine. The mosquitoes and the flies have begun to multiply and as soon as the water goes down there are hundreds of bodies and thousands of dead animals that will contaminate. There is no major city that escaped this disaster. The whole city of La Lima is under water. Whole developments were covered with water in seconds and so many had no chance to escape. Ninety percent of Hondurans do not know how to swim. In Comayagua two avalanches destroyed over 100 houses. Two days ago the men rescuing people found over 45 families on their rooftops, but their rescue craft were full. . . . Then men went back yesterday as soon as light came and the water went over their roofs and the rapid water took over 400 people. I can't go on because there is no end to the suffering and agony."

While surveying his city Sunday, the popular mayor of Tegucigalpa, César Castellanos, was killed in a helicopter crash.

Mitch, now a tropical depression, left Honduras and petered out in the Guatemalan mountains on Sunday, November 1, its winds dropping, its pressure rising. By Sunday morning the National Hurricane Center centered it 75 miles west-northwest of Guatemala City and said it was moving west at 6 knots. The pressure was up to 1005 millibars. Circulation was "poorly defined," and at 4 P.M., Richard Pasch declared Mitch dead.

"The system has been over land for about three days. Although there is still a general turning of the cloud pattern around an apparent center near the border of Guatemala and Mexico, surface data show little evidence of circulation. Mitch is dissipating and the remnant low and area of disturbed weather will be monitored for signs of redevelopment in either the Gulf of Mexico or the eastern Pacific. This is the last advisory unless regeneration occurs."

The *Miami Herald's* Sunday edition reported that the fate of the thirty-one *Fantome* crewmembers remained a mystery. "So far we have not found squat of this vessel," said Scott Carr of the U.S. Coast Guard. "We haven't found debris. We haven't found life rafts. We haven't found bodies. Now that is a good thing."

A hot tip Sunday that the *Fantome* was in Puerto Cortés pulled a Coast Guard C-130 off its search pattern to circle around the port. The ship was not there. The plane then flew from Puerto Cortés to Belize, essentially retracing the *Fantome's* route the week before, with negative results. Conditions for searching had improved. One plane spotted the slick from a dead whale at a distance of 5 miles, which "reinforced the notion that debris should have been sighted from a sunken/capsized vessel," according to a trip report.

Sometime on Sunday, the HMS *Sheffield* learned of the stair banister and the stenciled life jackets at Posada del Sol. Windjammer was informed, along with the U.S. Coast Guard, but the company did not want the information released, according to Jeff Murphy, a public information officer with the Coast Guard in Miami. "The company was rather touchy." Windjammer denied the first suggestions from reporters that the debris was from the ship. The company did not believe that the life jackets, probably knocked from deck cabinets, constituted significant proof of a disaster, and their Sunday press release made no mention of it.

Although a London newspaper quoted Paul March as being "very worried" about his brother, Windjammer wouldn't confirm that Guyan March was captain or give out the names of any crew, a silence the company would maintain for three weeks. The company said later it was trying to protect the privacy of the crew's families.

Late Sunday, Dean Dey's *Fantome* Web site crashed from so many hits. When he got it running again, he forwarded a message from Windjammer that a private ship from Holland had joined the search. "As the weather improves, so do the chances of finding *Fantome*," said the company's message. "Six U.S. Coast Guard planes and two chartered airplanes we have hired are all busy looking. Hope springs eternal so let's pray for some good news."

Waiting in Miami, Laura-Jo Bleasdale, the evacuated activities mate of the *Fantome*, pulled from her luggage the wad of notes hastily scrawled by crewmen and handed to her in Belize. In a haze of uncertainty—half despair, half hope—she tried to fulfill their wishes. A year later, she went through the notes again and described her desultory efforts:

"Colin August: He asked me to call his wife and have her change her flight. I believe, but am not 100 percent sure, that she was due to come sailing with us. . . . I did not make the call to her. He also asked me to send money to her via Western Union. Of course, this was carried out.

"Brasso: I remember him giving me a long list. I told him I would see what I could do. Send money via Western Union. Done. Price up some mobile phones and international service lines. If I could find a good one that was a good price, would I be so kind as to buy it and he would pay me back. I never bought a phone.

"Onassis: He always managed to make me laugh. He wanted me to call his girlfriend, to tell her that he loved and missed her terribly. I remember sitting in the hotel room trying for a long time, but I never managed to get through. I regret not keeping my finger longer on the redial button. 'Ona' also wanted me to buy him a nail clipper as a present from Miami. Strange but true! I bought one and it sits on my dresser at home.

"Brusch (Vernon): He wanted me to price up some electrical parts for a Sharp product.

"Kevin Logie: For Kevin I was to send money via Western Union and also make contact with his brother. Both done. Something about Kevin, I remember as if it was yesterday, there was myself, Cathie, and I think Laurie in the office, Kevin had his video camera out and we were messing around with it taking funny footage of ourselves. This was about the time passengers would be watching the stars go by or eating at second seating for dinner. I remember Pope [Layne] popping up from the engine room to collect some notes he had made earlier. The reason I remember this so well is because we were laughing so hard our cheeks hurt. It's a moment that I will never forget. I just wish I had the tape.

"Eon Maxwell: Eon asked me to send some money via Western Union.

"Pope: I was to give some money over for him. If I needed anything at all, [I was] to call a couple of friends of his who I also knew. I was to tell his daughter how much he loved her and that he missed her. He also wanted a linen shirt, a white one. I remember spending one of those long days, waiting to hear something, in a mall with Cathie and Laurie. I looked in every shop for a white linen shirt and couldn't find one. I was so distraught. I think I thought it was a sign that he wasn't to return.

"That is the end of the list. It's strange to think of all the little things I have kept hold of over the years and the most important document, like the one you are meant to have forever, I throw away, but these little pieces of paper that are almost illegible I have kept hold of and will never throw away. The world is a strange place full of strange people, myself included."

BAY ISLANDS, GUYANA, GULF OF MEXICO, AND MIAMI
November 2–5, 1998

❧

S IX DAYS AFTER the *Fantome* disappeared, Guanaja revealed in its wreckage the first significant clue to the ship's fate. At 7:48 A.M. on Monday, Windjammer called the Coast Guard in Miami to pass along a new report of "debris" on the southeast shore, and shortly after, the helicopter "Monty" lifted off the HMS *Sheffield* and flew to Black Rock Point on the island's easternmost extremity. There, beneath ochre cliffs on a rocky, open, wind-blown indentation, the crew found a large life raft. It was "severely damaged and appeared to have been thrashed against the reefs," the Coast Guard reported. Sixty-two minutes later, at 9:57 A.M., Windjammer confirmed the serial number as one belonging to the *Fantome*. No bodies were found, but the news ripped through the company like a fish knife.

This point of Guanaja is dangerous and bleak, rarely approached by local boaters because of a close-by reef and almost constant swell from the trade winds. It is a lee shore virtually all the time, this day being no different, with 20-knot winds, 4- to 8-foot seas, and showery weather. Mitch had bashed this coast unmercifully, snapping a tubular steel navigation light atop the cliffs as if it were a toothpick.

The crew of the Monty began a low, slow survey of the shore in both directions, north past East Cliff, North East Bight, and Mangrove Bight, and south along the archipelago of cays and the island's shoreline to Savannah Bight and Posada del Sol. At the same time, in their single largest effort to locate the *Fantome*, four Coast Guard C-130s from the United States flew a huge search pattern from Belize to Nicaragua. At 1:45 P.M., one of the Coast Guard planes spotted a debris field with timber and "blue material," probably tarp, 30 miles north of Roatán. It could have been the tarp from over the *Fantome*'s party-deck bar. Ten minutes later, near Posada del Sol, the Monty crew found a second life raft, eight stenciled orange life vests, and the wooden staircase spotted a day earlier by Hector Castro. By 6 o'clock the HMS *Sheffield* had recovered the second raft. It was "severely mangled," perhaps vandalized by islanders for its emergency rations and tools. It belonged to the *Fantome*.

Colin Hamp, the captain of the HMS *Sheffield*, concluded that the *Fantome* was gone, and after two days as Guanaja's angel of mercy, the *Sheffield* prepared to depart the island Monday night. Hamp felt their presence had helped, but as a warship he didn't have the crew or supplies for long-term recovery. The British ambassador to Honduras came aboard and asked him to stay overnight, "so the islanders can see you go," and Hamp agreed to delay their departure fourteen hours. The ship's aircrew began to dismantle the helicopter for maintenance.

In Miami, Michael D. Burke acknowledged that one piece of wood recovered by the Monty's crew appeared to be from the quarterdeck bar and that the bannister appeared to have come from one of the ornate, original staircases rising from the "lobby" to the quarterdeck. These were indications of substantial but not fatal topside damage. None of the life jackets belonged to crewmembers, whose jackets were stenciled with their cabin numbers. But by now the Coast Guard had searched over 120,000 square miles—an area the size of Colorado—and Windjammer's dreams of finding an intact ship were severely deflated. Burke scheduled a news conference for Tuesday to discuss the ship's tactics in detail, and he and his staff set about re-creating a narrative of the *Fantome's* last known hours.

🦜

The news of the life raft discovery reached Guyan March's family in Cornwall on Monday, the very day, as it happened, that they buried his grandfather. "This news, especially on a day like today, has shocked us all," Paul March told reporters. "We are in constant contact with the office in Miami. All the families have their fingers crossed. We are very concerned."

That evening, in the soft air of New Amsterdam, Guyana, the families of missing crewmen gathered at Town Hall for a vigil organized by several pastors and the mayor. Eight of the crew were from New

Amsterdam, and the three-hour gathering was billed as a "solidarity watch" to pray for the crew's safety and to comfort the families. Athelene Brusch arrived with a photo of her son, Vernon. Dawn King carried a picture of Jerry, her brother. Roselyn Austin attended to pray for her brother, Rhon. Colin August's wife, Marcel, came, as did Shelly James, the wife of Carl James. Lynette Ramsudh, Deonauth's wife, carried his photo and a candle to light. They set the photos of the men together on a table and, surrounded by relatives and members of their churches, prayed and sang with accustomed fervor. At times, their separate prayers merged in a crescendo of woe, asking God to deliver their missing men.

"I do not know what to say. I tried studying a map to see where they could be," Marcel August told Calvin Marshall, a pastor at a prominent church in town and a correspondent for the *Guyana Chronicle*. "I am just living in hope." Dawn King said she didn't take the news seriously at first, "thinking the vessel might have been blown off course." Athelene Brusch still believed "the ship drifted somewhere and Vernon is alive."

At the vigil, Stuart Larcombe, a former *Fantome* captain sent by Windjammer, showed the ship's last location on a chart. Rhonda Epperson read a poem, "A Letter from Heaven." Their appearance, offering hope and two months' crew wages to the families, countered the gloomy news from Guanaja. Even so, several women picked up on the contradiction between their supposed hope and "A Letter from Heaven," which read, in part: "Here I dwell with God above / Here, there's no more tears of sadness / Here is just eternal love."

"We were still holding on," Dawn King said later. "But people got suspicious when Rhonda read a poem and the words were like a good-bye."

On Tuesday, November 3, at 11:45 A.M. in Miami, Michael D. Burke, Stuart Larcombe, and other Windjammer representatives stood before a dozen reporters and seven television crews. Burke read a straightforward account of the *Fantome's* moves and Mitch's unusual path. When pressed, he conceded that he feared the ship had sunk. "We believe the vessel either drifted out of the area—or it went down," Burke said. "We're having a very hard time." Captain Larcombe added, "All the right moves were made. Unfortunately, every time we made the right move, the hurricane made a different move."

The headlines from the news conference reflected the gloom: "Hope Fades in the Search for Missing Schooner, Survivors," the *Miami Herald* concluded.

Ten minutes after the Miami news conference began, two more Coast Guard C-130s arrived in the Bay Islands to continue the air search. Conditions were good: clear skies, winds southeast at 25 knots, 10-mile visibility, and 8-foot seas with whitecaps and spindrift. The sea around Guanaja was full of debris, most likely from mainland Honduras: trees, parts of homes, dead farm animals. In the channel between Guanaja and Roatán, a crew reported "white and occasionally blue planks of various lengths/widths, mixed in with trees, bushes, and other nondescript man-made material. Crew also saw 2–4 dead cows that could not have been mistaken for bodies. No rescue equipment was sighted in the debris field."

At 2:19 P.M., a Coast Guard C-130 buzzed over a collection of wood in the water about 20 miles north of Guanaja and spotted what looked like a body on a piece of corrugated zinc roofing. The body moved. The crew circled, dropped a transmitting marker buoy, and called the HMS *Sheffield*, which was more than 70 miles away and steaming east.

"We turned the ship around," said Captain Hamp, who chastised himself for writing off the *Fantome* and her crew. His flight crew crash-assembled the chopper in forty minutes and the Monty lifted off and raced the remaining 30 miles to the marker buoy.

When the chopper arrived and hovered, blasting the survivor with prop wash and terrifying noise, the person stood up. With the zinc roofing submerged in the water, it looked as if the survivor were standing on the water. As the winch man descended, he realized it was a woman. She lunged for him. "That's the mental image I have, of her standing on top of the water, almost like Jesus walking on the water," said Zach Miller, a sergeant with the U.S. Marine Corps, who was aboard the HMS *Sheffield* acting as interpreter.

As the woman was hauled into the chopper, half-delirious, mumbling in Spanish, the crew chief asked Miller—back aboard ship—to help translate questions to her. They placed a crew headset on her head. Miller was to ask her the question, and the crew was to watch her response and relay it back. It was the worst possible scenario for a conversation. The woman was terrified and in shock. The earphones were filled with air traffic instructions, crew chatter, and the roar of the military helicopter. Miller, who had learned Spanish in the army, shouted:

"Estaba por *Fantome*?"

The woman nodded yes.

"Are there other survivors?" he shouted in Spanish.

She seemed to nod yes and indicate the number "two."

Traveling at the speed of light, the news, delivered at 3:54 P.M., burst like fireworks at Windjammer headquarters. People ran through halls and down stairways to Michael D. Burke's office, shouting, "They found someone! They found someone!" They grinned, hugged, and wept. "Our hearts were pounding," said Polly Burke.

There was just one problem. There supposedly was no woman aboard the *Fantome*.

Windjammer's euphoria lasted two hours—until the woman, carried unconscious into the *Sheffield's* sick bay and given an IV, was stabilized enough to talk face-to-face with Sergeant Miller, the only person aboard who spoke Spanish.

"I started asking her about the *Fantome*. She had a look of confusion. That's when we found out."

Isabella Arriola had been washed out to sea six days earlier from her inundated village of Santa Rosa de Aguán. Aboard the *Sheffield* she became a patron saint of a Honduras whose death toll from Mitch was climbing toward ten thousand. According to Captain Hamp, the entire ship was energized. "It became a search for something—if one person could survive what she survived, then there could be somebody else, not necessarily from the *Fantome*, but somebody." Using words like "guardian angel," the British career officer described with awe how "something" delayed the ship's departure by fourteen hours. "If we hadn't been delayed, we would not have got there. She would have died." As Arriola recovered in sick bay, two dozen men volunteered to keep watch around the clock for other survivors in the waters around Guanaja. "It's something I shall never forget," said Hamp. "She touched everybody, really. Her strength of character—resilience does not describe it."

Nor did the Spanish word for miracle—*milagro*—do justice to Isabella Arriola's story, pieced together over the two days of her recovery aboard ship. As she slipped between delirium, sleep, fits of crying, and prayer, she described to Sergeant Miller how the Río Aguán rose during the night of Wednesday, October 28, and engulfed her house sometime after midnight, how she grabbed her youngest child and followed her husband and two other children into the black night through the rushing water. They were all washed away.

Hurricane Mitch, at the time a Category 2 storm, was centered only 16 miles from Santa Rosa. Arriola and her family had to be in the eye wall of the hurricane, swept out to sea both by the mad, dark river and by 105- to 110-knot winds that were pushing the water to the north. Where the river met the ocean, 100 yards from their house, huge standing waves chewed up all that came through them. With six-year-old Anderson in her arms, Arriola was washed through the maelstrom. "It tore him out of my arms," she later told Agence France Press. "I saw a wave swallow him and afterward I never saw him again. I wrestled around in the water and afterward stuck my head out to breathe. Later I was floating and I swam and I swam and I swam until I found three sticks. Later, I came upon a *balsa* [raft of debris] and I was vomiting all the water that I swallowed." By dawn on Thursday, October 29, Arriola had been swept out of sight of land.

The doctor aboard the HMS *Sheffield*, Sue Davies, said Arriola was dressed in black denim shorts, a bra, and a red T-shirt and was "remarkably unscathed. She must have had five cuts, on her shins and between her toes." Her blood pressure was low and she was hypothermic. Her lips were badly chapped, her skin encrusted by salt, and her hair tangled. "We cut her clothes off, put her in a warming envelope, gave her antibiotics and fluid."

Zach Miller sat and talked with Arriola, comforting her when she would pause in her story and sob quietly. At some point she asked for a Bible, and the ship produced a New International edition in English. With Miller translating and Arriola following the words with a finger, they recited a favorite psalm, "which is kinda difficult to do," Miller said later. Periodically the schoolteacher would scold Miller for his Spanish.

Arriola described how, from her perch on the roof raft, she grabbed floating coconuts and chewed the husks off with her teeth to eat the meat and drink the milk. She sang to seabirds, and she described watching Coast Guard planes go overhead five or six times. "The first few times I waved and they flew away."

Dr. Davies issued Arriola a set of emergency clothing: dungaree pants, shirt, and black knit watch cap. Then Davies remembered the woman's own clothes, which had been patched and cleaned in the laundry. When she handed them to her, Arriola began fumbling in a pocket of the shorts. During their evacuation, Arriola's eight-year-old daughter, Elizabeth, had handed her an earring for safe-keeping. The ship's Chinese laundryman had found it—a tiny, gold, dolphin-shaped loop. Davies retrieved it and handed it to Arriola. "That set off an absolutely hysterical crying. It was horrible to witness," the doctor said.

By Tuesday, November 3, Arriola and her *balsa* had drifted 60 miles from her village, up and around the east side of Guanaja, past the beach where debris from the *Fantome* had been tossed. Left undiscovered, she might have journeyed to Belize or been caught in the North Equatorial Current. After Isabella Arriola was flown to Trujillo's hospital, Honduran officials reported that 4,615 people were isolated in the coastal zone where she had been pushed into the sea. Many had not eaten since October 28, when she and the other inhabitants of twenty-five coastal communities were given up as "disappeared."

"I just wanted to have wings to fly," Arriola later told Agence France Press. "Only God saved me."

❧

As Isabella Arriola's story played out, a resurrection of another sort was on the mind of forecaster Richard Pasch at the National Hurricane Center. Mitch, which he had written off as a "low" on Sunday, November 1, "regenerated" as a tropical storm on Tuesday in Mexico's Bay of Campeche, west of the Yucatán Peninsula. "Mitch in no way resembles the intense hurricane that it was," he wrote in a Tuesday afternoon advisory. The system was traveling east-northeast at 5 knots, and Pasch expected it to weaken back to a tropical depression when it moved over the Yucatán. He called the convection "unimpressive" but said Hurricane Hunters had found a 997-millibar central pressure and winds of 50 knots at 1,500 feet.

By Tuesday night, Mitch was crossing the Yucatán Peninsula at 7 knots and the center's computer models were again in a catfight over its future. "The dynamical track guidance takes Mitch towards the northeast either across the Florida peninsula or the Florida Straits, except the GFDL which dissipates the system. There is a wide range of speeds forecast, with 72-hour points stretching from the northwest Bahamas to the Azores." There was now a 24 percent chance that Mitch would strike Key West, Florida, by Friday. By dawn on Wednesday, November 4, the storm had cleared the Yucatán and warnings were flashed to the Florida Keys. The storm was moving northeast at 12 knots.

Mitch was a warped-looking storm at this point, its area of thunderstorms and gale winds stretching from northeast to southwest ahead of the low-pressure center. The computer models predicted that once across Florida, Mitch would fuse with a cold front and become "extratropical"—a nicety lost on the public. Once "extratropical," Mitch would be out of the hair of the "tropical" prediction center and its sobered hurricane specialists in Miami.

On Wednesday, November 4, the day after the HMS *Sheffield* left Guanaja, Louise Reece and Dave Penny of Windjammer flew to the Cayman Islands and chartered a flight to the Bay Islands. Reece, who was British and the company's shore excursions manager, and Penny, the engineering chief, had the unenviable task of confirming the ship's demise. Reece knew the crew and the Bay Islands, having set up agents and excursions there. Penny knew the ship inside and out. Their most gruesome task was to track down reports of "hundreds" of bodies washed up on Roatán. They carried with them photos of the crew.

One rumor of thirty bodies proved to be thirty cow carcasses, but Penny and Reece spoke to police and a local judge who had looked at six male bodies in the harbor of Oak Ridge. Islanders had buried the bodies immediately, treating them like lepers, really, in one case throwing a rope around a foot and dragging it to shore. "Their feeling was the bodies had come across from the mainland, where the river swept out the villages. One had a Seaman's Book [a log of hours at sea] identifying him as being from one of those villages. Port Royal had found two bodies, a man and woman, but the man didn't fit the description. He was enormously obese," unlike any of the crew. "We showed the pictures of our men to the judge. We looked at a video of the bodies they had taken." Five other bodies had been found at Jones Hole near Leo

Woods' house. One caught on videotape looked bleached, except for the black skin down the backbone. He was floating facedown near shore, his arms overhead as if in surrender. Curious children looked on from shore.

"You wanted things to match, but every time it was wrong. There were only a couple of very tall guys, but neither was black. They were Indian—light skinned. Every time you initially heard a description, something didn't match. The judge was determined that we were barking up the wrong tree. It's harrowing. Everybody tells you this stuff. Then it turns out not to be true," said Reece. At the Roatán airport, for example, the British ambassador told them that the HMS *Sheffield* had found twelve empty life rafts and that he was very sorry. "I lost it," said Reece. "Then, it turns out, it was completely untrue. Twelve life vests— that's where it came from. It was very irresponsible."

Reece and Penny flew to Guanaja, where three more bodies had been found. "You couldn't tell. One had limbs missing, the other was so overly bloated—it was Latino—so disfigured you couldn't tell who they were." One fell apart when its arm was lifted and was burned where it lay. "They looked . . . Aguán—dark brown, Indian types," the mayor said.

By this time, a week after the storm, scavenging was under way, and Reece and Penny followed a report of a wheelbarrow full of life preservers to a spot near the airport. "The jackets belonged to a previous wreck or someone else's misfortune," said Reece. Reece and Penny boated to Posada del Sol to view the life jackets, stairwell, and other debris found there. Among the dozen orange jackets from the *Fantome* was one numbered 31—the life jacket assigned to Chrispin Saunders.

"It was quite an emotional moment," said Reece. "We were at Posada, a beautiful hacienda with wonderful Spanish tile. The concrete was destroyed, the roof half gone. It was battered. You would assume that the crew would have their own jackets on. It's important to wear your own crew number. It is part of our training. But they might have opened a passenger door and grabbed one. Chrispin—he probably picked up a passenger jacket. I know him. It wouldn't occur to him to get his own jacket because he's a steward."

At Posada they also viewed a large, 6- to 8-foot section of caprail, the heavy, wooden finishing strip atop the steel bulwarks that had been leaned on by countless passengers. "We found other wood from the ship—benches from all over the top deck, most of it in bits on the beaches. They were varnished splinters. You could see where they were from—I used to store snorkel gear in them." Though indicative of a badly smashed ship, the debris left Reece, Penny, and the Windjammer family without the closure they'd hoped for. There still was no clear picture of what had happened to the steel ship and its men.

※

Tropical Storm Mitch was more than halfway across the Gulf of Mexico, barreling toward Florida at 20 knots, when it caught the *Victoria*, a 58-foot coastal freighter, 300 miles southwest of Clearwater Wednesday afternoon. In 6- to 8-foot seas and 37-knot winds, the ship lost its steering and two of the six crewmen became incapacitated. They abandoned the drifting ship and were picked up by the 500-foot bulk carrier *Starman*. Just then, the Coast Guard received another Mayday from a 46-foot sloop, *Seeker*, 30 miles to the west. *Seeker* had blown out its mainsail and was taking on water, its power and bilge pumps out. Responding to the Coast Guard's call, the *Starman* found the sailboat, put it in the ship's lee, and tried to get the four crewmen aboard. One succeeded, but in the tumult, the sailboat's mast broke off. After several failed attempts, the remaining three sailors abandoned ship in life rings that were tethered to the *Starman*. Finally they were hauled aboard in good shape.

With the look and fury of a squall line, Mitch slammed into the Florida Keys Wednesday afternoon with heavy rain, lightning, and wind gusts of 60 knots. Shaped like a badly wrapped cigar, the storm stretched over a 300-mile slash of the Gulf of Mexico and blasted the islands through the night with tornadoes and rain bands. Dozens of structures damaged by Hurricane Georges thirty days before collapsed in the second pounding. Boats overturned and blew ashore. As dark enveloped the Dry Tortugas, the fishing boat *Miss Donna* began to founder and called for help. The *Karefree*, a fishing vessel manned by Don Atkins and Paul Knight, radioed that they were coming to help but could not get through a pass because of rough seas. The *Karefree* radioed that it would turn back and find another route. At 2:36 A.M. on Thursday, the Coast Guard received a transmission from a 406 EPIRB registered to the *Karefree*.

At first light a Coast Guard plane spotted the overturned hull of a

40-foot blue-and-white fishing boat and a nearby life raft. It searched the water and found a body facedown with no life preserver. Army divers checked inside the hull and identified it as the *Karefree*, but they did not find the other man. The boat's propeller was fouled with rope.

The storm that blew across Florida Thursday morning was not really a tropical storm, but the National Hurricane Center maintained the name Mitch to keep the public's attention. Hurricane Hunter planes had to search for a low-pressure center—they found 993 millibars—but as Max Mayfield, the center's deputy director, wrote: "The center is not the most important feature but rather the severe weather threat." Gusts of 63 knots, tornadoes, and nasty weather blew ashore at Fort Myers and rolled across central Florida. The system spawned five tornadoes across the Florida peninsula. It sank several more boats in the Keys, injured sixty-five people, and destroyed 645 homes. By 10 A.M. it was exiting Florida on the east side, smacking the Bahamas and bearing down on Bermuda.

At the Coast Guard station in Miami, the phone rang nonstop with vessel emergencies in Florida and the Bahamas. Two American boaters were rescued by helicopter after they abandoned their sinking 60-foot motorboat, *Endless Summer*, 12 miles northeast of West End in the Bahamas and jumped into a life raft. When a coastal freighter from Belize ran aground off Bimini in a 40-knot gale, the Coast Guard hoisted two Haitian crewmen to safety. Another helicopter found two persons clinging to the capsized hull of an 18-foot lobsterboat near Memory Rock in the Bahamas. And a Coast Guard boat rescued the crew of the 37-foot sailboat *Domas*.

At 4 P.M. on Thursday, November 5, after fifty-four advisories and a "named" life of fourteen days, Mitch was abandoned by the National Hurricane Center. It had lost its circulation and become "extratropical." The center issued its last advisory and handed the storm to another office of the weather service.

But with winds of 50 knots and a freight-train motion of 28 knots on a track of 70 degrees, Mitch still had punch. Gale-force winds spread over 230 miles of ocean. Several hundred miles off the Florida coast, the storm bellowed through a rally of sailboats headed to the Caribbean for winter cruising. It knocked boats over, broke masts, convinced two crews to abandon their boats, and scared the living daylights out of yachters who had been told on Sunday that Mitch was dead and the weather looked idyllic for the crossing.

"It seemed impossible that it could reach us," said Steve Black, a Rhode Island yachter who organized the Caribbean 1500 rally, a group crossing of a hundred yachts—half from Newport, Rhode Island, half from Hampton, Virginia—to Virgin Gorda in the Virgin Islands. Sponsored by West Marine, a marine retailer that supervised safety equipment and training before the start, the rally included amateur but experienced coastal cruisers in boats ranging from 28 to 65 feet. Because the rally required a single sideband radio on board, the fleet was aware of Mitch's havoc as it plowed into them Thursday and Friday.

"We were in winds of 40 miles an hour for twelve hours or more, periodically higher," said Black. With seventy-two hours of warning, the boats scattered, some turning back, others trying to beat the storm to the south. The Newport fleet took refuge in Bermuda, where several boats were beat up at anchor. Among the Hampton fleet, the seasick crew of the *Circa* abandoned ship and were rescued by a freighter. The 35-foot *Chalets* lost its anemometer after a gust of 68 knots. When another sailboat was knocked down, a crewman broke a vertebra. A commercial ship and a Coast Guard helicopter rescued them.

"When you listened to reports afterwards, it was surprising, you could see the area of 40- to 60-mile-an-hour winds included nearly the whole fleet," said Black. "The blessing in all this was the fact that it was moving as fast it was. It was covering 1,000 miles a day. It crossed the Atlantic in three days."

The U.S. Coast Guard stopped looking for the *Fantome* on Wednesday afternoon, November 4. By that time its planes had searched for seven days over 145,000 square miles, an area the size of Montana. As the last two C-130s flew home to Florida, the northwestern Caribbean was calm. The weeklong search had cost the Coast Guard $650,000 just for airplane time. Not once did the Coast Guard raise the issue that it had been looking for a ship registered in a foreign country. "We do the same thing for cocaine smugglers," said Lieutenant Commander Paul Steward, a search-and-rescue coordinator. "But then we arrest them."

If the men had been in rafts, decorated with the orange and silver colors of distress, they likely would have been seen. If they were in the water, they were likely dead of exposure. The Coast Guard's final situation report said, "Personnel from *Fantome*'s parent company stated they will conduct the necessary next of kin notification."

Michael D. Burke extended his "deepest gratitude" to the U.S. Coast Guard. "Being a close knit, family organization, we are devastated by this nightmarish event," he wrote to Rear Admiral Norman Saunders in Miami. "However, in saying this, we can feel some consolation in the fact that every effort has been made to locate these men who courageously fought for their lives. We thank the men and women of the Coast Guard and wish them fair seas."

And still the families of New Amsterdam prayed. At the evening vigils, "we had the whole town with us," said Norma Jean, mother of Jerry King. "They never told us that they had found stuff." The termination of the search was on the news, however.

"It was very emotional. We cried and cried," said Suzette August, sister of Colin. "Sometimes you go there, the hymns, the . . . we were so sad. We just cried and cried and cried. A relative said to me, 'You haven't slept, have you?' My eyes had shadows."

Several families remained in almost daily touch with Windjammer personnel in Miami. Alisa Maxwell, wife of chef Eon Maxwell, said the company was "really good" about keeping her informed. But as word of debris came through, hope was replaced with anger. "I don't think you are telling us the truth," Suzette August exploded on the phone. Remembering the conversation later, she was still troubled. "They kept saying, 'We don't know.' I think they knew all along."

In Omoa, Honduras, the girlfriend of Jesús Hernández made up a "wanted" poster with his photo and took it to the Bay Islands in hopes of finding him. In Belize, Faith Herrera miscarried Chrispin's baby. "I couldn't cope with it," she said. "I freaked out."

In Cornwall, England, Jenny March, the captain's mother and commandant of the club where he learned to sail, said she gave up hope when the Coast Guard called off its search. But at her parents' home in Wales, Annie Bleasdale sat down and added more lines to a letter to Guyan March. "I couldn't finish it until I knew he was safe. It went on and on. I was in total denial. I refused to give up hope. I cried. I begged. I prayed. I would have given up my own life just to see him again. I couldn't understand why, why!? He was such a magic person, such a pure human being, how could this be happening to him? I always thought that I was magic. Like I could wish or ask for something and it would happen. Now it was like I had run out of magic spells. It was like I couldn't step outside myself and watch me being upset. . . . It was me hurting, it was real, and no matter what I did, I knew I couldn't make it go away.

"Later, I found out that people had called our home with gossip that the *Fantome* had been found, beached, etc. . . . Dad didn't pass this on to me until much later, when he found out that it was just gossip. Two nights later, I was in bed, I couldn't sleep, so I got my letter out. I cried uncontrollably while writing to him. Just then, my bedside light started flickering. I stared at it, I stopped crying, I stopped writing, the light stopped flickering. I turned back and started writing and sobbing again, the flickering started once more. I stopped, it stopped . . . this went on and on four or five times, until I spoke out loud to Guyan telling him how much I missed him and loved him. After that I sensed him near me many times. I sensed him in the wind in the trees, the birds in the sky, the smell of cut grass, everything beautiful. I just couldn't believe that I hurt so much and that I was still living. I couldn't believe that I had been left here without him. Why wasn't I on that ship with him? I imagined the whole crew drifting in life rafts, they would be found soon. I imagined the ship beached somewhere and the crew on land trying to find help. I imagined the ship, with no communications, limping its way towards Trinidad. I couldn't give up hope. I couldn't let go. After just one week of not hearing anything, my friends started preparing me to think the worst. . . . I couldn't believe that they were giving up hope. All I could think of was flying to Miami to be there when they were found and brought home."

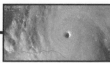

BAY ISLANDS, MAINLAND HONDURAS, EASTERN CARIBBEAN, MIAMI, BRITISH ISLES

November 6, 1998–Year's End

🐚

O NE WEEK AFTER the search ended, the *Fantome*—its photo, its sailing schedule, its myth-laden history—was erased from the Web site of Windjammer Barefoot Cruises, and marketing clerks rescheduled a year and a half of *Fantome* reservations onto Windjammer's five other ships. A telephone call to the company was still answered by a bright jingle of Caribbean music, but inside the headquarters building, the shell-shocked staff retreated from a barrage of questions, criticism, and second-guessing. "I feel like I lost a child," Michael D. Burke told sister Susan. After fifty years of mostly positive press, the hard-line inquiries of major newspapers and networks startled the Burkes, who found themselves on the receiving end of widespread public scrutiny. They hired a public relations firm and announced the establishment of a trust fund for the lost sailors' families. Passengers were encouraged to donate, and Windjammer contributed proceeds from sales of memorabilia.

Images of the *Fantome* from its earliest days to its most recent trip, with snapshots of the crew, sprang to life on a dozen private Web sites created by Jammers. Bill Graf's Fortogden.com displayed a virtual scrapbook of the *Fantome*'s entire history, from donated snapshots. Dean Traiger created a bulletin board that collected hundreds of love letters. Bill and Trudy Willison's site featured the *Fantome* floating on the illusion of rippling water. Several sites attached audio files of "Amazing Grace" to play as one viewed the photos.

"I am heartbroken," wrote one passenger. "Nevertheless, my husband and I have no intention of ending our love affair with Windjammer cruises. Hurricane Mitch was something no one could have foreseen or fought, under the circumstances."

Laura Marshall, still holding her boarding card for cabin number 37, remembered her first sight of the *Fantome*: "She moved slowly up to the concrete pier, all 300 feet of her—slowly, majestically, even theatrically. Her bowsprit was the upturned nose of a duchess; her transom an immobile bustle. She turned, once, as if to show off her dress, then came in to the dock all grace and style. We have pictures of that moment—me in shorts and hat, watching her dock, turning to the camera smiling— but they still don't capture the excitement, the heart-lifting anticipation—we're going to stay on board a ship like that—all the little-kid dreams of being a pirate spring to the surface; you can feel yourself sprouting an eye patch, feel one leg turn into wood."

Kathy Ptasnik, another Jammer, described how she haunted the Internet after the disappearance, first trying to find the ship, then looking for comfort from fellow passengers. "It would have been much harder to deal with if not for our support of each other who have one thing in common, the love of the *Fantome*, Guyan, and the crew. Us WJ lovers have prayed our hearts out and mourned so much for our loss and the families and loved ones they left behind. . . . please understand the feelings that we have. . . . For every person that questions his decision there are a hundred standing behind him. How absurd that anyone could question the loss of a ship in a class 5 hurricane."

David Horne, the California veterinarian who had spent one week on the ship as Mitch developed, said he went into clinical mourning— depression, anxiety, talking incessantly about the crew—as if he had known them all his life. "When you're on a boat, it's like this little community gets created," he said later. "People start relating as if it were a small town. It was this tropical paradise. The crew knew how to create something that was magical. And then to have the ocean swallow it up, like it didn't happen, was a surreal experience. She *is* a phantom."

❧

On Monday, November 9, one month to the day after Tropical Wave 46 left the African coast, a gale once known as Mitch struck the British Isles. Gusts of 93 miles an hour overturned cars, disabled fishing boats, blew down trees, and damaged electric utility grids, blacking out thirty thousand homes in the western and northern counties of Ireland. For more than ten hours, prolonged winds of 40 to 50 miles an hour whistled in the west of Ireland, creating waves of 20 to 30 feet. On the Irish

Sea, ferries stopped running to England, and scores of endangered seal pups were washed away from their mothers and stranded on coastlines. On the western coast of Scotland, a trawler with a crew of five lost its propeller and drifted in large seas until the coast guard, working twelve hours to rig a tow, rescued them. On the east coast, south of Aberdeen, a couple out for a Sunday walk suffered hypothermia when caught in the storm in a remote glen. "The mist came down all of a sudden and we got completely disorientated," the man told the *Scotsman*.

Weather officials tried to explain that the storm was not Mitch but tropical remains trapped in a temperate-zone depression. Still, in the press and the public's minds—and in the hearts of the Bleasdale sisters, Annie and Laura-Jo, both now at home in Wales—Mitch had "blown itself out" with one last swipe.

Guanaja's airport opened on Tuesday, November 10, and Tony Solomon arrived to find her parents, Mary and Doug, looking like "Robinson Crusoe, but happy to be alive." Mary was handing out food to islanders. When she discovered that somebody had taken her own bag of rations, she broke down. "I just couldn't keep it together anymore," she bawled. "I felt quite abandoned." Tony brought baby powder for her father, and he fondled it as if it were myrrh. They scoured the dead mangroves for bits and pieces of their former lives, found an air mattress, blew it up, and slept outdoors. "For the longest time, they refused to sleep under a roof," she said.

People everywhere were living under tarps, which were valued like gold. The island "was brown. Hot. Eerie," said Julius Rensch, an American resident who was in the States during the storm. When he flew from the mainland, he saw whole housetops still bobbing in the sea. His own small hotel, next to Alex Patterson's vacation home, was gone. "You could hear sound differently. There was no vegetation to absorb noise. The light was harsher. The acoustics changed. Everything became brash. Even outboard engines sounded noisy." At Rensch's home, the closest one to Black Rock Point, Mitch had spun a ceiling fan so hard the arms had been flung off. Wind-driven salt water had permeated every nook and cranny, ruining wiring, electronics, computers.

Surveying what was left of his Bayman Bay Club, Don Pearly noticed that the birds were gone. Forty yellow-naped parrots that had flown over each night had disappeared. "One hole in the storm window had feathers around the hole. It looked like a hummingbird went through it at 95 miles an hour. We also had a scarlet macaw named Pepito. I had put him in the men's room with some food and nailed the door shut. Nine days later, I opened it up. He was skinny. He had never talked before. He began saying, 'Hello. Hello. Hello.'"

All the bees kept on North East Bight by Dave Hyde, a blind bee-keeper, blew away. On Roatán, four dolphins trained by Anthony's Key Resort disappeared. In the Río Aguán delta, eco-tour operator Paul Laman found cormorants hanging dead in the mangroves, their claws in a death grip around branches. Meanwhile, hundreds of vultures circled over Tegucigalpa, which was still buried under mud.

Fisherman Daniel Díaz and members of the twenty-seven-boat Moderpesca fleet hauled food and water to villagers stranded by a completely transformed Río Aguán delta. They also searched the Mosquito Coast for signs of villages that had disappeared. The fishermen estimated they had rescued seven thousand people from the flooded delta. Díaz personally rescued five hundred. Haunted by people he could not reach, Díaz tried to find bodies in the sea, but he ran out of gasoline. Rationing gave first priority to taxis.

After a week of doing what he could to help the residents of Santa Rosa, Peace Corps worker Patrick Cleary noticed a helicopter landing in the school yard. In his two years in the village, Cleary had carried on a running joke with his students over their perception of the United States. "They were always saying, 'You're magic. You're American.' 'No,' I'd say, 'I'm a poor, dumb kid.' 'No, you're rich.' 'I'm not. I'm a loser. I'm a fucking volunteer. I go to the States and I'm shit.'"

As the helicopter landed, his students came running. "'It's for you,' they yelled. I go out, a hand reached out from the chopper and pulled me in, and we flew off. I had no clothes, no passport, no money, no good-bye, no thank you. I was filthy dirty. An hour later, I'm in the Pizza Hut in La Ceiba. The kids were right. Everything they thought of me was true. A big giant bird came out of the sky and totally whisked me away."

Hurricane Mitch was the most destructive hurricane in the history of the Western Hemisphere. Its dead or missing toll of 18,207 people ranked second behind an unnamed hurricane that struck the West Indies in 1780, killing an estimated 22,000. If the missing were declared dead, it outstripped the Galveston, Texas, storm of 1900—the so-called Isaac's Storm—which killed 12,000. Another 3.2 million people were what in Spanish are called *damnificados*—injured ones.

In terms of sheer damage to a nation, Mitch outweighed any storm, as detailed in mind-numbing statistics for Honduras alone: 92 percent of the bridges and 52 percent of the roads were destroyed, while 21 percent of the people lost everything they owned. One-third of the country's population were *damnificados*. More than 33,000 homes were destroyed and 49,000 damaged. More than 3,000 schools and 300 health centers were wrecked. Most of the coffee and banana crops, and 70 percent of the grain, were washed away. City centers were buried up to 3 yards deep in mud that was filled with sewage, body parts, and pathogens. The cost of infrastructure loss alone was estimated by the United Nations at $8.5 billion. In dollars, that was one-third of the damage Hurricane Andrew did in Florida, but Honduras would need twenty years to rebuild.

"Mortally wounded," said President Carlos Flores Facusse. "We have before us a panorama of death, desolation, and ruin throughout the entire country."

Relief efforts great and small flooded Guanaja, Roatán, and mainland Honduras. Jean Greatorex, wife of David Greatorex of the West End resort, "maxed" her credit cards at Winn-Dixie grocery stores in Tampa for over one hundred cases of food. They were loaded on the *Caribbean Star* and sailed to Guanaja. The Spring Branch Presbyterian Church in Houston delivered sixty-five boxes of clothing and food to Galveston, where Tidewater Marine shipped it to Honduras. Steve Hooper of Calgary, the good-time Jammer from *Fantome's* October 4 trip, was moved to act after reading about a local Hispanic church that had collected supplies. Hooper arranged for his employer, Canadian Pacific Railway, to ship an oceangoing container free to Vancouver. He also set up donation hampers at the railroad's office and got local publicity. "We ended up filling three containers with over 150,000 pounds of food, medicine and clothing" he said on his Web site. "Financial donations totaled over $65,000. The Catholic Church distributed the aid. The money purchased water purification units." Hooper said he received hundreds of e-mails from Jammers all over the globe supporting the project and donating money.

One of the greatest single-handed relief efforts came from Karsten Honack, a German, who filled up three 40-foot ship containers with supplies. "This is like a drug. You want more and more," Honack wrote the Caribbean Hurricane Page. Chiquita Brands International donated the containers, and a cargo company transported it free.

"We never ate so grand," said Julius Rensch on Guanaja. "There was a constant churning of church groups, the Red Cross. Some people hoped for another storm." Private yachts also "poured in like fleas," said Bonacca's mayor. "Everybody was looking for 'mitch'"—the name given to handouts.

On the Honduran mainland, the Mennonite church sent squads of builders. Vermont's Rotary Clubs sent a team. The Web business GardenWeb.com sent seeds. President Clinton also announced an increase in aid, from an initial $3 million to at least $66 million, including help from the Defense Department.

After tasting Mitch, the Irish jumped early to aid Honduras. On November 9, the day after the gale at home, the government doubled its official relief to IRL 400,000. Liz O'Donnell, a junior Irish foreign minister who threatened to resign unless her government helped, urged Western countries to suspend debt payments from Central America. "The capacity of heavily indebted countries such as Nicaragua and Honduras to meet their debt obligations is now hopeless," she said. The *Irish Times* criticized the world—particularly the United States—for an effort that it called laughable. "Despite the predominance of U.S. firms in the region's economy, its government has so far demonstrated a lamentable unconcern. If one compares the loss of life and damage to that visited on southern U.S. states by recent hurricanes, the contrasts can readily be seen. . . . This mirrors the collapse of interest in the region's problems after the end of the Cold War." Mitch, said the newspaper, "cruelly exposes the vulnerability of these societies compared to more advantaged ones."

Also on Monday, November 9, the first lawsuit was filed against Windjammer Barefoot Cruises by the families of Colin August, Jerry King, Vernon Brusch, and others. Miami attorney William Huggett, who specialized in representing injured seamen and their families, had sent an investigator into the Caribbean to sign up clients in an attempt to cre-

ate a class-action suit. He claimed the crew had 150 dependents, though he represented only 10 families. Windjammer said the crew had "32 or 33 children—that we know of." The suit alleged that the company "carelessly and with incredible negligence sailed the ship directly into the approach of a known hurricane of extraordinary high winds." It claimed the ship was unfit, the crew untrained, and the *Fantome*'s foreign registrations "phony," designed to avoid U.S. taxes and American jurisdiction. To drum up clients, Huggett recorded a television commercial and broadcast it across the Caribbean. "They wanted to save the ship, not the lives of the men," he said in the ad. "My God! Why didn't they just beach the ship and let the men get off? They would be safe at home today."

Dawn King, whose family was one of the first to hire Huggett on a contingency-fee basis, said, "It's not the money. No money could give my mom's son back. It's that people should accept responsibility. They murdered him."

Just as quickly, the case sank into the quagmire of admiralty law, which did not favor crewmen on foreign-flagged ships. The lawsuits sought only $1 million for each family because the Death on the High Seas Act limited a seaman's loss to lost wages, with nothing for pain and suffering.

Windjammer's lawyer, using a legal formula, posted a bond equal to the company's estimated liability under admiralty law—essentially, the value of the ship divided by the number of sailors. Because the ship was virtually worthless on the bottom, the company estimated its potential payout at about $280,000, or about $9,000 per man. Windjammer also argued that because of the ship's offshore incorporation, U.S. law did not apply. In an affidavit, Michael D. Burke said *Fantome*'s crewmember contracts placed them under the laws of Honduras at the time, and that all contracts were aboard the ship and lost. Burke said he would seek to hear the case in Honduran courts.

The lawsuit had the effect of villainizing Windjammer, and forced the crews' loved ones, still in mourning, into one of two camps. Families split over it. Common-law wives stopped speaking to mothers. Separate "wives" in different nations claimed conflicting dependency on the crewmen. Jenny March, Guyan March's mother, declined to sue and settled with the company. "Guyan wouldn't have sailed if he didn't think it was safe," she told the *New York Times*.

The restless sea washed bits of the *Fantome* onto shores of the western Caribbean for many weeks after the storm: bottles of spices, a lime squeezer, shards of angelique cupboards, blue vinyl deck pads, life preservers. Scavenged by islanders, they were often recycled. A salmon-orange ring buoy, which once hung in the ratlines and could be seen bearing the words "*Fantome*" and "Malabo" (the port of registry in Equatorial Guinea) in the backgrounds of hundreds of photographs, became a wall decoration at Hank Connor's new bar in Bonacca Town. Julius Rensch found a one-foot square piece of tongue-and-groove cabinetry, scratched "*Fantome*" on the back, and put it in his den. In North East Bight, Pearl Hyde, eighty-four years old, who lost her home in the storm, recycled a carved, hardwood handle for the door of her new "home"—a plywood box.

A week before Thanksgiving, Louise Reece made a second trip to the Bay Islands, stopping first at Belize, where a life jacket with an Admiralty Suite cabin number had washed ashore. Anthony's Key Resort loaned her a dive boat and dive master Kevin Brewer to circle Guanaja. Windjammer had posted a $10,000 reward for information leading to the *Fantome*'s discovery, and Reece was bombarded by destitute islanders.

"When I got there the woman with the life jackets started yelling at me, 'You're the Windjammer woman! They found the mast! They want $10,000!' She took us to this beach off Black Rock Point." As the boat approached, Reece could see a *Fantome* life ring on the rocks. "On that beach we found what they said was a mast—an aluminum mast from a small yacht. There was obviously the remains of another small pleasure boat that had kids on it—children's toys and a broken Windsurfer. We didn't have one. There was a surfboard. They found a wave runner in the mangrove. It wasn't ours."

Then Reece found one of the belaying pins on which the *Fantome*'s staysail halyards had once been secured. Picking her way over the debris-laden shore, where mementos from the ship were interspersed with animal remains, she stepped on a dead cow. "It was horrible. I found the cooler from the bar. A Windjammer flag. Parts of the horse-racing set, stick horses with bases. That was stowed on B Deck." Picking her way through the flotsam, she also found one of the saloon

doors, heavy wood with brass handles. "Lots more life jackets; some were from B Deck, cabin 41 or 44. There were life jackets from one of the Commodore Deluxes." She found one from cabin 26, the forward portside cabin on B Deck. There were other things on the beach: a small plaque given to the *Fantome* by the Aruba Tourist Board. "That was on the wall when you walked down the stairs, on the bulkhead at B Deck."

Much of the *Fantome's* debris from Black Rock Point had been taken to Mangrove Bight by islanders hoping for ransom. Men demanded $1,000 for a life jacket, said Brewer. Reece was approached with a life ring, life jackets, a door to an Admiralty Suite, and other objects once belonging to the ship. Among them was a huge, heavy canvas flag stored in a cupboard in the bridge deckhouse. Brewer said the islanders irritated him with their demands for money. "They were fighting for it— 'Don't give her any stuff until she gives you the money.'" Reece paid about $250 for debris.

On Moon Key, Reece found another cabin door and a piece of wood from the Sea Chest. At Southeast Cay, the last and biggest in the archipelago on Guanaja's southeastern side, Reece and Brewer walked all the way around. "We found round rail uprights, mahogany. We found at least one or two more doors, and part of a banister," said Brewer. Pieces of angelique, presumably from the top deck and deckhouse, were all over the island. Reece took much of the debris—enough to fill a pickup truck—to Roatán, where it was stored. She took home several bits of wood. She gave the belaying pin to Captain Guyan's mother, to take to his memorial service. She also gave a piece of a bench to Brasso's mother. "She wouldn't believe anything had happened. I kept a piece, too, but threw it away. It was making me too maudlin."

On December 6, the day he was due home for Christmas, Guyan March was memorialized in Cornwall. Nearly 150 people came, including 45 from the Island Cruising Club in Salcombe, where he had begun his career. Bob Dearn, a longtime sailing friend, spoke, as did Michael D. Burke.

Six days later, on Quarantine Point in Grenada, Windjammer held a memorial service for the crew's families. They set up a tent with white plastic chairs. On a corkboard, they posted snapshots of all the men along with a large photo of the ship. Several women broke down crying when they saw the board. Their grief rose to loud cries of "Oh, God" as the service began. Captured on a videotape shot by investigator Nelson Ayala of the Huggett law firm, whose presence created additional tension, the service was painful to witness. Father Clive Thomas of the Grenada Council of Churches presided. An organist on a synthesizer played requiem music and a local choir sang a hymn, but the wailing and sobbing of Caribbean women pervaded the gathering. Children dressed in their Sunday best looked around bewildered and sucked their thumbs. Michael D. Burke, Susan Burke, and other members of the Windjammer crew, in dress whites, sat isolated in their chairs, curled in pain and regret.

Captain Paul Maskell read a passage from Rudyard Kipling's *Captains Courageous*, a favorite of owner Mike Burke, who didn't attend. When Maskell read the line "Sometimes they would not return," the wailing in the background rose. Then family members were invited to speak.

A male friend of Deodatt Jallim talked of Jallim's birth to a poor family. Rhon Austin's sister spoke: "I will do what Rhon promised. He loved the beautiful. He was a supporter of little people. He believed in happiness." The teenaged daughter of Deonauth "Django" Ramsudh read a poem that left everyone in tears. Through gritted teeth, the sister of Alvin and Alan George said a blessing. Colin August's sister Suzette broke down as she began speaking of her "charming . . . closest brother. I hope he had the opportunity to call on God. I'm sure he's with God." As she wept, other cries rose in response.

Chrispin's father spoke: "Many are the afflictions of the righteous, but the Lord will deliver. This is the will of God." Onassis Reyes' older brother said, "He looked up to me. I was a cadet, a sailor. Our task now is to make them proud. They're looking upon us, until we reunite." Cyrus Phillips' aging mother was helped onstage. In a quivering old voice, she sang an a cappella hymn.

Norma Jean King, Jerry's mother, then read a statement: "I will not be able to replace my son, but Windjammer can and perhaps will replace the *Fantome*. It will be business as usual. As a matter of fact, it is business as usual for Windjammer, but for me, in many ways, my life has stopped. . . . Officials of Windjammer, I implore you to dig deep down in your hearts and your finances and see what price you will pay for a human life. Is a ship, however large and luxurious, of equivalent or more value than a human life? Of what value are your lives? Have you thought of it?"

Father Thomas, sensing the pall the statement created, reminded the group that they were gathered to "honor the men."

Michael D. Burke, looking sick and white, stood and talked about the ship's final hours. "The *Fantome* put to sea to put as much distance between itself and the storm's forecasted track as possible. Then the unthinkable happened. It stalked the ship and its crew. Each time the ship changed course, the storm changed course. Twice in the next six hours the storm changed course. As if to track the ship and cut off her escape. Then, as if to assure her complete destruction, it stopped, and for the next thirty hours the storm lay right on top of the *Fantome*." He called the crew "remarkable men" and described how they created memories and goodwill for passengers. He quoted Joseph Conrad: "The sea has never been friendly to man."

As the memorial service came to an end, the name of each of the thirty-one men was read, accompanied by a single stroke on a ship's brass bell. Wreaths were laid in the ocean, a cannon was fired, and "Amazing Grace" was sung. "Why?" someone wailed. "Oh God, Oh God, Oh God. Come back. Come back."

"Everyone had roses to throw over the cliff into the sea," said Annie Bleasdale. "I couldn't throw mine—I just stood there, blinded by tears until I was alone. I kissed them, said a private prayer, then threw the flowers as far as I could. Right at that moment, the sea became alive with fish dancing on the surface. They seemed to swim towards the cliffs where I was standing, with the roses below being tossed in the surf. Then they turned and swam back out and stopped dancing. It was so incredibly symbolic. The next day I was talking with a local fisherman from Carriacou. He took my hand, looked me in the eye, and said, 'Annie, did you see the fish?' He said that in all his years, he had never seen anything like it. He said that it was Them. That was exactly how I felt."

Hanging over the memorial like a poisonous cloud were attorney William Huggett's aggressive solicitation and lawsuit, and the company's hurried attempt to sign and pay settlements. Huggett's $1 million per crewmember claim stood in stark, if unlikely, contrast to the company's first offers of five years' pay—about $20,000—for some of the men. And while Huggett's firm spread rumors of "unidentified bodies" on the Bay Islands, Windjammer flew some families to Disney World.

Windjammer's initial offers incensed Rhonda Epperson, Burke's now former human resources manager, who was also angling for a settlement for her child—fathered by engineer Pope Layne. She downloaded the men's salary schedule from the company computer and began working for Huggett. At the memorial service, she said, a Windjammer executive let it be known that a $100,000 check was "waiting for me" in Miami.

Before the memorial, a company representative brought Athelene Brusch 150,000 Guyanese dollars—$750 U.S.—and promised to continue her son's monthly paychecks. They stopped, she said, and she later rejected an offer of $30,000. Francis Morain's wife continued to receive $350 per month, and Windjammer offered her $100,000 as a final settlement. She was tempted, but under Grenada law, each of the six children would receive $14,000 in a trust, payable when they turned eighteen. That left her with only $14,000 to house and raise her children. Gilberto Reyes, father of Onassis Reyes, demanded $2.5 million from Windjammer. After Michael D. Burke negotiated a settlement with Reyes for around $275,000, Windjammer owner Mike Burke withdrew the offer.

❧

In the weeks after the tragedy, the founder of Windjammer spoke about the storm in his usual, blunt manner—true to the beliefs of a man who had "done what he had to do" to build a business from a sailing dream. He told a film crew that the tragedy made him hate boats and the thought of going to sea again. He said he was taking antidepressants. But he was finally persuaded to take his yacht, *Tondeleyo*, out to film an interview.

"My family is totally fucked up. You can quote me on that. The family's shattered. Because they knew these West Indians, too. All grown up down there. They lived on the *Fantome*. Used to piss on the deck. Changed their diapers on the dining room table. You saw Suzie? Michael? I've sheltered them all my life financially and emotionally. I can't help them with this. It just breaks my fucking heart to see them cry. Well, I cried. There's a bit of myth about the *Flying Dutchman*. You know? She's still sailing. I'll see her again."

Shortly after the memorial service in Grenada, Annie Bleasdale brought her last chain letter to Guyan March to a close. She put it an envelope marked to him. "I just didn't know where to send it to. I still have the letter. It's with all the letters and cards that he had ever written to me, along with the last four letters that I had sent to him. They were returned. He never received them."

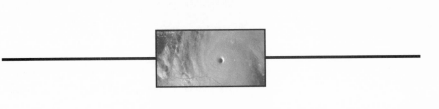

Coda

ALONG THE DOCKS and in the harborside bars of the Caribbean, in yacht clubs on the American coast, and wherever sailors
gathered, the story of the *Fantome* became the grist for a thousand de-
bates. Tempered by the refrain "There but for the grace of God go I,"
sailors nonetheless took sides.

In one corner were the fatalists, those who knew that sometimes, no
matter how good the decisions, the crew, and the ship, the storm wins.
Some viewed the chase as almost animistic—as Michael D. Burke put
it: "Like the storm went after the ship. Like the devil itself."

Hauling out charts, the mariners looked at other options: "Why
didn't they run east sooner Tuesday morning?" asked Hugh Sprunt, a
former watch officer with the National Ocean Survey. "The *Fantome*
should have anchored in the Bugle Islands," off Placencia, Belize, wrote
Phil Malter on an Internet news group. On the Internet's International
Marine History Information Exchange Group, Jim Donelson wrote:
"*Fantome*, in this case, should have never left port, all hands should have
been on the plane to Miami, and the ship written off. You don't guess
with a Cat 5 storm, especially one that had shown such an erratic track
(i.e., no strong steering systems). When NOAA's models yield no de-
finitive track, there is a damn good reason. And this is not hindsight—
the danger was clear as a bell at the time. Honest acts of nature and
circumstance do happen. This wasn't one of those."

Others, who had followed Mike Burke's career, and several who had
worked for him, felt that his past had caught up with him. "There is a
pattern to people's lives," said Harvey Schuster, who, as a young Coast
Guard marine inspector, boarded one of Mike Burke's boats as it arrived in Miami from Bimini. "Father Time finally caught up with him.
He ran ahead of the wave, and eventually the wave overpowered him."

Michael Youngman, the port captain for Hyde Shipping, whose
freighter left Belize when the *Fantome* did, said Captain March "made a
good decision. He ran south to cut behind the hurricane, not knowing

that it would do a 180." Wynn Jones, a master mariner and *Fantome* captain for a decade in the late 1970s and 1980s, could not fault Captain March. "I was disappointed with people who said they should have run aground and got off. We know that now. We weren't there. Given the information available at the time, I would have done exactly what he did. I compliment him and God bless him."

By inference, many blamed the storm's erratic path and the National Hurricane Center's forecasts for Captain March's wrong moves. Forecasters asserted that statistically speaking, their errors for Mitch were better than average. The National Hurricane Center produced a standard evaluation, calculated after every storm, that showed the center's 24-hour forecasts for Mitch were off by an average of 80 miles, down from the center's 10-year average of 88 miles. Its 48-hour forecast error was only slightly above average, 167 miles compared with 165. The 72-hour forecast was 11 miles below average, 237 miles compared with 248. But this "average" evaluation did not tell the whole story.

Early in Mitch's life, as it became a tropical storm and then a hurricane, the forecasts were wildly wrong, up to 200 miles in the 24-hour forecasts and 380 miles in the 48-hour forecasts. Forecasters also had trouble locating Mitch's indistinct center early on—missing it on three occasions by 53, 64, and 75 miles. Once the eye was fully formed, they pinpointed its location to within 20 miles. The average error was 13 miles.

The forecasts contained errors in intensity as well as predicted track. For the *Fantome*'s three decision thresholds—Sunday in Omoa, Monday in Belize, and Tuesday off Roatán—the National Hurricane Center both underestimated the storm's strength and expected it to go north of where it actually went.

On Friday, October 23, for example, as Tropical Storm Mitch meandered and threatened to fall apart, the outlook for Sunday called for a Category 1 hurricane making a gradual turn to the northwest. The fixes were off by 37 to 72 miles, but the forecasts completely missed the explosion of Mitch on Sunday to a Category 3 and 4 storm with winds of 115 to 130 knots.

On Saturday, as the storm grew and moved north and Guyan March began to worry, the forecasters predicted a gradual turn to the northwest. Their tracks for Sunday were off by 32 to 100 miles, but their outlooks for Monday were wrong by more than 150 miles to the north. They predicted a Category 4 storm, but not a historic, Category 5 storm.

Saturday's 11 P.M. forecast missed Mitch's dramatic turn to the west, but it was correctly called by 4 A.M. Sunday, and by the time passengers were arriving and Captain March and Michael D. Burke were making their critical decision about the cruise, the forecasts for Monday were within 50 miles of Mitch's eventual track. The 48-hour forecasts on Sunday failed to see the unprecedented turn south on Tuesday. Given the immensity of Mitch at the time, however, even if Mitch had gone where it was predicted, toward Belize, the storm would have filled the Gulf of Honduras like a whirlpool.

As the *Fantome* moved toward Belize on Monday, the forecasts for Tuesday morning were accurate to within 18 to 50 miles, and put a huge hurricane north of Guanaja. They missed the turn south toward the Bay Islands Tuesday morning, predicting it would pass 100 miles to the north.

On Tuesday morning, before the *Fantome* arrived in Roatán and tacked east and west, the 12-hour forecast put Mitch's center 60 miles north of Guanaja by 1 o'clock, and the 24-hour forecast placed it 95 miles north of Roatán, headed toward Cozumel. In reality, by 1 P.M. it had turned southward and was 40 miles southeast of the prediction. At 1 P.M., the National Hurricane Center predicted that by 7 P.M. Tuesday evening, Mitch would be 54 miles from Guanaja. In fact, it was 14.

Although GOES-8 was down from 2 A.M. to 9:45 P.M. on Tuesday, it did not seem to affect forecasters' ability to locate the storm. A Pacific satellite looked sideways on Honduras, and two polar orbiting satellites passed almost directly over Mitch. The shot from NOAA-15 at 8 o'clock that morning, in fact, showed Mitch crossing the 85th meridian and smothering the Bay of Honduras with boiling white wrath.

Model performance varied widely. The empirical CLIPER, projecting from a database of past storms at the same location, was wrong by more than 600 miles in its 72-hour forecasts. But the complex GFDL and NOGAPS models, based on atmospheric equations of motion and the best incoming data the world could provide, consistently did better than the human forecasters, averaging 71- and 70-mile errors, respectively, in their 24-hour forecasts. Unfortunately, because of their long computation times, neither was available for real-time forecasts and could only influence the next forecast six hours later. The hurricane specialists did much better than the models in predicting intensity but still underestimated Mitch consistently by a whole category on the Saffir-Simpson scale.

The error not summarized by the National Hurricane Center, though it can be calculated from forecast plots, was direction. Mitch deceived computer and human alike. And to a captain hanging on every word—particularly the storm's predicted track—this became the fatal error.

"Most likely it would have changed the course of action for the crew of the *Fantome*. Their decision had to be based on the forecast," said hurricane researcher Mike Black. In a rueful rumination the following spring, Miles Lawrence, the veteran forecaster, wondered if, maybe, he had called the storm "stationary" instead of moving "northwest slowly," Captain March would have made a different decision.

The real information gap was that forecasters knew they were wrong and were likely to be wrong by about 100 miles a day, but Windjammer didn't. Despite standard warnings that "errors could be large," Windjammer, in company with much of the maritime world, had the mistaken notion that because of science, satellites, and technology, hurricane forecasts could be counted on for accuracy. Captain March and Michael D. Burke had counted on science—on models and satellites—but also on the best possible outcome. They had gambled on everything going right. Grasping his heaving chart table Tuesday, Captain March had clung to "west-northwest" like a life preserver. He didn't act as if it was just a probability.

No one disputed Windjammer's experience. October hurricanes in the Caribbean usually do recurve to the north. But there were so many warning signs—computer models all over the place, contradictions between forecast and actual trajectory, a stalled storm with no steering currents—all pointing to uncertainty. James Franklin said later, "It is easy to ignore the uncertainty that was expressed."

Michael Black stated: "Personally, I can't understand their decision. Based only on my knowledge of hurricanes and sea state, they went totally in the wrong direction. They went into it. They thought they would slip around south. I thought it was an extremely foolish move on their part, knowing this kind of dangerous storm was out there. Plotting a storm, they see a dot. The storm is not a dot. What they failed to realize is just the size of the storm. Look at a satellite picture—there is nowhere safe. Nowhere in the huge circle. It is a tragic sequence of events."

Captain Andy Chase, a professor at the Maine Maritime Academy and author of *Auxiliary Sail Vessel Operations*, studied the *Fantome*'s maneuvers in Mitch and noted that too many sailors take the National Hurricane Center's forecast as gospel, while failing to take into account the center's wide error rate. "We take bigger risks now because we think we know where the edge of the storm is. Before, we knew it was out there, somewhere, and we better hunker down. Now we know where it is and think if we've got 10 miles we can scoot between." But cutting it close leaves no margin of error for breakdowns that could draw a ship into a large hurricane's eye, he said.

Chase urged mariners to adopt a neglected decision-making process regarding hurricanes, one first codified by the U.S. Navy in World War II. The first step is to circle the storm's fix with a radius of 34-knot winds as given in the National Hurricane Center's wind radii discussions. Ship handling deteriorates dramatically in 34 knots of wind, and a disabled ship can be sucked into the hurricane by its spiraling winds. Add to that radius the stated error in the fix—as much as 20 miles. For the 24- to 72-hour predictions add the forecast error radius of roughly 100 miles per day. The result is a 40-degree danger arc to either side of the forecast track. "In Mitch there were five occasions when it changed course by more than 30 degrees between advisories. I believe the fundamental mistake made by the captain of the *Fantome* was to underestimate the unpredictability of a hurricane. . . . Human nature is such that your mind will resist believing the worst-case scenario, and you will never allow as much margin as you should."

Plotting the known error rate onto the *Fantome*'s position on Sunday, October 25, while boarding passengers in Omoa, "it is clear that he was already hopelessly trapped in a situation with no safe way out," said Chase. "I firmly believe that his only option at that time was to find the best harbor he could and secure the vessel to ride out the storm in port."

❧

In their discussions of the *Fantome*—stimulated both by ghoulish fascination and the urge to salvage something from the disaster—sailors imagined the end. The few clues left behind by the *Fantome* were sifted and picked over in the effort to reconstruct those last moments—a vision those who loved the crew fought off as best they could. Yet even they, in unguarded moments, when water poured into their imaginations, found themselves on board with the men.

"I imagine you can't see a thing. You can't hear," said Paul March, the captain's brother: "The whole ship would be just droning. Water everywhere. I guess it was pretty dark. It probably capsized, whether it broached or not. I couldn't see the ship falling apart. I saw the [recovered piece of] stairway. For the sea to break that was incredible. I saw the caprail from the quarterdeck. It was a solid, solid piece of wood."

Captain Paul Maskell imagined the men "on their hands and knees. It's black. You can't see anybody else around. The ship is rolling. The wind blasts. The worst sort of nightmarish conditions. The sea is crashing all around."

Neil Carmichael, captain of the Windjammer ship *Polynesia*, said, "In the Caribbean generally, even with a hurricane, you'll get 20-foot seas, and the *Fantome* can handle it. But for this kind of situation, what ship could? A bloody submarine. She must have gone down quick. There was not a lot of debris. The bridge was high off the water. A big old wave came down and knocked it off, and maybe broke it. That's the only thing I can think of."

Captain Ed Snowdon thought the end came quickly after Guyan March's startled report of a "big one." "I don't think it was long after that the ship got broached. Ships have stability only so far. You get sideways on big waves and get knocked down and another lands on top of you, and another one, then the rig's in the water, and another big wave busts through every bit of—saloon doors, all the windows and stuff, and you have so much water on deck, the ship can't come back, because of the bulwarks it won't right, and another wave slams down on it. It doesn't take long."

Mike Burke, who had pulled the *Fantome* from mothballs twenty-nine years before, also believed she broached. "One (wave) grabbed her ass and turned her around and laid her over. Before she could recover, the next 50-foot wall of water hit her. I hope she went fast."

🐚

On her deathbed in Hurricane Mitch, the hulking, majestic *Fantome* was a helpless toy awash in monstrous waves. No one survived to bear witness. But Guyan March's words, the experience of Guanaja's residents 10 miles away, the ship's debris, and the eyes and instruments of the mad scientists who were inside Mitch when the ship disappeared paint a reasonably accurate description of her last moments.

At 1:15 P.M. Tuesday, when higher winds prevented Captain March from swinging the bow around for another tack westward under Roatán's lee, Hurricane Mitch had taken its sharp left turn and begun its slow drift south. Its center was 50 miles away, but winds of at least 50 to 75 knots—roughly Category 1 force—were coming over the island. At the ship's location, a mile or two south of the island, those winds were strong enough to prevent a course reversal, even though the hurricane's seas were partially blocked by the island.

As the ship moved east out of Roatán's lee and the wind increased gradually, sea conditions worsened rapidly. By 2 P.M. waves had jumped from the 10- to 15-foot range to around 30 feet. They also became "confused" as wave trains from different quarters of the storm collided. Waves generated by Mitch's outer winds were coming from the west-northwest around Roatán, behind the ship. In the open channel between Roatán and Guanaja, these seas met higher waves from the eye wall itself. The result would have been strange and erratic resonant combinations. The rolling and pitching grew violent. Waves higher than the exposed well deck struck the hull at right angles, periodically pouring several feet of seawater over the bulwarks railing into the "lobby," just forward of the dining saloon doors.

Over the next two hours, this chaos worsened because, unbeknownst to Captain March, the ship and the storm were on a collision course. The ship was moving eastward at 7 knots and the storm was moving southward at 2 or 3 knots. The wind speed rose gradually through Categories 1 and 2, from 65 to 95 knots—a 50 percent increase. But the wind's force, measured as the square of the wind speed, increased 125 percent. March reported the effects on both the sea and the ship. Cabinets on the top deck broke apart and cataracts of water washed back and forth as the ship heeled 30 degrees to one side, then 30 to the other.

March and his boss, Michael D. Burke, read the 4 P.M. hurricane fix with relief, believing that the ship was finally on the same longitude as Mitch's eye. March reported winds clocking westerly, directly on the ship's stern, an indication that the storm was passing to the north and the ship was entering the so-called navigable semicircle of the storm. They were wrong on both counts.

Radar images captured by the NOAA research P-3 turboprop and analyzed later by researcher Michael Black showed that the ship was about to enter the eye wall itself, on Mitch's southwest sector. The westerly winds that gave March hope were, in fact, surface winds spiraling in toward the eye, an area researchers call the "inflow channel." Rather than a beneficial wind blowing the *Fantome* east and to safety, the inflow was sucking the ship into the eye wall. This helped account for the ship's forward speed of 7 knots in those seas.

The outer edge of the eye wall is clearly delineated on the radar images shot from the plane at the time. In a space of 5 miles, the color changed from yellow to orange to an arc of reddish-brown reaching from the channel between the Bay Islands to southeast of Guanaja. The *Fantome*'s own radars would have shown this as a broad wall of dense green, the storm resembling a sonogram of a curled embryo. The eye would have been an oval mouth beyond the wall, coming toward the ship.

The P-3 plane burst into the eye at 4:30:45, the moment the ship's satellite phone went dead, and a moment when the brown arc glowed with the red and magenta "holy shit" colors marking the most extreme conditions. Looking at it, even a year later in a quiet laboratory, knowing that the *Fantome* had entered that maelstrom, a sailor's gut tightened with the sense of hell about to open.

In the eye wall, the sky turned charcoal gray-black with a density caused by the rain and convection. The base of the cloud cover was 500 to 800 feet above the ship, but the effect would have been like entering night.

Winds at the *Fantome*'s bridge rose quickly to 120 to 130 knots. The radar's red-magenta area was caused by boiling convection—thunderstorms with violent up- and downdrafts sucking and pummeling the sea surface. The stronger gusts were in the neighborhood of 156 to 169 knots. The wind alone exerted a force of 57 to 114 pounds per square foot, so the force on the hull, masts, and rigging equaled, at times, the dead weight of the ship. The jerking changes in pressure caused by the gusts would have worked on welds and fasteners, including the rigging that supported the masts. Shrouds and stays would have slackened and snapped, vibrating as if plucked.

The noise of the wind, described by people on Guanaja as resembling an F16 taking off or an express train blowing steam, blew through rigging and ratlines and around the structures and protuberances of the ship, turning the *Fantome* into Satan's calliope. The sound would have begun with a throbbing more felt than heard and risen through the audible scale to a continuous, metallic shriek.

The eye wall was saturated with water blown horizontally. Rainfall exceeded 10 inches an hour, but the majority of airborne water was ocean, blown from the tops of waves. Drops of water hit like bullets. Shards of waves struck as if shot from cannons. Periodically, "streamers" of seawater blasted the ship with fire-hose force.

None of which held a candle to the sea itself.

In his last report, Captain March described confused seas of 30 to 35 feet. But the area directly under the eye wall would have been far worse than that. The abrupt escalation would have been akin to that of a duckling caught in a swollen gutter suddenly disappearing under a street sweeper.

Because of Mitch's southward motion, according to researchers, the southwest quadrant of its eye wall created the storm's worst sea conditions—bigger and more chaotic than the northern half, which itself was generating winds still strong enough to qualify Mitch as a Category 5 storm. Large swells on the order of 30 to 40 feet were shoveled away from the eye wall at 45 degrees, both outward and inward through the storm itself. Directly under the eye wall, local waves were created and bulldozed around in a circular motion. These two trains would have met at right angles. Based on wave physics, their combined heights would have reached 38 to 45 feet. About one in ten was 48 to 57 feet high, and periodically a wave would reach 58 to 68 feet high, according to a wave model run by Dr. Steve Lyons of the Weather Channel. Theoretically, in these conditions, once every twelve hours a single wave of 74 to 90 feet was possible. Lyons said his calculations were conservative because his model "tends to underestimate wave heights in extreme hurricane wind situations. The dual direction of wave action would have made the sea state a horrible cauldron of destruction."

Because of the extreme wind force and the lack of fetch, or open sea, the waves were not mature, "fully developed" rollers like the 100-foot monsters of the Southern Ocean. Instead they were very steep, subject to collapse and collision, making them more dangerous to ships. And because of resonant combinations, the waves were not regular in any sense. Rather, they were a chaos of giant pyramids, domes, deep canyons, and overhanging cliffs moving at and around the ship at 25 knots. The distance between crests, at times, was no longer than the ship, likely causing her to bury her bow at some moments and teeter on crests at others. These waves struck the ship on the nose, on the stern, and amidships.

From this maelstrom came the most destructive force of all. "In an extreme hurricane, you see the tops of the waves actually ripped off. Not necessarily breaking. Just sheared off. It's a pretty spectacular sight," said Dr. Peter Black. "I'll watch a particular breaking wave crest to see exactly what's happening. It's almost like an avalanche. You see a front, several hundred meters long, begin breaking. It's not like these pictures you see of waves hitting the shore in Hawaii, with those nice curls. The leading edge is just a line of rolling water that is running downhill, down the wave slope, the size of a football field. It's like pictures of avalanches coming down mountains, with a sharp leading edge. It's just like that." Depending on the orientation of the wave to the eye wall, such an avalanche might blow along the crest of a wave and not just down its face. According to Michael Black, who flew into Mitch, the avalanches under the eye wall were as wide and long as city blocks. Fifteen to 20 feet high, these walls of foam and water would plunge at 40 knots from the tops of 38- to 68-foot waves that were themselves traveling at 25 knots. This water, weighing 64 pounds per cubic foot, would break, bend, and crush anything it struck. It is likely that "avalanche" seas bludgeoned the *Fantome*.

As the avalanches crashed, the water behind them would have turned turquoise blue, the beautiful color of shallow water over sand in the Bahamas. These striking patches covered the water under the eye wall, a serene illusion amidst calamity. Physically it was foam, water filled with air bubbles, which refracted the light in such a way as to look turquoise. There was no distinct interface between sea and air around the *Fantome*. The foam would have been so thick, said Peter Black, "you couldn't possibly breathe. You'd be breathing water."

A forensic study of her debris revealed few conclusive clues as to the actual cause of *Fantome*'s death. Most of the debris found on Guanaja came from the top deck and the well deck—life jackets, deck cushions, bits of deck furniture, splinters of angelique, a stairway between the two open decks, a flag stored in the bridge deckhouse, a door to an Admiralty suite, and a door to the saloon. Some of these things, located above watertight compartments, were coming apart as Guyan March watched. The likely destruction of the bridge deckhouse, almost certain death for March, Brasso Frederick, and Onassis Reyes, did not yet doom the ship. The saloon door indicated flooding of the dining sa-loon where the crew cowered, and subsequent flooding of the galley below. But if bulkheads held, the wallowing *Fantome* might still have floated. But several life jackets were from cabins on B deck, below the watertight doors at the tops of the stairs from A deck: two amidships on either side of the ship's store, and two forward, where the Admiralty suites butted against the forecastle. Louise Reece remembered finding life jackets from cabin 41 or 44, and some from the Commodore suites aft of the galley. A tourism plaque and the hobbyhorses stored on B deck were also found on Guanaja, suggesting that the ship opened up.

But the lack of debris remained the *Fantome's* greatest mystery. If the ship cracked open like an egg, why didn't more debris float out? What happened to the 406 megahertz emergency position-indicating radio-beacon stored outside the bridge deckhouse—whose silence kept hope alive for days—and what happened to the nine other life rafts racked on the top deck?

Cases of EPIRB failure on ships are rare if the EPIRB is attached prop-erly and charged "in date," according to Lieutenant Commander Paul Steward, the Coast Guard's search and rescue/satellite coordinator. *Fantome's* hydrostatic-release EPIRB had been registered with the gov-ernment in 1996 and had a battery life of 5 to 10 years. Steward listed four possible scenarios for the *Fantome's* silence: (1) EPIRB failure, per-haps from being smashed by debris; (2) the EPIRB wasn't on board; (3) the EPIRB was improperly installed or had been removed from its hy-drostatic basket by the captain to control its release in wild seas; or (4) the ship experienced a catastrophic capsizing and sinking in which the radiobeacon was trapped and went down with the ship. He deemed sce-narios 3 and 4 most likely. Captain March could have taken the EPIRB in-side the deckhouse to prevent it from deploying prematurely in a huge wave or going down with the ship. He might have hoped to take it with him in a life raft. Or the EPIRB might have deployed automatically as the ship foundered, but been trapped or tangled. "If [it was] mounted on the starboard side and the ship rolled to starboard, it could have been trapped on deck and washed into the pilothouse or caught in any other kind of rigging," said Steward.

The *Fantome's* nine missing life rafts were also designed to pop open under water. Burke said they were installed by a Florida firm, checked in July, and were "in date." Each twenty-five-person raft was 15 feet by 8 feet when inflated, very visible and extremely buoyant—prone to blowing away in strong winds. Tethered to prevent that, they, too, could have been trapped in a ship that "turtled," although several of the rafts were mounted outside the hull line. Michael D. Burke theorized that the empty rafts were in the mangroves of the Mosquito Coast. He dismissed speculation that Captain March strapped down all but two that he needed for the crew. Either way, in Mitch's conditions, survival in a life raft was unlikely. Any crewman who managed to get into one would have been thrown out in the tumbling.

The most crucial missing debris was any crew life jacket other than the one belonging to steward Chrispin Saunders. SOLAS-required PFDs—"personal flotation devices"—are buoyant for years and have twice the capacity needed to support one of the crewmen on the *Fantome*. Properly worn, they were not likely to be torn off, and even if stripped off by the seas, the jackets would have floated away. Some, at least, should have been recovered. This, too, suggested that the men and their jackets were trapped in the ship.

Since the *Titanic's* loss in 1912, ships built to SOLAS standards were designed to sink in a relatively upright position—with so-called damage stability—to give the crew or passengers time to get on deck and into lifeboats. Watertight bulkheads were designed to limit "free surface effect," or water running to one side, further heeling the ship, increasing its moment of roll, and reducing its ability to right itself. Navy experience in Halsey's Typhoon showed that even one foot of water reduced a destroyer's positive righting arm—the point beyond which it would capsize—from 80 degrees to 64 degrees. Two feet of water reduced it to 50 degrees, according to Captain Calhoun in *Typhoon: The Other Enemy*.

But the *Fantome's* forensics suggested no such thing occurred. If the ship had leaked slowly, become waterlogged, and slipped under, rafts and crew life jackets likely would have survived. The most reasonable scenario is that the ship sank in seconds, trapping EPIRBs, life rafts, lifeboats, and crewmen.

Steel hulls sink quickly when filled with water, and the *Fantome* could have filled quickly in any of three scenarios: (1) It broached or was knocked down by wind or waves, filled from various holes, turtled (turned upside down), and sank. (2) A catastrophic break occurred in the deck or hull. (3) A huge wave engulfed the ship and the sea swallowed her in one gulp, flooding her and causing further breaches under water. Most informed speculations center on one of the first two possibilities.

"At some point they were going to lose the rudder from the extreme torque on the boat from the seas," said hurricane researcher Peter Black, who was also a sailor. "After that they would not last long." Once broached, a ship tends to orient itself parallel to the wind and breaking seas, with waves crashing over the exposed side of the hull.

Michael D. Burke speculated that the ship was simply overcome by the wind. "Twin screws were trying to push a lot of windage. A gust turned it beam-to. Eventually that would happen, given the power of the wind. He didn't have enough horsepower. . . . That wind would have laid her over on her side."

Former *Fantome* captain Paddy Shrimpton believed the rigging went first. "It would have broached. At that angle, a mast came down," possibly holing the hull or deck. "She would start flooding and go down." John Taylor, the former *Fantome* captain who supervised the 1991 refit, when two beams were cut, speculated that with the bow and stern suspended between wave crests, the stress and distortion "broke its back."

Marine architect Andrew Davis, designer of modern SOLAS-standard schooners, said most ships sink from downflooding. "Whether the *Fantome*'s plating thickness was reduced, or framing was weak, it's kind of rare for a vessel of this size, even when very degraded, to have a catastrophic failure where it snaps in half because of weakness in plating. But deck plating could be gone and [water] could have just started to gush in through the deck—who knows? They drilled so many holes, willy-nilly, they would just cut a beam for some stupid reason. My basic belief is the boat sank fast. It sank because it didn't have sufficient stability. It could have been knocked down by a wind blast and laid down. [Once] a door [was] immersed, . . . it would flood rapidly and sink. It probably flooded through a bunch of points. That's the standard way boats sink."

Sheila McCurdy Brown, a professor at State University of New York Maritime College, where Onassis Reyes was once a student, said that an opening the size of a 4-inch pipe "doesn't look like much, but underwater it is a fire hose. So now you're putting hundreds of gallons of water below. As the boat heels, all that water is going to the lower side, making it more sluggish and pinning it to that side. The boat has a tendency now to heel farther. Now that 4-inch pipe is 6 feet under water. Now you have the pressure of 6 feet under and you have thousands of gallons coming below, and the boat just continues to roll. Obviously if it is [an opening the size of] a hatch, it happens a lot faster. These things happen to freighters and tankers. It can break a boat in two."

If, in fact, the wind and sea laid her on her side, the *Fantome* exposed her tenderest parts to the sea—the top two decks—which could account for most of the debris. Based on the saloon door found on Guanaja, water forced its way into the dining room, either through the doors or through the windows that circled the stern. It then would have poured down through the open stairs and dumbwaiter into the galley, a huge space. Downflooding would have begun through the engine fresh-air intake on the top deck. The hollow, top-heavy masts could have filled, helping to hold the ship down, but because their bottoms were closed they likely did not contribute to downflooding, said Michael D. Burke. Once she was on her side, breaking waves—avalanche water—also could have stove in portholes on B deck, or the watertight doors leading to B deck, in which case the downflooding would have happened quickly.

❧

Sailors are trained not to abandon ship until they have to "step up" into life rafts. In Mitch, the ship was still the best place to be—until there was no ship.

"I would imagine things got beyond being able to abandon," said Paul March. "At what point do you realize, 'Oh hell.' I don't know if you ever say that till it's over. By then, the life rafts were probably shredded."

"Guyan's final moments were totally futile. He was totally helpless, at such an angle, to do anything, much less have controlled launches of lifeboats and rafts," said Captain Shrimpton. "You wouldn't be able to hear a thing. You'd be giving orders. No one's hearing you. Blinded."

Jeremy Linn, March's first instructor, suspected that the captain "probably thought it couldn't happen to him. Like a lot of us. You hear about tragedies. But Guyan was so experienced, so good at his job. He was going through every single operation he could think of, how to get out, and if I can't get out, what's the next step. I think even until they were bobbing around in the water, he was probably thinking, 'Where are the life rafts? How am I going to stay alive?' I can't imagine him ever giving up, sitting in the corner of the wheelhouse saying, 'This is the end.' I can't imagine him doing that. I can only think of him trying to work out what his next step would be to stay alive. That's why I expected for a long time after. . . . It was very hard for us to believe he'd been lost that way."

In *Typhoon: The Other Enemy*, Captain Calhoun described how the wind laid the *Hull*, a destroyer, on her side and held her down "until the life went out of her and her struggles ceased. Now the seas came flooding into the pilothouse, and through every open ventilation duct into the ship. She remained on her beam ends, at an angle of 85 or 90 degrees, as the water poured into her hull and superstructure. Finally, she began to capsize." Men scrambled to the top of the hull like rats and then into the sea. They felt the suction of the sinking ship. They felt the concussion of exploding boilers. The violence of the sea held their heads under water. "Worst of all was the overwhelming sickness of heart that now must have blotted out every other emotion," Calhoun wrote. In the *Hull*, 100 men were trapped below decks. Another 160 men were in the water, tumbled head over heels by breaking crests. Men were pounded to pulp against the side of the ship. Water and oil blew through the air, choking them. They beat the water helplessly. Neighboring boats saw lights in the water and heard the cry of rescue whistles. Then the sharks came.

When the waters came for the *Fantome*'s crew, they likely took the captain and his mates first. Waves smashed or swallowed the top party deck, the bar, the horseshoe buffet, benches and cabinet, the loudspeakers that blared "Amazing Grace," the "ski slope" covers on the duke's stairways, and, finally, the bridge and deckhouse. Guyan March, Onassis Reyes, and Brasso Frederick may have gone overboard or been trapped in the deckhouse wreckage. Scores of orange life jackets and blue deck cushions sailed off into the whirlwind. A flag stowed in the deckhouse was whipped into the foam, to be tossed later onto the beach at Guanaja. The seas smashed or sank the whaleboats. Two of the canister life rafts popped open and blew away.

One deck down, Mitch smashed and flooded the sixteen Admiralty suites. It peeled away the staircases between A deck and the top deck and ripped the mahogany caprails from the steel bulwarks. It flooded the Sea Chest, shattered the mermaid in stained glass, burst open the saloon doors, and swarmed over the table where Chrispin Saunders had performed. The crew, presumably in their life jackets, some of them unable to stay afloat without them, would have felt the warm waters envelop them at the same moment they came to the sudden, panicked realization that the boat was sinking. In the tumult there would have been an attempt to arrest the mind, to focus on exits, stairways, and life rafts. There might even have been an attempt to reach others trapped in booths or against the ceiling or floor or the big windows.

The water poured down the stairs and dumbwaiters to the galley and dry stores and the Commodore Deluxe suites. It filled the space atop the dogged door leading to the engine room, where Constantin Bucur and Pope Layne were trapped. They could have been the last to die.

If the ship cracked open, as one or two life jackets suggested, water would have quickly flowed into the B deck cabins made of plasterboard. Broken in half amidships, the *Fantome* would have gone down much faster than the *Titanic*. Life jackets could also have floated out of broken portholes.

With the arrival of the waters, so warm and inviting the week before, there would have been the brief, thrashing struggle against drowning. If their eyes saw anything it was froth, then turquoise, then blue, then black.

❧

One small mystery of the *Fantome's* disappearance was the Mayday call reported by Winfil Alegría Palma, the trucker and fish buyer who was monitoring VHF Channel 16 from his home in Puerto Castilla, near Trujillo, on Tuesday afternoon. Almost precisely as the *Fantome's* phone went dead and the P-3 research plane penetrated Mitch's eye wall, Palma, according to his claim, heard a call from the *Fantome* saying, in Spanish, that a wave had entered and they were about to sink. He said the voice asked for a position. Palma, a man with a solid reputation among fishermen, was a believable source, but his report left lingering questions. The only Spanish speaker on the bridge was Onassis Reyes, the second mate. Spanish was his first language. He had access both to the ship's VHF radio and to a handheld radio, which likely was out of range. Why he would have asked for a position wasn't clear. Mayday callers are expected to report a position, not ask for one. Getting a fix on the ship from radar or the weak VHF signal would have been next to impossible and little help anyway. At the time, Alegría was himself in the hurricane. "Nobody could have helped them," he said later. "Castilla was flooded. My house, the water was up to here. I lost my roof."

Months later, when they learned that they had been directly over the *Fantome* as it fought for its life, the crew of NOAA's P-3 research airplane could only express wistful regret. "Not knowing in real time that a ship was foundering left me sorta feeling helpless, after the fact," said Michael Black. "If we had realized, if we had heard a distress call, we would have broken off our pattern and done a search. Even if we had located it, I doubt anything could be done in those winds and sea state. No rescue could have been attempted. No rescue aircraft or vessel would be likely to survive." Pilot Phil Kenul said he could have tossed a couple of life rafts—"whether it would do any good. In calm seas, they're tough to get in. I don't think there was a whole lot we could do." The crew also could have called out on the radio and searched emergency frequencies for a Mayday call.

The belly radar on the P-3 was capable of picking up a metal hull the size of the ship. Researcher Michael Black created an animation of the radar images over two hours of time and searched for a radar return that might have been the *Fantome*. Amidst the thunderstorm cells and magenta convulsions of the eye wall was one suspicious, brown blip in the vicinity of the *Fantome*'s last position. It didn't appear to be moving, which would have been consistent with a ship in trouble. It disappeared at 4:36 P.M., six minutes after the ship's phone went dead. It could also have been a thunderstorm. "It's inconclusive," said Black. The water beneath the blip was 2,600 to 4,300 feet deep.

❧

The violence and peace of the *Fantome*'s death informed the dreams and spirits of lovers and family members that night and beyond. From their *honduras*—the depths—the men flew home, stood in doorways, crawled into bed, asked for the children, held them and talked. Many loved ones described what happened in eerie detail that echoed the best marine speculation.

"You are doubting me," Colin August said to his sister Suzette in a dream during the first week of the families' vigil in New Amsterdam, Guyana. "Let me tell you what happened. Captain Guyan came and said, 'I don't think we are going to make it.' He was smoking. The wave hit me from the side. A wave came and we turned turtle." In subsequent dreams, she talked with her brother.

"Colin, are you OK? Did you have time to pray?"

"Yes."

"Did you have time to ask the Lord for forgiveness?"

"We all had time to pray. We prayed together. Don't cry, Sue. I'm OK."

In her grief, Heila Bucur, bank economist and wife of chief engineer Constantin Bucur, underwent hypnosis. "I was dreaming that I was on the ship when it was a hurricane. It was very dark. I go inside. I enter and I turn left in a small room where I found Guyan March and he looked very, very nervous. He was not alone. He was there with another officer, a black officer. He was very tall. I didn't know the crew at the time. I'm afraid. I feel that the ship will go down. I was on the deck. Nobody was on the deck. In a moment I feel that the ship go very fast to the coast—it was a reef. I saw the seamen, how they tried to leave the ship. They were somewhere on an island and it was dark out. Not many, only six or seven. It was only my husband, Guyan, and five or six black men. Guyan and another black were on the ship. The others and my husband were lying on the island. And this person [hypnotist] told me, 'We have to find this island.' So I became like a bird. I was flying. There were lots of islands. I was looking for a green, very nice, island which had a very big stone, something like a mountain. When I saw this mountain, I was so scared, because I feel I go down like a plane crashing." Guanaja is a mountainous island.

Shirlan Saunders saw her son, Chrispin, many times in the coming days. "Every time I dreamed about him he was in the water. Every time."

Pope Layne appeared in a dream to Laura-Jo Bleasdale. They were in a Roatán shopping mall. He came up behind her and spoke a four-digit number.

"Don't forget it," he said.

"What does that mean?" she asked him.

"You'll figure it out." The phrase was familiar to her. It was what Pope always said to her when her ship accounts didn't balance—"You'll figure it out."

"In the dream, we were walking and I turned around and he was gone," she said later. The next day, in Susan Burke's office at Windjammer Laura-Jo saw the same four digits on a pad on her desk.

"What is that?" she asked.

"That's the *Fantome*'s last coordinates."

"I went pale. I had never heard it before."

Glenn Parkinson, the girlfriend of Onassis Reyes and a trauma psychologist, agonized over his last moments. "This was the man I loved more than anything. It's so horrible to think of him with no one there that he trusted to share that fear. It's the most sacred part of love to be there when you're hurting or fearful, and I couldn't do it. If I didn't know what his death was like, I was missing a huge part of it. It was also so baffling. They just disappeared. No trace. There's no finality. I needed to understand, sort of, how it happened.

"I think it was hell. There have been accounts of people taping their passports to their bodies to let people know who they are when they are found. I can't imagine the fear and the horror. Just lying in your bunk. They couldn't do anything. Throwing up on themselves. Being incapable. My greatest hope was that he smashed his head on something so he didn't have to deal with the fear of drowning. My God, how horrible. I have no doubt that I was with him, in ways that he needed me to be. He had pictures of me, taped to the ceiling above his bed, so he could look up at me. If he was lying down there, that's what he would be looking at."

For a year after the tragedy, Jerry King's daughter in Belize, Princess, was sickly. Near the first anniversary of the ship's disappearance, her mother, Teresa Au Gustus, dreamed that she and King were quarreling. He took Princess. "He told me, 'You take Princess. I was going to take her from you but I will leave her with you.' She hasn't been sick since."

Kevin Logie's mother in Trinidad believed that at the end, in his most painful time, her son "must be calling my name. He's going down and calling me." Jerry King's mother, Norma Jean, reduced her boy's final moment to one agonizing cry. Jerry, she said, wasn't thinking of his children or girlfriends in three or four countries. She believed he reverted to her little boy, the one who tried anything and could do anything he set his hands to. In the end, in his worst need, she said, Jerry King shouted the name still used by West Indian men:

"Mommy!"

For many months after, Annie Bleasdale, Guyan March's companion, went back to the *Fantome* in her daydreams and night-dreams. "She was so beautiful. I was just walking from room to room, from deck to deck, crew mess to the bridge. It was as ever. I was on her for the last time and I had to take in every tiny detail of her. Even now, I can close my eyes and I'm there. So are all the crew, just doing what they did. Such great guys. I know they all suffered, they were trapped in the main saloon, in the crew mess, in the engine room. Guyan and his mates on the bridge. How had they been steering the boat? They must have been exhausted, terrified, angry. They must have taken such a beating, using all their energy just to keep standing, never mind keeping the bow in the right direction and navigating reefs. What was going through Guyan's mind when conditions were worsening, the dead of night, no sleep, no food, the thought that not only could he lose his life but his crew also? I know that's what he was thinking at the end—he couldn't save his crew. That breaks my heart in a million pieces. I know how much he cared for those guys and would have done everything possible to take them to safety. Guyan loved Windjammer. He loved the ships and the sea—it was all he knew. He loved his crew and his crew him. I truly believe that the storm chased them down—as if it was meant to be. Maybe someday we'll understand just why. WHY?"

Epilogue

🐚

THE FIRST ANNIVERSARY of the *Fantome* disappearance haunted the Windjammer family when three of the company's ships were threatened by Hurricane Jose, which swirled up the eastern Caribbean the week before the October 27 memorial date. While Jose was still 300 miles from Grenada, after a hurricane watch was posted, passengers on the *Yankee Clipper* and *Mandalay* were put ashore in hotels and the ships took refuge in bays on the southern shore. Several crewmen talked of abandoning ship, saying they "didn't want to be Fantomed." Several days later, Captain Pete Hall of the *Amazing Grace*, the company's supply ship, quit after quarreling with his Windjammer bosses over his attempt to approach the British Virgin Islands on the tail of Jose, by then a tropical storm. Marine Superintendent Paul Maskell told him he was getting too close to the storm. Hall, with seventy-two older passengers aboard in rough seas, was incensed to reach Michael D. Burke on his way to Disney World. "It sounds bad," Burke said later, but he was in touch with headquarters by phone. "Pete had reached the end of his rope. I was sorry to see him go. He has asked to come back." Hall wouldn't discuss the issue. On the anniversary itself, the company held a small memorial in Grenada. Few crew families attended.

After the loss of the *Fantome*, Michael D. Burke made substantial changes in company policies. He moved the majority of the fleet south for hurricane season, closer to the southern range of hurricanes, in order to calm nerves of crew, captains, and passengers. He purchased liability insurance for crewmembers—to cover potential company loss payments. He restricted "essential" crew to six deckhands, four engineers, and deck officers. Unless the captain overruled him, no hotel staff would be allowed aboard while evading a hurricane. Burke also established a new fleet hurricane evasion strategy based on a 100-mile margin of error for 24-hour hurricane forecasts and a 200-mile margin of error for 48 hours. Burke said Andy Chase's analysis influenced him. "I suppose it's not new science. I've never had access to it before. You assume today that the models are more accurate, that the forecasting is more accurate. Do we still need this much margin of error? Whether we do or not, we're going to."

The company settled with a dozen *Fantome* crew families for amounts ranging from $30,000 to $195,000. The *Fantome* trust fund, based in Trinidad, grew to $100,000. The company donated proceeds from the sale of T-shirts and other gift items to the fund. Most of the money came from passengers and those outside Windjammer.

For Windjammer Barefoot Cruises, Ltd., 1999 was a profitable season. Michael D. Burke said the *Fantome* disaster delayed his work on replacing the fleet's older ships by 2010, when new SOLAS regulations will outlaw all passenger ships that do not have fireproof cabins. "We've had a setback, so we've taken a year or two off. But we're looking for a new hull, and if we find the right deal, we'll bring it to Trinidad and get going again." Until then, he said, Windjammer would not carry insurance on the older hulls, except the *Amazing Grace* and the *Legacy*. "For the record, Captain Burke supports me with the upgrade in standards. Obviously [as] father and son, there are a lot of things we don't see eye to eye on, I being of the new generation that works in this environment that is somewhat alien to him in terms of the regulatory enforcement. The industry has grown. I see what's going on in terms of the popularity of new tonnage in the cruise industry. I have his support when it comes to the remodeling program."

Victor Jimeno of Maritime Inspection Corporation, who inspected the *Fantome* and reportedly signed its SOLAS certificate, said he did not plan to conduct an investigation of the tragedy, as required of flag nations by the International Maritime Organization. "What can we do? We have the Coast Guard and newspaper reports. That's all we have. It's impossible. It went to the bottom because of the hurricane." He declined to answer other questions about the *Fantome's* SOLAS certificate.

The *Fantome* disappearance diminished some Jammer enthusiasm, but Steve Hooper and Cathy Stumph sailed again with Windjammer on the *Polynesia* in the Antilles. Said Hooper: "I am regularly asked by people if we would travel with Windjammer again, and the answer is an emphatic YES." Deena Kaplan and Andrew Biewend, who were engaged on the *Fantome* before the storm, were married in April 1999 and honeymooned on another Windjammer trip. After returning home, they happened to hear a recording of "Amazing Grace" one night. "We stood in the living room, held each other, and bawled our lights out," said Kaplan. "We've decided, when we do have a baby boy, his name will probably be Guyan."

Several Jammers who followed the story worried that the overboard kitty, Tiki, retrieved by the *Fantome* crew off Belize, had perished with the ship. It turned out that after the 1997 rescue, American passengers took Tiki home with them.

The name "Mitch" was retired from use for tropical storms by an international weather committee, and Mitch joined other deadly storms in a hurricane hall of infamy. Officials at the National Hurricane Center also warmed to the idea of redesignating Mitch from a Category 4 to 5 storm at the hour the *Fantome* disappeared. They were urged to do so by flying researchers Michael Black and James Franklin, who had both the data to prove it and the desire to notch a Cat 5 storm in their "penetration" belts.

After looking at the data, Black said Mitch stirred up a lot of research issues. "We know less now than when we flew. Understanding why the numerical models kept sending Mitch off to the northwest, and Mitch didn't seem the least bit interested in the numerical models. And we have almost no skill in forecasting intensity, but being able to measure it better would be a start."

New analysis indicated that Mitch was part of a long-term climatic trend. After decades of relatively few hurricanes, there was growing evidence that in the mid-1990s the United States and the Caribbean Basin had entered a twenty- to thirty-year period of frequent and severe hurricanes. Based on "climate signals" from stratospheric winds and warmer currents in the North Atlantic, scientists reported at the National Hurricane Conference that changes in North Atlantic temperatures of about 1 degree Fahrenheit create twenty-year cycles of low and high hurricane activity. The record-setting storm activity between 1995 and 1998, with thirty-three hurricanes, could have signaled a return to a high-frequency cycle of two or three decades, they said. The last such cycle was seen in the 1940s and 1950s.

Christopher Landsea, a research meteorologist at the Hurricane

Research Division, said the 1970s and 1980s appear to have been one of the periodic lulls. "We've been lucky," he said. There were fewer hurricanes, and no major storm struck Florida between 1965 and 1992, when Hurricane Andrew caused $33 billion of damage. During that lull millions of people moved to Florida and other coastlines—the populations of Dade and Broward Counties increased 600 percent—and built expensive homes, which will make storm damage much more costly in the future.

The 1999 hurricane season was busier than usual, with eight hurricanes, five of them major and a couple of them as erratic as Mitch. Hurricane Floyd veered away from Florida but soaked the Carolinas with life-taking floods in September. Lenny moved backward through the Caribbean in November. Katrina, a tropical storm, went inland over Nicaragua and Honduras and exited into the Bay of Honduras between La Ceiba and Roatán. No one was reported killed. Tropical Storm Harvey was well charted by the National Hurricane Center as it moved east across Florida from the Gulf of Mexico. But when Hurricane Irene flooded Miami 50 miles closer than forecasters predicted, the Florida media decried forecasting accuracy.

Hurricane Floyd caught a large tugboat off Florida's east coast; an aircraft carrier that was putting to sea from Jacksonville rescued the crew. A Carnival cruise liner with twelve hundred guests aboard was disabled near Tampa in Harvey, but no one was seriously hurt. In St. Martin, Lenny, then a Category 4 storm, trapped the *Sir Francis Drake*, a 165-foot, three-masted schooner built in 1917 and flagged in Equatorial Guinea. The captain anchored the ship and put the passengers and crew ashore as the storm approached. The ship emerged from the rain and spume, still at anchor, when Lenny's eye came to rest over the island. Later, the ship's EPIRB went off and the vessel disappeared in 1,200 feet of water. No one was hurt, and the loss of the *Sir Francis Drake* made almost no news.

Long after Mitch's passage, one of the sailing yachts abandoned off Florida during the November 1998 Caribbean 1500 rally was found floating in June 1999. "It had sailed on its own from November until June," said rally organizer Steve Black.

Months after his lost contact with "Jack" of the yacht *Velella*, Caribbean Weather broadcaster David Jones learned that the boat had "ridden out the storm safely in the mangroves in Roatán but was unable to transmit." He also believed he had saved the lives of sailors aboard *Dreamcatcher* when he advised them not to head from San Andrés Island to the Bay Islands ahead of Mitch.

A week after the first anniversary of the *Fantome's* loss, the ship's battle with Mitch was presented as a case study in hurricane avoidance by the American Sail Training Association, a group that uses tall ships to train sailors. Andy Chase presented his paper on forecast errors, and new satellite-based navigation and warning devices were recommended for ship operators. Michael Carr of the Maritime Institute of Technology and Graduate Studies said that for less than $3,000 a sailor could download satellite images at sea using a satellite phone and an on-board PC. A new device, Seastation, provided weather fax from satellites. For less than $1,000, a sailor could receive faxed copies of wind radii forecasts. As of February 1, 1999, all merchant ships covered by SOLAS were required to carry a satellite-based Global Maritime Distress and Safety System which allows short e-mail emergency messages attached to GPS location readings.

※

From the East End of Guanaja, the idyllic paradise of the Bay Islands seemed unchanged on the first anniversary: the white curls of waves on the reef, the blue mountains of Honduras, and in between the deep blue of the strait where the *Fantome* disappeared. On this beach, Alex Patterson, the veterinarian, decided not to rebuild his seaside vacation home. But his sister's house, farther up the hill, was again habitable. Baby palm trees were beginning to grow around their property. Electrical power was finally restored in August 1999.

At Mangrove Bight no one rebuilt over the water, in spite of the desire to escape the sand fleas. The sea, thought of before as an occasionally ill-tempered child, had become a monster to be feared.

After sleeping for weeks under plastic on a found mattress, Doug and Mary Solomon began rebuilding. It took eight men two and a half months to haul their possessions back to the homesite. Their old, heavy lifeboat remained on a hillside, a reminder of the surge and strength of Mitch.

In Bonacca the mayor of Guanaja, Sherral Haylock, defended herself in a public meeting against charges that she embezzled relief aid. She said the charges were politically motivated by her enemies.

Guanaja looked like Yellowstone National Park after the great fires of 1988. Downed and dead trees, many lying north and south, recorded the direction of the wind in the eye wall. There were more flowers and the terrain was more open, sunny, and hot. Despite fears, not a single case of cholera broke out. The reef appeared to have rebounded, but fish harvests had declined 42 percent. "If there is no fishing, there are no beans," said the mayor. Oddly enough, rusting cans of pork and beans, sent as relief supplies by good-hearted Americans, piled up like unwanted guests on Guanaja. The pork violated the religious doctrine of the island's many Seventh-Day Adventists.

On mainland Honduras, crime rose in Trujillo. Bridges remained out or dangerously haphazard, and roads still were undercut, with asphalt edges looking like black serrated blades. From the air, wide arcs of mud outlined where the floodwaters had been. Banana trees were newly planted. Thousands of people remained out of work. The man who had barbwired his hands to the crotch of a tree held out his palms and shouted every time he saw Daniel Díaz: "My Salvador! I have nothing. But I've got two hands for you."

Along the roads to San Pedro Sula and Tegucigalpa, people still were living in homes made of shower curtains. "One woman even ran a tortilla-making business from her shower curtain home," reported *Honduras This Week*. In September 1999, German philanthropist Karsten Honack reported another container en route to Honduras loaded with "millions of wood screws and aluminum roof."

In the semiwild delta of Río Aguán, at what used to be Santa Rosa de Aguán, school buses remained toppled into what had become a new riverbed. The village, once so open and friendly, was striated by ugly currents of a river the villagers no longer trusted. The sea and surf were 200 yards closer. At the mouth of the river, dark chocolate waves foamed and roared through the night. The Catholic church was building a new cinder block village farther from the riverbank, and the people of Ireland erected and staffed a first-ever medical clinic. Former Peace Corps volunteer Patrick Cleary went back to Santa Rosa on his own and found an unending need for help. Many villagers went back to their sagging shacks on sand, but for months, kids wouldn't leave their houses. People wore small crosses made of toothpicks in their hair—protection, they said, from another flood. Olivia Batiste Norales, mother of Isabella Arriola, the woman rescued at sea because of the search for the *Fantome*, said her daughter was "not well" and was undergoing psychiatric care in Texas. Standing in front of her own house with her husband, Francisco Solano Arriola, she said, "The people feel unsafe. At any moment it could happen again."

❧

Without the bodies of their crewmen, the families of the *Fantome* slipped into a trancelike state of grief and spiritlessness, their acceptance of death incomplete. For those who dreamed, the 1999 hurricane season prompted a new round of nightmares.

Heila Bucur, the wife of Constantin, said she consulted ten gypsy psychics, each of whom said her husband was alive. The first psychic, contacted by telephone, said Constantin was "very ill and one day he will be back. He's somewhere in Malaysia. Maybe they told me to make me happy."

In Grenada, Christmas cards from 1998 remained on the mantle at Francis Morain's house. His six children still cried at random moments when speaking of their father. On the first anniversary of the *Fantome*'s disappearance, the oldest girl, studious and polite, came home from school in her neat uniform and said, "Mom, you know it's a year," and fell into tears. "It's not easy. It's hard," said his wife, Elizabeth. "To tell you the truth, sometimes I wish someone would come and take the kids. I have tears in my eyes all the time. I'm renting. I need a better home. If my husband were alive, life would be better. Even if they give me the money, and I blow it all on the kids . . . what's going to happen to my life? Who can I turn to? I can't turn to the kids. They have their own lives. I just trust that everything will go all right. I just wish I could disappear. I have nothing to count on. We're on hold."

Minga Maldonado, when called from her kitchen at the Bric Brac seaside café in Omoa, Honduras, to talk about her son, Pedro Prince, asked, "Is there any sign they are still alive?" She fingered an incomprehensible sheaf of documents from an attorney in Miami, suing on her behalf. She had signed up as a plaintiff, she said, after Windjammer offered her $12,000 for her son. Pedro's widow had gone to work to support their five children.

Annie Bleasdale left Windjammer with her new Yacht Masters certificate and signed on to a private yacht headed for the South Pacific. Paul

March, Guyan's brother, quit Windjammer to look for work on private yachts. Laura-Jo Bleasdale, after becoming increasingly distraught, took a long leave from Windjammer and returned to her parents' home in North Wales. She wanted to return to school, to study theater and acting. The other two female officers, Cathie de Koeyer and Laurie Fischer, returned to work on other Windjammer ships. Oxford Tuissant, a *Yankee Clipper* steward who didn't die on the *Fantome* because FedEx didn't deliver his tickets in time, shrugged his shoulders. "God wasn't ready for me," he said on a sunny dock in Grenada.

Kevin Logie's brother, Neville, an accomplished seaman on Mike Burke's private yacht, said that whenever he sailed it was like "working in a cemetery because that's where these guys are buried. Windjammer fired a gun and killed somebody. They didn't mean to, but they did. They saw it coming and didn't do anything. They kept going. As if a man with a gun were coming down the street and you didn't move."

The pain in mothers' eyes, one year later, was never far from the surface. "We were so close. He was like my baby," said Shirlan Saunders, Chrispin's mother. He would have been twenty-seven on February 7, 1999. His room had been left empty. She didn't go in, except to retrieve a folded apron, signed by passengers with inscriptions like "Dr. Salad—hope you have a good vacation." Many people had called and written to tell her that Chrispin had been the most popular crewmember on the *Fantome*. It was bittersweet music, making her feel warm and empty.

"Everytime I look at the pictures . . ." winced Margaite George, mother of Alan and Alvin George of Grenada, leaving the sentence unfinished. She sat on a porch of her mother's house with a long view across the Caribbean. She looked out, she said, still hoping that the ship would sail in. "I still can't believe it. I have belief that I will see the boat. I see boats and I start to cry. The *Yankee Clipper*. The *Mandalay*. I always cry." The company's settlement with her for her two sons helped her build a new cement home.

In Panama, the mother of Onassis Reyes fingered the newspaper clipping that first alerted her to her son's fate, and his last e-mail that began, "I love you very much, Vieja." His father, Gilberto, still angry over the way they learned about the tragedy and over Mike Burke's withdrawal of an agreed settlement, said, "If Onassis had been the master, his main concerns would have been first, his men, and second, his ship, and third, the company. You can't talk wrongly about the dead ones, but I knew my son. He wasn't wearing the epaulets just for show. He knows the responsibility for each one of those bars. They don't give a shit about the men. That's what I told Captain Burke."

On Vernon Brusch's birthday, October 30, when he would have been twenty-eight, Athelene, his mother, received a guest on the second floor of her neat home in New Amsterdam, Guyana. Wearing a blue-and-white bandanna, a red blouse, and purple slippers, Mrs. Brusch showed off a CD of Windjammer tunes that Vernon had brought home. Before church every Sunday, she played it. "I put on 'Amazing Grace.' Oh God, sometimes the tears come." Vernon's photo was shown on TV on the first anniversary. His three-year-old daughter saw it and said, "That's not Daddy. He's dead." Mrs. Brusch's lawsuit was pending, after the company offered her "$30,000—nothing much." After talking awhile about Vernon, his birth and childhood and fondness for taking radios apart, she sat empty, sucked dry by the interview, her hands folded in her skirt, the memories scattered about the living room with pieces of her heart.

"You take things for granted, that someone would always be there," said Dawn King, older sister of Jerry King. Long after the sinking, his collect phone calls from Honduras and Belize appeared on their telephone bills. "If there was a different government, they would pick up our story. If this had happened in Grenada with U.S. people, do you think the U.S. government would stay so quiet over it? If they had stood up for us, then we could get justice, but we are in a low class. Jerry said he wanted to come home and roll in the mud. My brother's rolling in all that mud now, wherever he is."

"I know they murdered my son," added Norma Jean King, Jerry's mother. "We're in a remote area and we saw that the storm was coming, a Category 5 storm. . . . They wanted to save an old ship."

"If they can save Americans, why not the crew?" asked the family of Deonauth Ramsudh.

As was their habit, Colin August's family gathered Sunday mornings for a devotion and took turns leading the prayers. On the anniversary of the tragedy, sister Audrey was leading and started to cry. Then everybody started to cry. "Who knows if they're alive?" said sister Suzette. "I haven't seen a body. I haven't buried him. This will live with me as long as life lasts."

Sherry Jallim, wife of carpenter Deodatt Jallim, said the company was good to her and she had settled. She said both her own family and Windjammer had comforted her. "I don't like to fight. They kept me informed. From the time of the accident they were at my side." On the first anniversary she had a private memorial for her husband. A woman from Windjammer joined her at the memorial. "I love him. I just miss him. He will always be in my heart. He was a loving husband, kind and loving. I just have to accept it."

In September 1999, Alisa Maxwell, wife of chef Eon Maxwell, flew to Miami to settle her claim with Windjammer. Their offer was reportedly $75,000. She described Windjammer as being "really good" to her. Mrs. Maxwell said her faith helped her through. "I'm a strong person. My mom was supportive. My son kept me going. He really looks like his father."

🐟

For the *Fantome* "family," the tragedy opened a window on the Caribbean cruise business as practiced by Windjammer Barefoot Cruises, Ltd., and its founder, Mike Burke. The bigger cruise companies couldn't distance themselves fast enough from Windjammer's loss, even as they exploited island economies and Third World flag registries just as Burke did.

Cap'n Burke made no effort to soften his words or gild his character for the sake of public relations. In rambling soliloquies he spoke his mind, even when his words seemed painfully insensitive. He talked more about the ship than the men, and maintained the illusion of the *Fantome* and its crew as experienced "men against the sea." While Burke's own captains called themselves "drivers" who were almost always in sight of land and tried to avoid bad weather because of their passengers, Burke remained the incurable romantic, painting for himself a life of "going to sea" while he sat in his castle and remembered.

"When I started this business, I was a happy guy, carefree. I used to brag that the soles of my feet were quarter-inch thick. I could walk on tacks, on hot decks. I never wore shoes. I could climb a palm tree. After all the probing and digging, the one question that comes to mind is, 'Why, Mike, did you go on to expand to the largest fleet of tall ships when you enjoyed life as a simple sailor?' I have thought about this often. It sure as hell wasn't the money, because I had more free money in my pockets when I was a beach bum to piss away on playmates and booze than I've had since. Now it's payroll, maintenance, advertising, legal fees, worries, etc., etc. Not much left to play with. But have you ever flown into a Caribbean port and looked down to see five tall white gleaming sailing ships that you've created? Or when was the last time you got a letter from a passenger, 'Mike, I wish to make my final trip on a Mike Burke Windjammer'? This from a former passenger, and he's not alone. That makes it worthwhile. Whatever mistakes I have made, and there have been many, it's been well worth it."

Burke said that after years of trying to avoid U.S. taxes, by registering and operating ships outside U.S. jurisdiction, he made a "voluntary disclosure" to the Internal Revenue Service in 1992. "I gave them back income tax. I wanted to make things legal and comfortable for my family, to deal with the inevitable probate. I didn't want my kids burdened with answering a lot of questions. They don't need it. They're not like me. Now I have nothing to hide. I can wave the American flag. I can die comfortably."

None of the probing would have occurred, he said, "if Mitch hadn't happened. Let 'em talk. When I started they were talking. When it flourished, they found out something else to say. These people who talked are underachievers. I never had a successful guy knock me.

"I don't know of any ship in the world that could stand 200 knots. I've been in a hurricane with 80 to 100 knots. The salt water hits your eyes. You can't see a thing. I've been in 20-foot seas, but not 50. I always felt good in a storm. Me against the wind. Me against the sea. Shorten sails. Put up a trysail. I wonder how I would have felt aboard the *Fantome*. It must have been an awful feeling, to be totally at the mercy. Seas so steep. How can you steer? The poor shit. I'm sure they were huddled in the saloon. They're sailors. They knew you had to be in the highest part, in case of abandonment. Some nights I have visions of them. I can't sleep. They were friends of mine. I've lived with these guys. I can image them huddled together. I wish I'd been with them.

"We had a good lee for four or five hours. We didn't drop the hook. We wanted to be free to run. Everything was just great. I told Mike, 'Don't worry.' I predicted the direction of the wind perfectly. First north, then west. Keep the boat moving around the island and take her where you can. And it didn't happen that way. And after she wiped us out, she went back on her course. Hey, does that make you believe in God?

"I'm a sailor. You get close to a hurricane, you're close to God. I've been at sea with a hundred passengers and in a lee storm and I learned to pray. When you get caught your asshole quivers. I don't say I'm the greatest. He pulled me through. Maybe He would have spared the ship if I had been there. Because He always spared me. He came right at me. Dumped me out and went on His way. I hope He's happy. This is the one time, fifty years of sailing, I didn't get that break. It's almost as if there were a purpose, the way it acted. I'm not that important. Why would He do that to me? I've drunk a lot and fucked a lot. But I don't go around killing people. Sometimes I can't sleep. I wake up and say, 'Why did you do that?' Maybe I was too cocky. Why would He turn that storm from northwest to south? It couldn't have been an accident. The sad thing is, it happened in the twilight of my life. How can I ever replace the ship or make amends to the world for a loss like that? I don't have time or energy. I could never replace her. She was a piece of glorious history. I almost wish, I do quite often wish, I'd been aboard. It would have been a climax. And now it's an anticlimax."

Acknowledgments

THIS BOOK IS NOT MINE ALONE. Hundreds of people contributed. I was never aboard the *Fantome*, and I did not know the crew. They were brought to life through interviews, e-mails, photos, and videotapes provided by loved ones and friends. The families of the crew were generous to a probing stranger, and willing to reopen a painful subject. Mike Burke, Michael D. Burke, and the Windjammer family endured hours of difficult quizzing unattended by PR spokespeople or lawyers. Those named or quoted in the book should know how much I leaned on them. I will not repeat all their names here.

Many thanks to the Jammers who introduced me to the joys of a Windjammer cruise and provided heartfelt memories of the men: Kathy Ptasnik, Melody Filarey, Ruth Kuehn, Rebecca and Fred Baird, Steve Hooper and Cathy Stumph, Ted and Margaret Mesch, Melissa Fryback, Janet Jemelka, Jim St. Leger, Valerie St. Claire, and Don Heller. "Jammer Don" Conyngham's crew profiles were, in many cases, quoted verbatim. Dean Dey spread my call for help, and his Web site, along with Dean Traiger's Jammer Web site, were gold mines. Sara Sommers' e-files were invaluable. Nancy and Steve Tharp copied their video of the Belize trip made two weeks before the ship disappeared. Watching it was akin to watching the movie *Titanic*, in which a sunken hull comes to life with smiling crew.

In my travels, I camped with hosts Calvin Marshall in Guyana, Katie Lyons in Key West, Jerry and Darlyn Stockfish of Madeira Beach, Florida, Atheleny Woolnough and Amy Carrier in Boston, and the crew of the *Tondeleyo* in Miami.

Professional mariners who educated me: Paddy Shrimpton, David Wood, Ian McCurdy, Peter Stanton, Joe Maggio, Ken Lewis, James Stevens, Bob Gable, Wynn Jones, John Rains, Neil Parker, Niels Thomsen, Paolo Scanu, Peg Brandon, Phil Richards, Ray Ashley, Doug Rabe, Chuck Hawley, Dave Buchard, Steve Black, Jim Gladson, Mike Elder, Ricardo Jimenez, and Mike Alford.

Weather experts not quoted in the text: Lee Chesneau, Sam Brand,

Bob Sheets, Frank LePore, Hugh Willoughby, Bill McCracken, Dr. Abdoulaye Kignaman-Soro, Steve Renwick, Sim Aberson, Michael Carr, Chris Velden, Doc Radawski, Patricia Viets, Wassila Thiaw, and Terri Gregory.

Among other contacts not quoted, but who added to my knowledge: Don Nugent, Judith Balfe, Frank Gleberman, Linda Coffman, Bill Graf, Gert van Dijken, Dale Miller, Nelson Ayala, Dawn Shelburne, Deb Martin, Joan Ritzenthaler, Alcide Doyon, Akosua Garcia Yeboah, Barbara Leonard, Andre Guevremont, Ray Auxillou, Roger Kohn, Don Nugent, Ludovick Scotland, and Amy Simpson.

Thanks to my colleagues in the news and writing business who shared their contacts and information: Calvin Marshall of the *Guyana Chronicle*, Eric Avram of ABC, John Vaillant of the *New Yorker*, Curtis Morgan of the *Miami Herald*, Reese Palley, John Dupuis of Honduras.com, Jeff Hammond, Michael Grey, and Neville Smith of *Lloyd's List*, Sally Erdle of *Caribbean Compass*, Jim Gilbert of *Showboats International*, Leslie Pierre of the *Grenadian Voice*, Scott Marshall of the *Atlanta Constitution*, Robert Schachner, Barb Strauch, and Henry Fountain of the *New York Times*, Carol Frierson-Campbell, Megan McFarland, and Trish O'Kane of Red Shoes, Inc. Winston Burrell, publisher of the *Island News* in Key West, provided an office for my first interviews. Sebastian Junger, author of *The Perfect Storm*, was generous in advice and encouragement.

Thanks to Morris Dees and the staff of the Southern Poverty Law Center, who gave me a long rope and superb facilities to research and write the book.

My sailing mentors Buie Seawell, Sarah Cavanagh, Jim Cook, Sam Chapin, and Dave Pfautz taught me caution at sea. Mates Katie Lyons, Sally Ranney, and Susan Biddle brought pleasure.

Thanks to Carl Brandt, my literary agent, with emphasis on literary. And special kudos to editor-publisher Jon Eaton. I am tough on editors, and our partnership felt, at times, more like mud wrestling. But I trust the process, and came to admire Jon's intuition and sharp eye, and the book we jointly created.

Thanks, finally, to Trish, who saw this book emerge one ragged paragraph at a time, and cheered each one, even at 4 A.M. on weekends when I abandoned her to be with my new love.

About the Author

A JOURNALIST FOR 34 YEARS, Jim Carrier has been a radio newsman, AP editor and correspondent, newspaper managing editor, roaming columnist, and project writer. For 13 years, readers in the American West knew him as the Rocky Mountain Ranger for the *Denver Post*, a job that took him through 500,000 miles, 7,665 sunsets, and 87 pairs of Levis while roaming the Rocky Mountain states. In 1997, Carrier set off to pursue a lifelong dream of living and writing aboard *Ranger*, his 35-foot sailboat. Writing for the *New York Times* and *Sail* magazine, Carrier encountered Hurricane Georges and the remnants of Hurricane Mitch while "living on the hook" off Key West in 1998.

A native of the Finger Lakes Region of New York, Carrier has written eight books, among them *Letters from Yellowstone* (1987), and *West of the Divide* (1992), which won an award for the best nonfiction book from the Colorado Center for the Book. His writing has also appeared in the *National Geographic*.

Carrier currently directs Tolerance.org, a Web project for the Southern Poverty Law Center in Montgomery, Alabama, devoted to fighting hate and teaching tolerance.

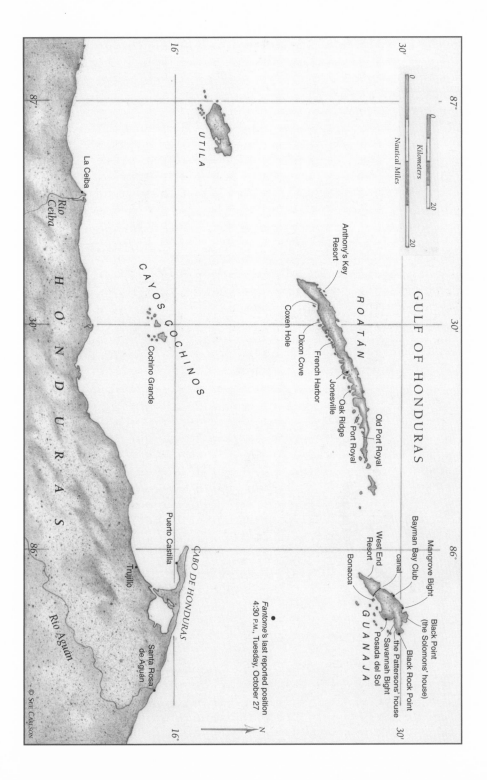

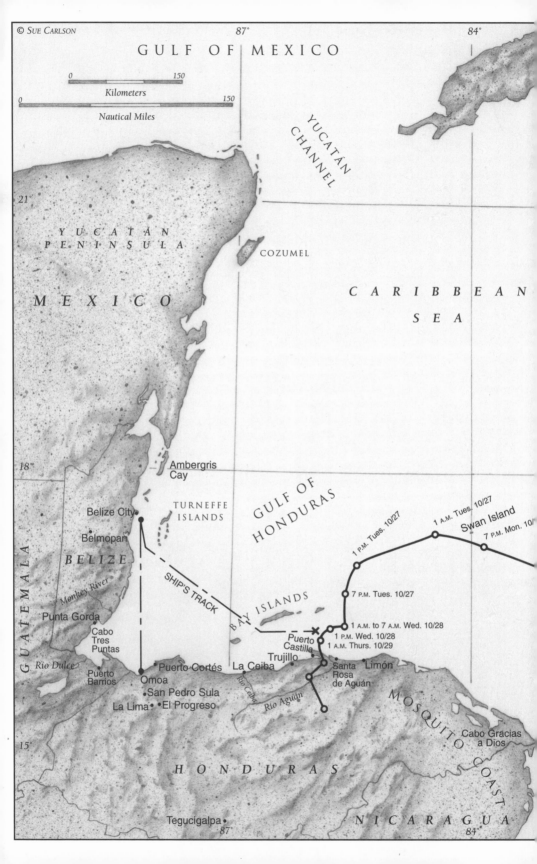